HOUSTON
SIMPLY SPECTACULAR

▲ CAROLYN BROWN

TOWERY PUBLISHING, INC.

HOUSTON
SIMPLY SPECTACULAR

BY

Ron Stone

AND

Maria Moss

★

PROFILES IN EXCELLENCE BY

Molly Glentzer

★

ART DIRECTION BY

Brian Groppe

NEARLY A MILLION COMMUTERS HEAD HOME EACH EVENING TO HARRIS COUNTY'S VAST SUBURBS; FOR THOSE WHO WORK IN DOWNTOWN HOUSTON, THE REARVIEW MIRROR CAN YIELD DRAMATIC IMAGES AT SUNSET (ABOVE).

▲ © ELLIS VENER

SESQUICENTENNIAL PARK, DESIGNED IN 1986 TO COMMEMORATE HOUSTON'S 150TH BIRTHDAY, SPILLS DOWN THE BANKS OF BUFFALO BAYOU NEXT TO THE WORTHAM THEATER CENTER. IN RECENT YEARS, INCREASED ATTENTION TO DOWNTOWN'S PUBLIC SPACES—AND TO THE STREAM THAT FLOWS ALONG THE EDGE OF THE CITY CENTER—HAS SPURRED PLANS FOR A STRING OF SUCH WATERSIDE PARKS (PAGE 1).

PAGES 2 AND 3: JAY STEVENS

LIBRARY OF CONGRESS CATALOGING-IN-PUBLICATION DATA

Stone, Ron, 1936-

Houston : simply spectacular / by Ron Stone ; corporate profiles by Molly Glentzer ; art direction by Brian Groppe.

p. cm. -- (Urban tapestry series)

Includes index.

ISBN 1-881096-32-7

1. Houston (Tex.)--Civilization. 2. Houston (Tex.)--Pictorial works. 3. Houston (Tex.)--Economic conditions. 4. Industries--Texas--Houston. I. Glentzer, Molly, 1956- . II. Title. III. Series.

F394.H85S76 1996

976.4'1411--dc20   96-28646

CIP

Publisher: J. Robert Towery
Executive Publisher: Jenny McDowell
National Sales Manager: Stephen Hung
Regional Sales Manager: Michele Sylvestro
National Marketing Director: Eleanor D. Carey
Marketing Coordinator: Carol Culpepper
Project Directors: Carolyn Delmar, Henry Hintermeister, Quentin Jungheim, Thom Singer

Executive Editor: David Dawson
Senior Editor: Michael C. James
Profiles Manager/Associate Editor: Mary Jane Adams
Associate Editors: Lori Bond, Lynn Conlee, Carlisle Hacker
Editorial Intern: Jennifer Larson
Editorial Contributors: Barbara Brown, Sandra Cook, Chris Kelly, Victoria Lightman, Anne Seltus

Profile Designer: Laurie Lewis
Technical Director: William H. Towery
Production Manager: Brenda Pattat
Production Assistant: Jeff McDonald

URBAN TAPESTRY SERIES

TOWERY
PUBLISHING, INC.

CONTENTS

9

HOUSTON: SIMPLY SPECTACULAR *By Ron Stone*
"Houston was an invention! One of the great ones of the 19th century.
It was a classic leap of faith that became simply spectacular."

PROFILES IN EXCELLENCE *By Molly Glentzer*
A look at the corporations, businesses, professional groups, and
community service organizations that have made this book possible.

PHOTOGRAPHERS

271

INDEX OF SPONSORS

SURROUNDED BY A SPIDERY NETWORK
OF BAYOUS, STREAMS, AND RIVERS,
HOUSTON SITS WHERE THE GREAT
SOUTHERN FOREST GIVES WAY TO THE
GULF COASTAL PLAINS. THE NEARBY
WETLANDS, GRASSLANDS, AND PINEY
WOODS ATTRACT MORE MIGRATING AND
RESIDENT BIRD SPECIES THAN ANY
OTHER LARGE AMERICAN CITY (PAGES 6
AND 7).

HOUSTON'S VERDANT SURROUNDINGS
HAVE ALSO ATTRACTED PLENTY OF
PEOPLE. CIRCA WORLD WAR I, A
CROWD OF PROPERLY ATTIRED HOUSTO-
NIANS SLOGS THROUGH THE MUD ALONG
BUFFALO BAYOU TO WITNESS THE
LAUNCH OF A STEAMER (PAGES 8 AND 9).

PAGES 6 AND 7: STEPHAN MYERS/TEXSTOCK
PHOTO INC.

PAGES 8 AND 9: COURTESY HOUSTON
METROPOLITAN RESEARCH CENTER,
HOUSTON PUBLIC LIBRARY

By Ron Stone

HOUSTON EXISTS TODAY WHERE NOTHING ELSE EVER WAS. WE were not once an Indian village, a crossroads, a sacred burial ground, or even a place where old buffalo went to die. There was nothing here but the edge of the Great Southern Forest, a maze of bayous, and enough mosquitoes and alligators to cause anyone with sense to go someplace else. ★ Houston was an invention! One of the great ones of the 19th century. It was a classic leap of faith that became simply spectacular. ★ Houston was the vision of two New York land speculators who decided to build a town in the middle of nowhere—and did it. If that sounds improbable to you, welcome to Houston! ☞

IN APRIL 1836 GENERAL SAM HOUSTON LED AN UNDERSIZED ARMY against the forces of Mexican dictator Antonio Lopez de Santa Anna at a strip of land north of Galveston called San Jacinto. In an 18-minute miracle General Houston changed the direction of the Republic of Texas and, eventually, the United States. ★ Popular history says it really did take just 18 minutes to end the Texas Revolution, although we've never

thought to ask who in the devil was there with a stopwatch. We're also told that General Houston led his army on a charge that day as generalissimo Santa Anna was "resting" in his tent with a lovely mulatto lady whom history remembers as the "Yellow Rose of Texas." Caught off guard, the generalissimo fled in his silk shorts, and his army followed.

Chasing them through the scrubland of San

ENRICO CERRACCHI'S 1924 BRONZE SCULPTURE OF GENERAL SAM HOUSTON CASTS A FAMILIAR SHADOW AT THE ENTRANCE TO HERMANN PARK (ABOVE). THE GENERAL POINTS EAST, TOWARD THE SAN JACINTO BATTLEFIELD WHERE HIS TROOPS DEFEATED THE ARMY OF MEXICAN DICTATOR SANTA ANNA AND SECURED TEXAS' INDEPENDENCE.

HOUSTON IS AN INTENSELY GREEN CITY, THANKS IN PART TO ITS WARM MOIST CLIMATE. AMONG ITS MOST TREASURED CITIZENS ARE ITS LIVE OAK TREES; THE ELDERS PICTURED HERE FORM A MOSSY TUNNEL ALONG SOUTH BOULEVARD NEAR RICE UNIVERSITY (OPPOSITE).

Jacinto were men and boys from Tennessee and Kentucky, from Virginia and the Carolinas, from up and down the eastern seaboard. The soldiers, who now called themselves Texans, all screamed with pride, "Remember the Alamo!"

Sam Houston, who had been a congressman and governor when he lived in Tennessee, as well as a full-time drunk when he lived with the Cherokee Indians, became a national hero that day.

Meanwhile, the Allen brothers—John and Augustus—came from New York later in the 1830s with a horde of land speculators just itching to move into the Texas territory. There was no question about the name of their new town. Some suggested "Sam's Town," but the brothers settled on Houston.

The Allens had two things going for them:

There was a good, deep stream called Buffalo Bayou that ran through their property, which meant ship traffic was possible, and there was plenty of room to grow.

They had one other thing going for them: They were shameless promoters! They advertised in eastern newspapers that a new town was being formed in the Republic of Texas. One of the ads proclaimed, "There is no place in Texas more healthy, having an abundance of excellent spring water, and enjoying the sea breeze in all its freshness."

The ad was accompanied by a wildly inaccurate rendering of the new city, with houses, bridges, and hills that looked like the Côte d'Azur. However exaggerated those images might have been, Houston has welcomed promoters with open arms ever since.

The Allen brothers landed a boat on the south bank of Buffalo Bayou and set about laying out a town with the help of Gail Borden, a surveyor, newspaperman, and all-around tinkerer. As Borden surveyed the forest and helped plan the city, he also figured out how to condense milk in a vacuum. Traffic jams and Elsie the Cow: not a bad legacy.

In January of 1837 the steamer *Laura* chugged up Buffalo Bayou following a yawl that was hunting for the city. The yawl got stuck in some brush, and when the crew got out to chop up the flotsam that was holding up progress, they discovered they had passed by the new city.

The folks on the *Laura* that day didn't miss much—a collection of tents and a saloon or two. But before long, there were log cabins and more saloons. And when Sam Houston finally arrived, he noted, "All was bustle and animation. Hammers and axes sounding, trees falling." From the very beginning, the city flourished. One traveler wrote home that "houses could not be built as fast as required." He continued the letter by saying that about half the people in town worked; the rest drank and gambled.

When the great naturalist John James Audubon visited Houston City, as it was then called, he wrote of wading in water above his ankles in the mud of what passed as a street. Thus, from the forest, a town began to grow, and it never stopped growing. ☛

ABOUT THE TIME HOUSTON WAS BEING BORN, ROBERT BROWNING was somewhere in England writing, "Ah, but a man's reach should exceed his grasp, / Or what's a heaven for?" That could be the credo of this town. Rarely has any city in the world gone from nothing to something so fast. ★ Today Houston is America's fourth-largest city. It is also one of the hottest—in all senses of the word. When then President

George Bush brought the leaders of the free world here for the economic summit in the middle of a scorching Texas summer, skeptics guffawed. Some boosters printed up T-shirts proclaiming "Houston's Hot," and no one missed the point. Yes, the weather was hot, but Bush and Margaret Thatcher and Helmut Kohl and their friends all came here because the only thing hotter than the weather is the business climate. People who don't mind a little sweat have found the good life among the pine trees and the mosquitoes.

Houston is a city with a world-class symphony; an innovative, nationally recognized ballet; an opera company that is widely renowned; and a professional theater that routinely sends actors and shows to Broadway. As for the visual arts, more than 50 galleries are scattered throughout the city. And clustered around the Wyndham Warwick Hotel near downtown, the Museum District features a half-dozen art, science, and history museums.

The view down South Main from the dining room on the roof of the Warwick is one of the finest in the city. Ancient live oak trees shade the boulevard and guard the entrance to Rice University. To the left, you can see the wide green expanse of Hermann Park, the zoo, and one of the hundreds of golf courses that dot the landscape.

Houston's educational opportunities are worthy of note as well. Rice takes only the best for its small student body and maintains its reputation as one of the nation's finest universities. The University of Houston (U of H) is on the cusp of becoming a great center for urban studies. St. Thomas University is one of the finest private universities anywhere, while Houston Baptist University's Master of Liberal Arts program is the envy of colleges around the country. Texas Southern University, near the U of H, is yet another excellent source for advanced education. ☛

© ELLIS VENER

MANY PEOPLE WHO LIVE NEAR MOUNTAIN RANGES CAN NAME EVERY PEAK IN SIGHT OF THEIR HOMES. LIKEWISE, PLENTY OF HOUSTONIANS CAN TICK OFF THE NAMES OF THE SKYSCRAPERS THAT DOMINATE DOWNTOWN'S PROFILE. HERE, A STEAMY SUMMER SUNSET IS REFLECTED IN (PAGES 12 AND 13, FROM LEFT) ONE SHELL PLAZA; FIRST INTER-STATE BANK PLAZA; THE 1100 LOUISI-ANA BUILDING; TEXACO HERITAGE PLAZA; AND ONE, TWO, AND THREE ALLEN CENTER. ANOTHER RECOGNIZ-ABLE STRUCTURE, THE DECADES-OLD HOUSTON INDUSTRIES PLAZA, ON THE RIGHT, IS CROWNED BY A NEW MULTI-STORY "LANTERN," COMPLETED IN 1995 (OPPOSITE).

PAGES 12 AND 13: F. CARTER SMITH

HOUSTON'S POPULATION IS RICHLY DI-VERSE, AND ITS CULTURAL LANDSCAPE IS WORLDLY AND VARIED. HERE, A PAIR OF YOUNG DANCERS PERFORM AT THE AN-NUAL CARIBBEAN FESTIVAL (LEFT).

HOUSTON'S FATE WAS SEALED IN THE FIRST 15 YEARS OF this century. Oil was discovered in 1901 at Spindletop near Beaumont, 90 miles to the east. Later wildcatters discovered that east Texas was atop a sea of oil and Houston, as it turned out, was the closest big town to all the action. ★ In 1900 and again in 1915 massive hurricanes ripped Galveston, located southeast of Houston, to shreds. Shipping

and transportation were disrupted, but local business leaders had made a gutsy move. They dredged out Buffalo Bayou (on which the Allen brothers had first traveled to get to the city) and in 1914 created a ship channel that ran from Houston to the Gulf of Mexico.

When the folks from Dallas heard about that, they suggested, "If the people in Houston could suck as hard as they could blow, they could just pull the gulf up to them!" The Dallas bankers quit laughing, however, when Houston boomed with oil and chemicals and shipping. Because of the ship channel—and the guts of a lot of businesspeople—

Houstonians figure they can beat Dallas at everything they do, except football (weep on, Oilers fans). Unfortunately, winning at football in Texas is second only to making money as our state pastime.

Houston solidified its bond with the ocean on August 14, 1952, when the Gulf Freeway linking Houston and Galveston was dedicated. That stretch of concrete has become a metaphor for Houston: It is a road that is constantly a work in progress. Like Houston, it's often too fast, sometimes painfully slow, but in the end it still offers a great ride for those who persevere. ☛

THE WORLD'S FIRST GUSHER BLEW INTO THE MASSIVE SPINDLETOP FIELD ON JANUARY 10, 1901, SEALING HOUSTON'S FATE AS AN OIL TRANSPORTATION AND REFINING CENTER (OPPOSITE).

THE GOOSE CREEK OIL FIELD BEGAN PRODUCING IN 1908 (RIGHT). TWO FISHERMEN HAD SPIED GAS BUBBLES RISING TO THE TOP OF BLACK DUCK BAY AND FORMED AN OIL COMPANY ON THE SPOT. THEY DRILLED AND STRUCK IT RICH.

1922
COPYRIGHT
F.J.SCHLUETER

FOR SO MANY YEARS, THERE WAS NOTHING YOU COULDN'T DO, nothing you couldn't try in this town. Houston's successes and its failures were always spectacular. Because the town never had any form of zoning, it grew like a crazy quilt. Recent efforts to bring in zoning ordinances have failed; the locals love their freedom. ★ Such freedom has resulted in a lot of money being made in Houston. Another reason for such

riches is, of course, oil. During the last oil boom, people moved to Houston at the rate of 1,000 families a month. For every oil rig working in the free world, more than 200 jobs were created here. The Humble Oil and Refining Company was founded here, and quickly became one of the world's largest. We know it now as Exxon.

Not all oil ventures were so grand. There were the independent wildcatters, like the legendary Glenn McCarthy. After first hitting a few dry holes, McCarthy finally hit some very rich ones. In fact, McCarthy was the model for Jett Rink, Edna Ferber's character in *Giant*. If you remember James Dean stepping off his land and being drenched with oil in the movie version, you know what McCarthy was like.

Medicine, also, is a prominent feature of Houston's identity. Denton Cooley, who grew up in the area called the Heights, wanted to be a doctor, so he became one of the best in the world. Cooley performed the first human heart transplant in America. He conducted the surgery at the Texas Medical Center, one of the world's largest concentrations of doctors and hospitals and widely considered to be a medical mecca.

In the early 1960s a local judge named Roy Hofheinz visited the Coliseum in Rome and decided to come back home and build a replica with a roof on it, so major-league baseball could come to Houston. He dubbed his Astrodome the Eighth Wonder of the World.

That may be a stretch, but it changed the way stadiums were built and gave the world Astroturf and air-conditioned baseball and football. Oilers and Astros fans learned you could at least be comfortable while the home team lost.

More recently, some engineers doodled on a napkin at lunch one day and designed a computer. They quit their jobs, borrowed a few bucks, and started the Compaq Computer Corporation.

Meanwhile, a fellow named Giorgio Borlenghi came over from Italy and built two giant apartment towers in the Post Oak area. Borlenghi created a minor scandal by doing this *without* borrowing any

money. He just wrote checks out of his own bank account and was considered a novelty 'round here for quite a while.

Then there is the Galleria, a second "downtown" built by a former car salesman named Gerald Hines, where there is more shopping and office space than you will find in downtown Denver. The pricey shops have become a magnet for international shoppers. And the Galleria is just around the corner from River Oaks—one of the great neighborhoods in America—where the old money and this week's new money live in baronial splendor. In March or April the streets of River Oaks (as in the city's other great neighborhoods) come alive with pink and white azaleas that add to the natural beauty of the pine and oak trees that crown green manicured lawns.

(Speaking of blooming things and pretty lawns, because of our climate Houston is green year-round. It may freeze a couple of times a year, but a flake or two of snow is so rare as to merit headlines in the papers. The few months of extreme heat are worth the eight or nine months of grand weather.)

Most of the beautiful people—the ones who live in neighborhoods like River Oaks—dine at Tony's, a posh French-Italian eatery that is *the* place to see and be seen. If Houstonians want to just pig out, they go to Ninfa's, a chain of Tex-Mex restaurants that Ninfa Laurenzo started 25 years ago when her husband died and left her with no money. Mamma Ninfa introduced the world to the stuff she had been cooking for the kids for years—fajitas—a delight that has become a standard part of Tex-Mex fare all across America.

Young Robert Del Grande opened Cafe Annie for the haute cuisine lovers, and the Rio Ranch for the upwardly mobile wanna-bes who still crave an occasional helping of that Texas staple, chicken-fried steak. You can also join former President Bush for a hamburger and barbecue at Otto's, a hole-in-the-wall Houston favorite near Memorial Park. ☞

OIL AND PETROCHEMICAL REFINERIES ARE A FACT OF HOUSTON'S ENVIRONMENTAL AND ECONOMIC LIFE. THESE COKING UNITS APPLY TREMENDOUS HEAT TO EXTRACT THE LAST RESIDUES OF CRUDE FROM HEAVY ASPHALTIC COMPOUNDS (OPPOSITE).

IN HOUSTON THERE'S ALWAYS BEEN A DISTINCTION BETWEEN OLD AND NEW MONEY. MAINLY THE TWO HAVE GOTTEN ALONG JUST FINE. PICTURED AT LEFT, WILDCATTER, FORMER OIL-FIELD WORKER, AND FLAMBOYANT NEW-MONEY MILLIONAIRE GLENN MCCARTHY IS EMBRACED BY *Houston Chronicle* PUBLISHER, OLD-MONEY FINANCIER, AND POWER-BROKER-AT-LARGE JESSE JONES IN THE LATE 1940S.

ASA IS REALLY WHAT PUT HOUSTON ON THE MAP. WHEN the space agency was looking for a place to locate its fledgling Manned Space Program, Senate Majority Leader Lyndon B. Johnson, who got his start as a high school teacher in Houston, convinced Exxon to donate some land for a center. So the astronauts packed up their rockets and moved to town. ★ When President John F. Kennedy

A MOCK-UP OF A CARGO BAY GIVES VISITORS TO SPACE CENTER HOUSTON A LOOK INSIDE A SPACE SHUTTLE (BELOW).

"PLANET HOUSTON" AS SEEN FROM SPACE (OPPOSITE): THE CONFLUENCE OF THE BUFFALO AND WHITE OAK BAYOUS, WHERE THE CITY BEGAN, IS VISIBLE IN THE PHOTO'S SOUTHEAST QUADRANT.

came here to look the facility over, he promised Americans the moon. Lots of presidents have done that, but Kennedy delivered.

When Neil Armstrong sent back the first words from the surface of the moon, he said, "Houston, Tranquility Base here; the *Eagle* has landed!" Sam Houston would have been proud, and the Allen brothers would have been astounded that their little promotion had become a name on everyone's lips.

Houston remained, through all the glitz of the space program, a southern city—more like magnolias and mint juleps than cowboy hats. Still, the

Houston Livestock Show and Rodeo changes that image for one winter month each year when it takes its place as the biggest rodeo in the world.

The Livestock Show operates with 10,000 volunteers who take a couple of weeks off from their jobs as CPAs, lawyers, and corporate VIPs to pull on their Wranglers and "go Texan." Once the show ends, the jeans go into storage and out comes the three-piece suit. In truth, many Houstonians moved here from farms and ranches because they couldn't make a living off the land. But then they worked like hell so they could buy themselves a farm to escape to on the weekends. ☞

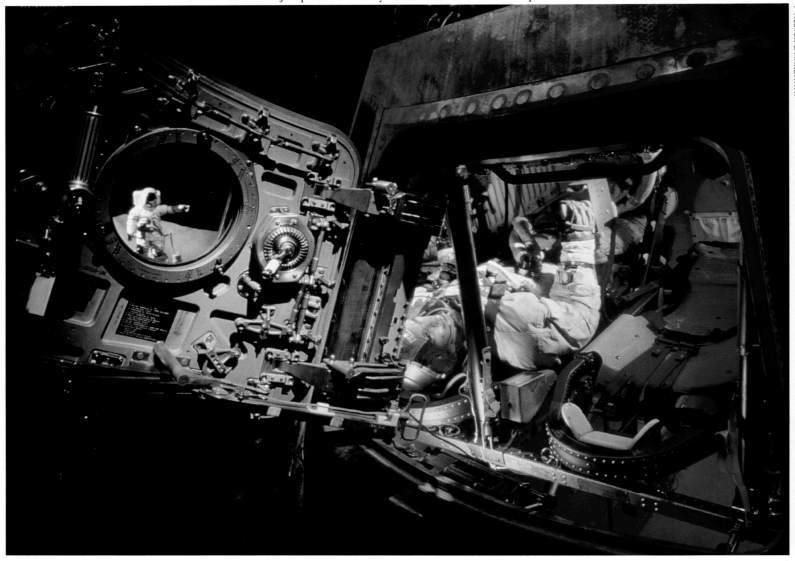

IN THE 1970s OUTSIDERS BEGAN BRANDING HOUSTON AS A KIND OF Redneck Heaven, a reputation that was bolstered by the 1980 release of a John Travolta movie called Urban Cowboy. It was the story of refinery workers who went to a beer joint named Gilley's to two-step with the ladies and ride a mechanical bull for eight seconds to prove their manhood. The refineries are still there, but Mickey Gilley's club has since burned down, and the urban cowboys have gone back to wherever they came from. The oil boom has busted too, but amazingly, Houston continues to grow. ★ We are a service town now, and more of us seem to be using our brains rather than our brawn. And most of us maintain a pride in this town that should have never succeeded, but that just kept defying the odds by always being a place that embraced the entrepreneur. ★ After all these years, the feeling remains: If you try, you can make it in Houston. ✒

Until recently, Houston has never cared much about being a pedestrian's city; it's a driver's town, with more than 675 freeway miles inside the city limits (PAGES 22 AND 23).

Houston's central business district is majestic day or night (above and opposite). Although downtown has long been a flurry of activity during working hours, a lively theater district and a spate of newly refurbished lofts and apartments are also making the area a hot spot at night.

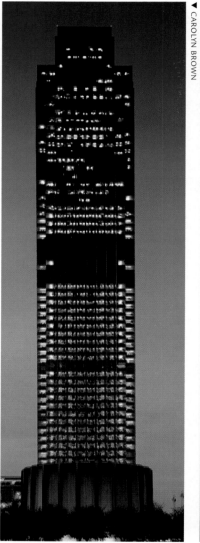

THE LIGHT FANTASTIC: A westward view from an oilman's downtown aerie (PAGE 26) and a look into the skyline at sunset (PAGE 27).

PAGE 26: JAY STEVENS
PAGE 27: PAUL SCHMIDT/TEXSTOCK PHOTO INC.

HOUSTON'S ARCHITECTURE stands as a metaphor for the city's role as a giant in business, culture, education, and space exploration. The Transco Tower, designed by patron saint of Houston architecture Philip Johnson and his partner John Burgee, looms imperi-ously above the Galleria area. At night the beam from its rotating beacon can be seen for up to 20 miles (OPPOSITE, LEFT).

Obelisks stand at the entrance to the University of Houston's main campus. Johnson's imposing College of Architecture building is visible in the background (OPPOSITE, CENTER).

From a distance, and from almost any direction, the Transco Tower appears as a solitary marker at the western edge of the 610 Loop. At 64 stories, it's the world's tallest build-ing located outside a downtown business center (OPPOSITE, RIGHT).

Tranquility Park (ABOVE), with its shimmery cylindrical fountains, is a downtown reminder that the city's name was the first word spoken from the moon. "Houston," an-nounced astronaut Neil Armstrong as the world listened, "Tranquility base here. *The Eagle* has landed!"

HOUSTON

THE PAVED TRAILS OF Buffalo Bayou Park (TOP) are beloved by scores of runners, cyclists, and urban hikers. The greenbelt stretches along the sloping banks of Houston's seminal waterway, winds through grassy picnic areas and past the occasional sculpture, and leads into downtown.

The view from the Transco Tower's observation deck (BOTTOM) highlights an undeniable fact of Houston's topography: The gulf coastal plain is startlingly flat, undistinguished by so much as a minor hill. The area's elevation rises consistently at about one foot per mile inland from the gulf, which means the city peaks at 60 feet above sea level.

THE HOUSTON AREA HAS more than 191 million square feet of general-purpose office space. In recent years the occupancy rate for commercial office space has topped 80 percent, up from a record midrecession low of 69.8 percent in July 1987.

Portrait of a superdeveloper: Real estate mogul Gerald D. Hines is largely credited with placing Houston near the center of architecture's bold new universe from the late 1970s through the 1980s. Hines was the first developer to bring internationally celebrated architects to town; with them, he helped turn the downtown skyline into a display of eye-popping modern and post-modern designs.

FOR ALL THEIR INFAMOUS braggadocio and exuberant pride of place, Houstonians know better than to take their town's wonders too seriously. Here, a "skating skyline" featuring replicas of downtown's most familiar forms—and one unfamiliar form—makes its way through the streets in Roadside Attractions: The Artist's Parade, an annual celebration of rolling artwork.

CORPORATE AND INSTITUTIONAL
Houston have helped personalize the city's public spaces with a wide variety of sculpture. Pictured here are (CLOCKWISE FROM TOP LEFT) James Surls' *Points of View* in downtown's Market Square, Joan Miró's *Personage and Birds* at Texas Commerce Tower, William King's *Collegium* at the University of Houston, Mel Chin's *Manila Palm: An Oasis Secret* at the Contemporary Arts Museum, and (OPPOSITE) Jean Dubuffet's seven-part *Monument au Fantôme* at Louisiana and Lamar.

TRANQUILITY PARK'S iridescent fountains are a splendid example of making art out of necessity—they disguise the air vents for a parking garage underneath.

STEPHEN FOX, HOUSTON'S preeminent architecture critic, calls the Transco Water Wall "a stunning work of hydraulic engineering." Situated at the base of the Transco Tower and designed by the building's architects, it mesmerizes crowds of out-of-towners and locals alike.

WHILE PLENTY OF LOCALS consider the Transco Water Wall to be the most romantic spot in town, others prefer the romance of Houston's many cultural events.

Maestro Christoph Eschenbach conducts the venerable Houston Symphony Orchestra. Founded in 1913, the orchestra plays more than 170 performances annually in downtown's Jones Hall and in other venues throughout the community, including free summer concerts at the Miller Outdoor Theater.

Houstonians love to point out that their city is one of only a handful in the country that support resident repertory theater, ballet, symphony, and opera companies. The Houston Ballet, directed by Ben Stevenson, garners international hurrahs for its performances of classical and contemporary works, and for its commitment to bold up-and-coming choreographers.

HOUSTON'S STAGES ARE HOME to at least 10 theater companies, including The Ensemble, one of the nation's most respected African-American theaters. Examples of the diverse fare offered on local stages are (CLOCK-WISE FROM TOP LEFT) the Houston Shakespeare Festival's *Othello*, with James Black and Richard Lawson; Houston Grand Opera's *Rigoletto*; Houston Grand Opera's *Mephistopheles*; and the Alley Theatre's *Macbeth*, also with James Black.

KNOWN INTERNATIONALLY as one of the opera world's shrewdist impresarios, Houston Grand Opera (HGO) General Director David Gockley has guided his company to major-league status. He challenges audiences by interspersing avant-garde works with classic grand opera while at the same time rewarding them with first-rate productions. Houston has responded in kind: Along with the Houston Ballet, HGO makes its home in the magnificent Wortham Theater Center, funded entirely by private money raised during the 1980s oil recession.

THE ALLEY THEATRE, winner of a 1996 Tony award for outstanding regional theater, is Houston's only resident professional repertory theater company. Its castlelike building in the Theater District houses two stages, where a dozen or more productions are mounted each season. Director Gregory Boyd schedules a broad range of work, from dramas such as *Angels in America* (TOP) to the "horror musical" *Jekyll & Hyde* (BOTTOM), which originated at the Alley before its Broadway run. *Jekyll & Hyde* was coproduced with Theatre Under The Stars, Houston's ticket to first-rate productions of Broadway musicals.

Angels aren't seen only on the stage in Houston: A host of 1920s angels preside over Washington Avenue's Glenwood Cemetery (OPPOSITE); Howard Hughes is buried there.

Houstonians are inveterate weather watchers. The summer storms that blow in off the Gulf of Mexico are often dramatic—especially when seen from a high-rise office building—and occasionally dangerous. Houston gets an average of 46 inches of rainfall annually, and thunderstorms occur about 64 days a year.

Only the threat of a hurricane can affect life on an oil rig (opposite). The Houston area accounts for about 27 percent of all U.S. jobs in crude petroleum and natural gas extraction—a total of more than 40,000 jobs. (That's not counting another 40,000 or so jobs in oil and gas field services and oil-field machinery manufacturing.)

THE VAST COMPLEX OF OIL refineries and petrochemical plants along the Houston Ship Channel never sleeps (PAGES 46 AND 47). The Texas Gulf Coast has the facilities to turn out 3.347 million barrels of refined petroleum products every 24 hours, almost 22 percent of the U.S. total. Refineries provide petroleum feedstock to more than 340 Houston-area chemical plants; the Houston-Gulf Coast region comprises almost half of the nation's base petrochemicals manufacturing capacity. In other words, when it comes to polypropylene and polyethylene, we rule.

PAGE 46: DOUG HICKMAN

PAGE 47: RAY SOTO/TEXSTOCK PHOTO INC.

SAFETY DRILLS ARE SERIOUS
business in the petrochemical industry. Most of Houston's
Ship Channel industries belong to a
mutual assistance program, through
which they can share emergency
resources such as first aid teams and
equipment to fight fires and contain
hazardous materials.

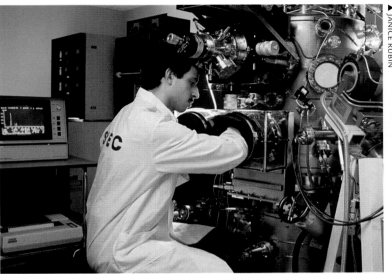

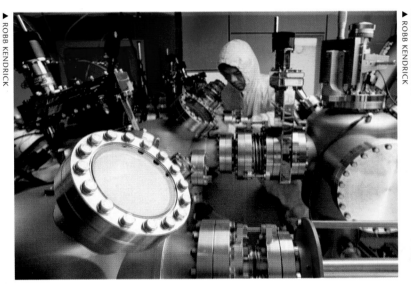

AFTER PLUMMETING OIL prices brought a painful recession in the 1980s, "economic diversification" became the mantra of the Houston business establishment. Today city leaders point with pride to robust growth in energy-independent industries like medical research, computer manufacturing, and biotechnology. In fact, there are now more than 50 biotech companies here. Meanwhile, new drilling technology has made energy exploration profitable despite low oil prices.

EVER SINCE HOUSTON welcomed the original seven astronauts with a parade and barbecue in 1962, the space program has been a profound part of the civic psyche. NASA's $1.2 billion Johnson Space Center, 25 miles from downtown Houston, manages the space shuttle program, trains astronauts, develops technology for human-piloted spacecraft, oversees many of the experiments conducted during shuttle missions, and is host center for the International Space Station.

OUSTON ALSO IS CENTRAL in NASA's program for the commercialization of space. Ongoing research toward that end ranges from medicine and agriculture to engineering and pollution control. The space program, which employs some 3,300 federal workers and 11,000 contract personnel, has helped draw a powerful "technology brain trust" to the area. Space science is now prominent at Rice University and the University of Houston-Clear Lake. The Lunar and Planetary Institute, a research consortium of 76 U.S., Canadian, British, and Israeli universities, is headquartered in Houston.

ROBB KENDRICK

HARD AT WORK IN Houston: High-altitude window washers have a lot in common with mountain climbers—strength, agility, and a taste for adrenaline highs. Houston's glass towers are the Himalayas of the trade (PAGE 52). Known as the "spaghetti bowl," the miles-long pipeline network that connects hundreds of chemical plants and refineries along the Texas coast provides many job opportunities for Houstonians (PAGE 53).

PAGE 52: GEORGE D. HIXSON
PAGE 53: JANICE RUBIN

OIL AND PETROCHEMICAL storage tank "farms" dominate the landscape around refineries in nearby Baytown, Pasadena, and Texas City. Keeping the tanks in good repair is dirty dangerous work, yet it's a crucial part of safe plant operations (ABOVE AND OPPOSITE).

T HE TRANSCO TOWER'S 51st-floor observation deck gives visitors a dizzying view of west Houston and the busy Westheimer corridor.

HOW DID AN INLAND CITY become a major international seaport? The Houston Ship Channel, opened in 1914, turned the lower section of sleepy Buffalo Bayou into a waterway that the world's biggest ships could navigate. The Port of Houston ranks third in the country and eighth in the world in terms of tonnage.

HERMANN HOSPITAL'S
15,500-square-foot
emergency center provides state-
of-the-art crisis care. Hermann is
one of two Level I trauma centers in
Houston; the other is at Ben Taub
Hospital.

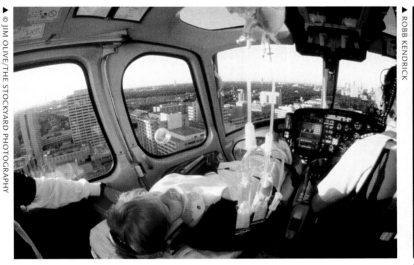

THE HOUSTON FIRE Department is the nation's third largest, with 3,002 firefighters based at 81 fire stations. Its Emergency Medical Services program averages a response every three minutes.

Hermann Hospital's Life Flight air ambulance service flies more than 2,800 missions annually, responding to calls within a 150-mile radius. Life Flight's three helicopters cost about $3 million annually to operate; Hermann, a nonsectarian charity hospital, relies on community support and fund-raising efforts to help pay for the service.

PATIENTS FROM AROUND THE world come for treatment at the Texas Medical Center, the largest concentration of medical technology on the planet. Established in 1942 with funds from wealthy cotton broker Monroe D.

Anderson, it now occupies some 100 buildings on 675 acres. Almost 50,000 Houstonians work at the center, staffing 13 hospitals and 28 other member facilities, including hospices, medical schools, and research institutions. The Texas

Medical Center has undergone a startling growth spurt in recent years; its physical plant space has almost doubled since 1982, jumping to nearly 20 million square feet.

▲ © ELLIS VENER

HOUSTON HAS BEEN HOME to many influential doctors in the medical profession, including Denton Cooley, M.D., who performed the first successful heart transplant in the United States at St. Luke's Hospital in 1968. Cooley still practices cardiovascular surgery at the hospital (ABOVE).

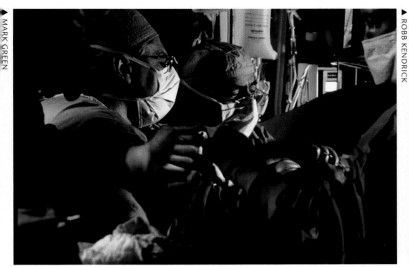

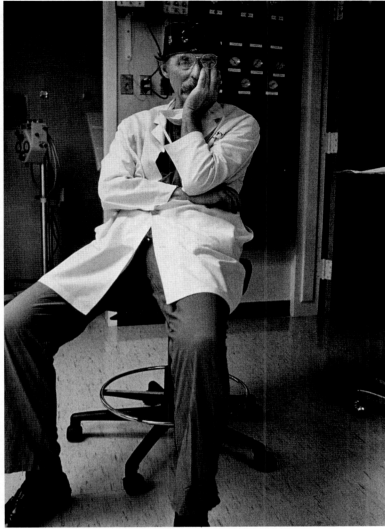

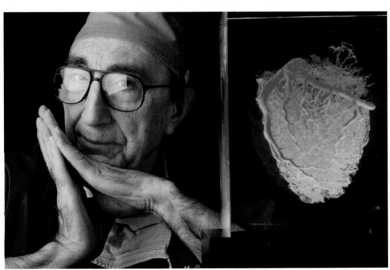

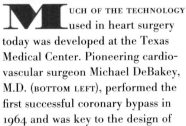

MUCH OF THE TECHNOLOGY used in heart surgery today was developed at the Texas Medical Center. Pioneering cardio-vascular surgeon Michael DeBakey, M.D. (BOTTOM LEFT), performed the first successful coronary bypass in 1964 and was key to the design of the artificial heart. As president, he helped make Baylor College of Medicine one of the country's most respected medical schools.

The camera caught trauma spe-cialist James "Red" Duke, M.D. (RIGHT), after a long night in the ER. Duke founded Hermann Hospital's Life Flight air ambulance service in 1976; he's known nationwide for his down-to-earth televised medical commentary and in medical circles for overseeing Hermann's flight emergency care.

DOMINIQUE SCHLUMBERGER de Menil (BOTTOM) and her late husband, John de Menil, helped bring Houston into the late 20th century in terms of contemporary art and thought. Their philanthropy helped to build the Media Center at Rice University and the minimalist Rothko Chapel; and to foster the careers of young artists and community leaders, including the late U.S. Representative Mickey Leland.

Passionate and astute collectors, the de Menils amassed more than 10,000 artworks, ranging from surrealist and cubist pieces to Byzantine artifacts. To house the still-growing Menil Collection, Dominique de Menil built a private museum in a residential neighborhood (OPPOSITE) and opened it to the public, admission-free. She also hosts the annual Carter-Menil Human Rights Awards with former President Jimmy Carter, and is helping fund construction of a Byzantine chapel to showcase a group of early frescoes. John de Menil commissioned Max Ernst to paint his *Portrait of Dominique* (TOP) in pre-World War II Paris; it now hangs in the Menil Collection.

THE MUSEUM DISTRICT is home to some of Houston's best-loved artworks and cultural institutions. Alexander Calder's *The Crab* (TOP LEFT) keeps watch over the entrance to the Museum of Fine Arts. Exhibitions at the Holocaust Museum (TOP RIGHT), like its architecture, are gripping. The bays and barrier islands of the Texas Gulf Coast are portrayed by the fountain outside the Houston Museum of Natural Science (BOTTOM LEFT). A stunning gem and mineral collection, a petroleum science exhibition, dinosaur skeletons, a planetarium, and a breathtaking butterfly house make it the most visited museum in the city.

Across town on the banks of Buffalo Bayou is the Houston Police Memorial (BOTTOM RIGHT); the sculpture and earthwork by Houston sculptor Jesús Bautista Moroles commemorate the lives of officers killed in the line of duty.

THE ROTHKO CHAPEL (LEFT), which holds 14 of abstract expressionist Mark Rothko's shadowy paintings, is as meditative a public place as you'll find in Houston. In the reflecting pool stands Barnett Newman's *Broken Obelisk*, dedicated by art patrons John and Dominique de Menil to the memory of Martin Luther King Jr.

The serene C.G. Jung Educational Center (RIGHT), a longtime presence in the Museum District, offers classes and lectures based on Jungian psychology and hosts introspective gallery exhibitions.

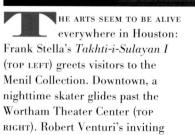

THE ARTS SEEM TO BE ALIVE everywhere in Houston: Frank Stella's *Takhti-i-Sulayan I* (TOP LEFT) greets visitors to the Menil Collection. Downtown, a nighttime skater glides past the Wortham Theater Center (TOP RIGHT). Robert Venturi's inviting design for the Children's Museum includes "caryakids" (BOTTOM LEFT). Generations of Houstonians get their first taste of postimpressionism at the Museum of Fine Arts' John A. and Audrey Jones Beck Collection (BOTTOM RIGHT).

THE MUSEUM OF FINE ARTS, founded in 1900, was Texas' first art museum. In 1999 the Beck Building—a 185,000-square-foot addition—is scheduled to debut.

Music producer Randall Jamail (opposite) is a study in young entrepreneurial Houston; he founded his fast-growing label, Justice Records, to go against the grain of traditional record-factory practices. He's coaxed critically acclaimed CDs, such as Willie Nelson's Grammy-nominated "Moonlight Becomes You," out of independent-minded jazz, rock, and country artists.

Houston's glitzy charity ball scene helps keep dozens of vital organizations afloat; every season, attendees funnel millions of dollars to social services, medical research, and the arts. Here, ball chairperson par excellence and undisputed first lady of fund-raisers Carolyn Farb chats with Houstonian and ZZ Top band member Billy Gibbons (top).

Gallery exhibition openings also bring out the local bright lights: Menil curatorial visionary and art eminence Walter Hopps (bottom, at left) with a friend from out of town, actor Dennis Hopper.

A MEL CHIN SCULPTURE
stands tall at the Menil
Collection (PAGE 72). In the 1930s
the distinctive cupola atop the Niels-
Esperson Building dominated the
Houston skyline (PAGE 73).

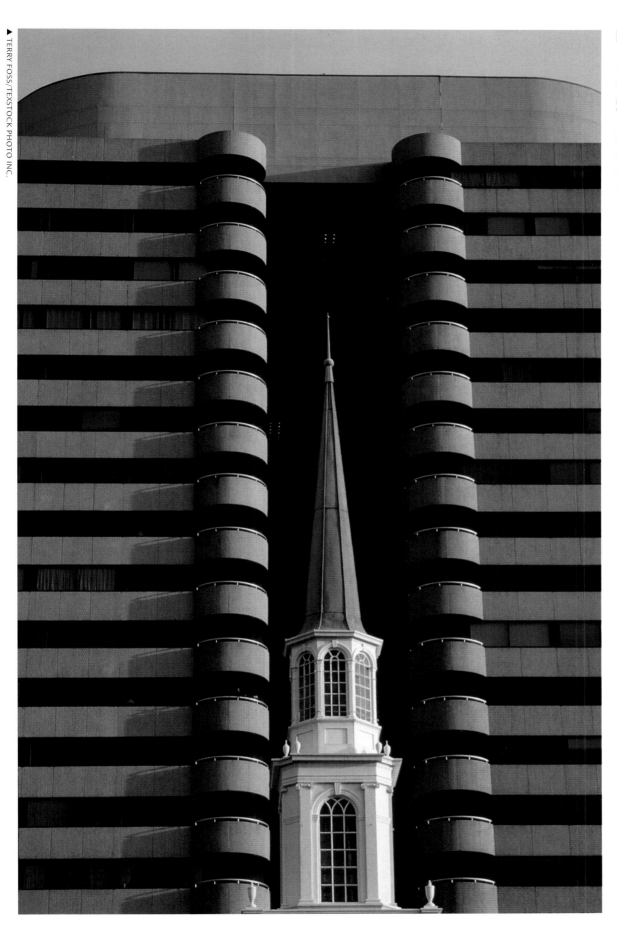

Then and now: The Cotton Exchange Building, a vestige of Houston's first days as a major agricultural trade center, has graced the downtown corner of Travis and Franklin streets since 1884 (OPPOSITE). Sleek and stately Houston stand side by side on Montrose Boulevard: The 5000 Montrose condominium tower and Fourth Church of Christ, Scientist.

HOUSTONIANS ARE ARDENT gardeners—balmy weather means something's in bloom almost every day of the year—and many local yards become wildly original personal palettes (TOP AND OPPOSITE, TOP).

EQUALLY AS INTERESTING AS Houston's gardens is its architecture. Architect Frank Zeni (OPPOSITE, BOTTOM) is part of a small design revolution in his West End neighborhood; Tempietto Zeni, his imaginative metal-clad home, is among a dozen or so "tin houses" in the area. Only Zeni's, though, boasts columns made of culvert pipe. The Niels-Esperson Building was constructed in 1927 as a memorial to a Danish-born real estate and minerals speculator. Commissioned by his widow, Mellie Esperson, it is crowned with a tiny templelike structure and covered with Italian Renaissance details (BOTTOM).

THE BEER CAN HOUSE: Retired railroad-car upholsterer John Milkovisch never understood why folks made such a fuss over his answer to expensive aluminum siding. He flattened some 50,000 beer cans, covered every inch of his exterior walls with them, hung shimmery can-top curtains from the eaves, and turned this modest dwelling at 222 Malone into a folk-art dreamscape.

RETIRED POSTAL WORKER Jeff McKissack built his whimsical Orange Show from found objects and concrete as a monument to the orange (TOP). Its balconies, tunnels, and pocket theaters make up Houston's most famous folk-art environment. The Orange Show Foundation, formed after McKissack's death to preserve his creation, has flowered into a vibrant arts organization that documents other such works and stages events that encourage the artist in everyone.

The Fan Man's House, now largely disassembled, is among the sites brought to wide attention by the Orange Show Foundation (BOTTOM).

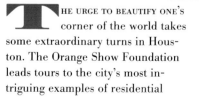

THE URGE TO BEAUTIFY ONE'S corner of the world takes some extraordinary turns in Houston. The Orange Show Foundation leads tours to the city's most intriguing examples of residential self-expression. Favorite stops are the homes of Cleveland Turner, aka the Flower Man (TOP AND BOTTOM LEFT), and the late Bob Harper, aka the Fan Man (TOP AND BOTTOM RIGHT).

BEYOND THE MAINSTREAM museums and galleries, an edgier kind of art culture also flourishes in Houston. Scenes from the art scene (CLOCKWISE FROM TOP LEFT): Zocalo Theater's art car parade entry; Heights Theater, lov- ingly restored and used for exhibitions and performance art; "lawnmobile" and driver in repose, postparade, in Market Square; and painter Jim Pirtle at work in his studio.

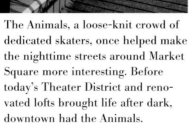

THE SPRUCED-UP McKEE Street Bridge (LEFT) reflects the beginnings of the movement to develop Buffalo Bayou. Warren's (TOP RIGHT) is a Market Square denizen. Scott Prescott (BOTTOM RIGHT), one of the original Urban Animals, takes the McKee on eight wheels.

The Animals, a loose-knit crowd of dedicated skaters, once helped make the nighttime streets around Market Square more interesting. Before today's Theater District and renovated lofts brought life after dark, downtown had the Animals.

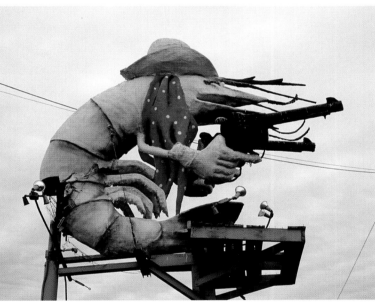

Urban animals of other sorts: Okay, so maybe Gulf Coast seafood restaurants exaggerate a bit, but not much. A giant blue crab touts the hefty platters at Christie's (TOP), while a gunfighter shrimp (BOTTOM) points the way to Gaido's.

And on a completely different subject, reports of the infamous cockroach, bane of Houston cupboards (RIGHT), are grossly exaggerated.

HUNGER ACTIVIST CAROL Porter (TOP) and her husband, Hurt, founded KidCare Inc., an acclaimed food distribution program, in their own kitchen. As a nonprofit corporation, KidCare bought government surplus food with donated money and served it to hungry children. Now the Porters' program is being heralded nationally as a grassroots model.

The city's reputation for reasonable rents and good value in the home market is well deserved. In many areas, though, affordable housing remains among Houston's toughest challenges. Pictured here is a now-completed effort to create affordable single-family homes within an existing Fifth Ward neighborhood (BOTTOM).

DURING THE 1992 Republican National Convention, thousands on every side of almost every issue exercised with vigor their right to free assembly, taking to the streets in scores of demonstrations, organized and otherwise. Here, a drum corps from the Women's Action Coalition beat a rhythm in Market Square, while thought-provoking images are screened on the side of a parking garage (TOP).

Housing activist Lenwood Johnson (BOTTOM, AT LEFT) led—and lost—a controversial fight to save Allen Parkway Village, a historic, once-exemplary public housing project, from the wrecking ball. Thanks in part to Johnson's efforts, however, plans are in place to renovate a small number of the more than 900 original units; new "scattered-site" housing will be built throughout the city.

H O U S T O N

HOUSTON HOLDS CLAIM TO several prominent politicians. Former State Highway Commissioner Robert C. Lanier (OPPOSITE) also served as Houston's chief executive from 1992 to 1996; the mayor and 14 city council members are limited to three terms in office. Early on, "Mrs. Mayor" Elyse Lanier translated her husband's love of roses into spectacular city plantings; she now serves on the University of Houston Board of Regents.

The city's most famous nonnative son: former President George Bush (TOP) stretches for the camera outside the house he and first lady Barbara Bush built after the 1992 election. U.S. Representative Sheila Jackson Lee (BOTTOM), longtime Houston political player, makes a point.

ALLAS MAY HAVE THE LOCK on megachurches, but Houston's religious culture is gloriously diverse. From simple neighborhood structures such as St. Matthews Baptist Church (TOP) to soaring modern spaces like Lakewood Church (BOTTOM) to Sri Meenakshi (NOT PICTURED), a painstakingly reproduced scale model of an Indian Hindu temple, opportunities for communal worship abound.

The neo-Gothic entrance to St. Paul's Methodist Church (OPPOSITE) dwarfs a visitor.

Since 1839, when Epis-copalians founded Houston's first congregation, Christ Church has occupied this site on Texas Avenue. The present building was erected in 1893.

Houston's large Asian population has brought a variety of Buddhist organizations to the city. The Taiwanese Tien Hou Temple, run by the Sino-Indochinese Association of Texas, is a Taoist site.

MUCH OF HOUSTON'S strength comes from the fact that it embraces a multi-ethnic population. The city's business, artistic, and educational landscapes are deeply influenced both by the individual contributions of its various cultures and by the unique ways in which they merge with each other.

Chinese New Year, complete with firecrackers and dancing dragons, is celebrated in many parts of Houston; Greek food steams at a Houston International Festival booth; and a would-be bullfighter hones his elegant form in a north Houston parking lot.

MEXICAN HERB SHOPS known as *yerberias* offer traditional Latin American remedies as well as prayer candles and other talismans and religious articles. Each November 2, as it is in Mexico, *Dia de los Muertos* is widely observed in Houston. Altars adorned with mementos honoring the dead are often highly creative personal works of art. Many galleries and shops feature locally made "Day of the Dead" altars during October and November.

HOUSTON HOSTS MORE THAN a dozen annual outdoor festivals that honor its myriad cultures, including Greek, Italian, Jewish, Egyptian, and Caribbean celebrations; the Juneteenth Blues Festival; Cinco de Mayo and Fiestas Patrias gatherings; and the annual Oriental Cultures Festival (TOP RIGHT). The massive Houston International Festival (TOP AND BOTTOM LEFT; BOTTOM RIGHT) spotlights a different country each spring, turning downtown into a street fair with arts-and-crafts booths, tantalizing food, an art car parade, and hundreds of stage performances.

HOUSTON SCULPTOR PAUL Kittleson's nutcrackers prance in front of the Wortham Theater Center each Christmas season, while inside, the Houston Ballet does a monthlong marathon of performances of Tchaikovsky's classic.

Northeast of the city, Mercer Arboretum's 252 thoughtfully landscaped acres show what grows in east Texas' Big Thicket ecosystem. Pictured is one of the botanical garden's iris bogs.

HOUSTON BLOOMS SPEC-
tacularly in the spring:
Wildflowers splash color along
neighborhood streets; bluebonnets,
Texas' state flower, blanket highway
medians; and azaleas show off in
shades from white to crimson pink.
(A tour of the River Oaks Garden
Club's annual Azalea Trail is a hal-
lowed ritual in some circles.)

Cut flowers dazzle year-round at
the Fannin Street flower markets
(TOP RIGHT), where late hours and
bargain potential tempt passing
drivers. Nearby, at the Museum of
Natural Science's Cockerell Butterfly Center, a rice paper butterfly
pauses amid tropical blossoms

(BOTTOM CENTER).

Planted early in the 20th century, Houston's giant live oaks are
genuine civic treasures (PAGES 98
AND 99).

PAGES 98 AND 99: MARK GREEN

A S IT DOES WITH JUST ABOUT everything else, Houston has its own exuberant take on Christmas traditions. Santas show up wearing cowboy hats and riding longhorn steers, skyscrapers sport wreaths of lights 20 stories tall, and church pageants feature lasers and live camels.

Some neighborhoods, like Candlelight Estates (воттом), put on such a jaw-dropping display of Christmas lights that carloads of delighted gawkers fill the streets every night in December. Others, such as the Heights, favor a more traditional approach (тор).

When River Oaks Shopping Center greets the season, palm trees are swaddled in lights, while downtown, in Tranquility Park, Houston artist Andy Mann's video Christmas tree makes an annual appearance.

Suburbs have long been part of Houston's civic composition. The Heights, developed in the 1890s, was the area's first master-planned community; developers arranged a direct trolley line for the two-and-a-half-mile commute to downtown. The growing city eventually swallowed the Heights, which was officially annexed in 1918. Many of its turn-of-the-century Victorian homes and pre-World War I bungalows have been lovingly restored, though, giving the neighborhood the feel of a small separate city.

Simple shotgun houses, like the ones pictured above, are among the historic structures still found in Freedman's Town, Houston's oldest African-American neighborhood where many emancipated slaves settled in the late 1860s. The community now stands in the shadow of downtown's looming skyscrapers, but the congregation of the nearby Antioch Baptist Church, founded in 1866, has in recent decades staunchly resisted overtures by real estate developers.

COMMUTER FACTS: HUNDREDS of outlying subdivisions mean Houstonians think about traffic a lot. In 1994 vehicles traveled almost 27 billion miles in Harris County, while average peak-period freeway speed was 49 miles per hour. Many downtown workers commute on METRO buses or in vanpools, but Houstonians, especially those who work in areas other than downtown, cherish their cars.

About half of the 1,053 freeway/expressway miles planned for the metropolitan area are now in operation. Houston has more miles of high-occupancy vehicle (HOV) lanes than any other U.S. city; when completed, the HOV system will cover 104.2 miles. The Houston Intelligent Transportation System, a $500 million plan to increase highway capacity, has begun to use computers, fiber-optic cable, video, and embedded road sensors, among other technologies, to measure and control traffic flow.

THERE HAVE BEEN NOISY public debates over whether Houston needs a rail transit system; the ruling opinion has always been that it doesn't. Of course—like many American cities—before the sweeping highway programs of the late 1940s, Houston had one.

HOUSTON CAN EASILY declare itself the "Art Car Capital of the World." It makes perfect sense—the city prizes individuality; eccentricity is out and out embraced; and automobiles are treasured. The Orange Show Foun- dation and Houston International Festival put on the annual Roadside Attractions: The Artist's Parade, an event that showcases this home- grown phenomenon. Entrants drive from across the country to join in the fun.

SKATERS, CYCLISTS, AND AD HOC vehicles also get to roll for the wildly appreciative crowds; the art car parade is grounded in the idea that everyone is an artist inside. The *Fruitmobile* (BOTTOM LEFT), created by Jackie Harris, is the grande dame of Houston art cars; it's never missed a parade.

Immobile car art: Billy Blues club commissioned Dallas sculptor Bob Wade to build its big saxophone sign (RIGHT); the upside-down VW Beetle makes it Houston.

United Community, A MURAL at St. Joseph's Catholic Church, was painted by Pio Pulido and Sylvia Orozco. The work was sponsored by Multicultural Education and Counseling through the Arts (MECA), which provides arts instruction and social services to inner-city youth and their families.

WITH HELP FROM corporate donors, charitable foundations, and volunteers, artist Rick Lowe transformed two city blocks of run-down row houses into one of the nation's most innovative community arts projects (TOP LEFT). Project Row Houses, in Houston's Third Ward, marries art and neighborhood revitalization with community services. This unique site addresses the whole neighborhood with art installations, housing for young single mothers and their children, after-school programs, a community garden, and other services.

Elsewhere in town, some works are in progress: an artist outside the Midtown Arts Center (TOP RIGHT) and students at MECA (BOTTOM LEFT AND RIGHT).

LAWNDALE ART AND PER-
formance Center began
life in a former fan factory as part
of the University of Houston's art
department. Eventually, Lawndale
put down its own roots and now
thrives as an independent nonprofit
gallery in a renovated building on
Main Street.

THE COMMUNITY ARTIST'S Collective (TOP) helps nurture art that reflects African-American culture with classes, workshops, exhibitions, and community service projects. DiverseWorks' loading-dock entrance (BOTTOM) at a north Houston warehouse is deceptive; inside, a 4,000-square-foot gallery and theater are venues for fearless cutting-edge contemporary art and performance.

A TALENTED COMMITTED GROUP of artists chooses to live in Houston—in part because of reasonable rents for studio space and the sense of comunity fostered by alternative arts organizations. The Core Fellows program at the Glassel School of Art, the teaching wing of the Museum of Fine Arts, has also brought top-drawer talent to town. But more fundamental, Houston's emphasis on self-invention means it's a good place to make art.

Here, painter Rachel Hecker poses with her 1990 *Censorship* (LEFT). A painting by John Peters, another Houston artist, covers the back door of the Commerce Street Artist's Warehouse (CENTER).

THE UNIVERSITY OF Houston's creative writing program put Houston on the literary map. It's often ranked among the top two or three graduate writing programs in the country, and competition for admittance is blistering. Novelist Paula Webb (RIGHT) is among the many strong voices that have come out of the program.

TOOTSIES

Houston's richest, thinnest, blondest women get their Gautiers, Muglers, and Mizrahis at Tootsies, while out-of-towners head for Neiman's and Saks Fifth Avenue.

At the other end of the retail spectrum, bargain hunters browse for vintage band uniforms, lava lamps, and distressed picture frames at Texas Junk, where it's hard to guess what proprietor Bob Novotny (BOTTOM LEFT) might dig up. Buy a ring at Kipperman's Pawn Shop and Wedding Chapel, and ordained minister Ted Kipperman (BOTTOM RIGHT) will probably throw in the ceremony for free. He also offers drive-through wedding services, as well as guns, violins, and exercise equipment.

Lawndale Art and Performance Center stages Houston's most self-conscious annual fund-raiser. The Hair Ball (OPPOSITE) honors Texas Big Hair and pokes some affectionate fun at our predilection for overdone dos.

Cowboy hats and manly footwear: Hometown heartthrob Clint Black (TOP LEFT) and Houston Astros owner Drayton McClane (TOP RIGHT) obviously know Houston headgear. World-class boot maker Rocky Carroll (BOTTOM LEFT) shows off a little number he whipped up for former President George Bush.

EVERY FEBRUARY, TRAIL RIDERS gather in small Texas towns, mount up, and follow covered wagons for days or even weeks, all the way to Houston's Memorial Park. They camp there, some 6,000 of them, and the next day they hoist flags and converge on downtown in a grand clattering parade, just to kick off Houston's rodeo season. Sometimes it rains, and it's usually cold, but it's tradition. Even the Houston Police Mounted Patrol officers, who get to ride their horses downtown every day, polish bits and spurs and boots for the parade.

ICE STADIUM'S 71,500 seats can accommodate the biggest rock shows (TOP), not to mention Rice Owl football games.

Houstonians love fireworks, the bigger the better. (Many of them haven't stopped talking about Rendezvous Houston, a 1986 extravaganza staged on the downtown skyline by French musician Jean-Michel Jarre.) The fireworks display inside the Astrodome during the Houston Livestock Show and Rodeo (BOTTOM LEFT) never fails to elicit oohs and aahs. Each Fourth of July, the Houston Symphony plays Tchaikovsky's *1812* Overture at Miller Outdoor Theater while the sky overhead explodes (BOTTOM RIGHT).

HOUSTON

▲ JIM CALDWELL

HOUSTON BECAME "TWO-STON" in 1995 when the Houston Rockets won their second NBA World Championship title in two years. Led by center Hakeem Olajuwon, the team plays home games in the Summit, where euphoria ruled after the final 1995 play-off game.

HOUSTON RESPONDED TO the Rockets' NBA World Championship wins with all the exhilaration you'd expect from a city that had never seen a professional sports team reach the top.

People poured into downtown for victory parades featuring players on fire trucks, and parking garages boosted the view for thousands of cheering, streamer-waving, confetti-tossing sports fans.

SINCE 1959 THE HOUSTON Oilers have toyed with the hearts of Houston sports fans: Super Bowl hopes have been repeatedly dashed, while the mighty Dallas Cowboys continue to define Texas football. But fans have shown a dotty devotion—"Oiler Blue" fright wigs and face paint have appeared at every home game.

THE SUMMIT CAN SEAT 17,000 for concerts and some 16,275 for sports events (TOP). Besides the Rockets, the Houston Aeros hockey team and the Houston Hotshots, part of the Continental Indoor Soccer League, also play there.

The Astrodome (CENTER) launched a new era in stadium construction when it opened in 1965. It's been home to the Astros baseball and Oilers football teams ever since, and a venue for every sort of entertainment from tractor pulls to the 1992 Republican National Convention.

I N FEBRUARY HOUSTON BOHEMians and buttoned-down types alike "go Texan." The Houston Livestock Show and Rodeo, held at the Astrodome complex (TOP AND BOTTOM LEFT), is the largest such exposition in the world and the whole city gets involved. The show is also one of the city's biggest charity fund-raisers, providing millions of dollars in scholarships and endowments. Many rodeo traditions originated on Mexican *rancheras*; Luis Jimenez' molded fiberglass *Vaquero* (BOTTOM RIGHT) salutes that legacy at Moody Park.

TOP RODEO COWBOYS COMPETE at bronc and bull riding, calf roping, and steer wrestling for shares of more than $600,000 in prize money. But auctions are the real business side of the stock show; bloodstock buyers who want to im-prove their herds come to Houston from around the world. When student exhibitors' champion animals go on the block, local bigwigs bid huge sums; much of the winning bid money goes into scholarship funds.

A s RECENTLY AS 1990, MORE than a quarter of the land in Harris County was devoted to farming and ranching. In fact, there are more horses in Harris County than in any other major urban center in the United States. Quarter horses and Appaloosas dominate the local equine population, but Thoroughbreds, Arabians, American saddlebreds, and most other breeds are well represented. At the Houston Polo Club (TOP AND BOTTOM LEFT), a horse gets new shoes, while another takes a shower.

THE TEXAS LONGHORN IS A tough temperamental breed descended from cattle imported by Spanish explorers. Its genetic resilience helped sustain the early Texas cattle industry; today longhorns are the pride of "preservationist" cattle breeders.

IN SPITE OF ITS HIGH-TECH SELF, Houston has deep ties to agrarian life. Nursery crops in Harris County account for more than $60 million annually, and agricultural income approaches $100 million.

Before oil, cotton drove Houston's economic engine. Today nearly 30 percent of Port of Houston export tonnage is agricultural products, including rice, which loves the Gulf Coast's soggy fields.

Enterprising organic farmer Camille Waters (BOTTOM LEFT) grows herbs and heirloom vegetables on inner-city plots and sells them, fresh picked, to restaurants.

MEXICAN BAKERIES—CALLED *panaderias*—in the Heights, Spring Branch, East Side, and other neighborhoods sell mouthwatering breads and pastries that taste almost as sweet as they look.

IF IT'S GROWN IN THE AMERICAS, you can buy it in Houston. The Farmer's Market on Airline Drive is the place to find cactus pears, fresh tamarind, endless chile varieties, and anything else that's in season, polished and artfully arranged. If you're looking for durian melon, though, you'll have to go to Chinatown.

TWO WAYS TO BEAT THE HEAT: Icehouses—friendly open-air neighborhood beer joints—and *raspa* stands, which sell shaved ice drizzled with fruity syrup.

▼ ROBB KENDRICK

▼ © ELLIS VENER

LOCATED IN OLD TOWN SPRING, Wunsche Brothers, a tavern established circa 1902, lives the family life now as a German-Texas country café.

ZYDECO MUSIC FIRST MIGRATED to Houston from south Louisiana with oil field workers, and Houston will be forever grateful. When Wilfred Chevis plays at venues like Pe Te's Cajun Barbecue, sitting still is not an option.

Accordion player Little Willie Davis (TOP LEFT) performs his brand of zydeco, while dancers at the Continental Ballroom dip and spin to another zydeco band (TOP RIGHT). Lovers of the "chanky-chank" sound also watch for zydeco church dances at St. Philip Neri.

Houston's place in blues music is often overlooked; America's first major African-American-owned record label, Duke-Peacock, was formed in Houston in 1948 and recorded the likes of Bobby "Blue" Bland and Junior Parker. Artists such as "Texas" Johnny Brown, Joe "Guitar" Hughes, Milton Hopkins (BOTTOM LEFT, at the Reddi Room), and I.J. Gosey (BOTTOM RIGHT, at C. Davis Barbecue) keep a rich Houston blues tradition alive.

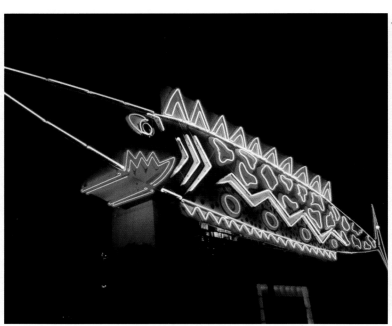

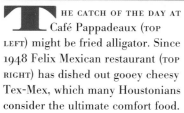

THE CATCH OF THE DAY AT Café Pappadeaux (TOP LEFT) might be fried alligator. Since 1948 Felix Mexican restaurant (TOP RIGHT) has dished out gooey cheesy Tex-Mex, which many Houstonians consider the ultimate comfort food.

Literary readings are given somewhere in Houston almost every night—either at a Poetry Slam at a local bar (BOTTOM LEFT) or at Brazos Bookstore. Brazos owner Karl Killian supports good local writers, and smart touring authors

usually touch down there.

The River Oaks Theater (BOTTOM RIGHT) is the last of Houston's art deco movie palaces that still show films. Modified to accommodate three screens, it's close to the hearts of Houston cinemaphiles.

TONY VALLONE'S RESTAURANT is where well-heeled Houstonians go when they want to be seen looking fabulous. After more than two decades and a two-year hiatus, the Continental-Italian kitchen is still among the best in town, but the food is pretty much beside the point. *Houston Chronicle* gossip columnist Maxine Mesinger has held court at Tony's for most of its life. Although the restaurant closed in 1993, it reopened after a face-lift in 1995 to the fierce delight of Houston high society.

ACCORDING TO THE ZAGAT restaurant survey, Houstonians probably eat out more often than people in any other American city, enough to keep more than 8,000 eateries in business. Houston's culinary culture is marked by the way longstanding regional styles—Mexican, Cajun, cowboy, and southern soul food—blend or collide with recent arrivals like Vietnamese, Thai, Indian, and South American. Barbecue restaurateur Jim Goode (TOP) is Houston's god of smoke. At 8.0 (BOTTOM LEFT), murals by local artists and healthy southwestern fare draw a moderately hip crowd. Nicaragua native Michael Cordua's Americas (BOTTOM RIGHT) and Churrascos restaurants sizzle with South American flavors.

Competition among bright young chefs makes for a vibrant restaurant scene. Meanwhile, Cafe Annie's Robert Del Grande, who pioneered new southwestern cooking more than a decade ago, remains Houston's most respected "star" chef. Fajitas (TOP) were invented here by Mamma Ninfa Laurenzo; her chain of Mexican restaurants has reached all the way to Germany. With Kim Son, the La family first educated Houston palates in the delicate pleasures of Vietnamese cuisine (BOTTOM LEFT). Louisiana's contributions are sometimes as simple as boiled crawfish, perfectly spiced of course (BOTTOM RIGHT).

IMPASSIONED LECTURES BY RICE University's J. Dennis Huston (TOP), a national Professor of the Year, electrify his English-literature students.

Empire Café (BOTTOM), a neighborhood favorite for its knockout layer cakes, looks out onto Westheimer's lively street scene; the clutch of nearby antique shops keeps the sidewalks primed for people-watching. Brasil, an art-smart Montrose coffee bar, occupies a former bicycle repair shop (PAGES 142 AND 143).

PAGES 142 AND 143: JAY STEVENS

JANICE RUBIN

JIM CALDWELL

BEFORE NASA, THE SKYLINE, or the artificial heart, Houston looked to Rice University to bolster its civic self-esteem. With typical humility, city boosters for years referred to Rice as "the Harvard of the South." They need not have worried about Rice's Ivy League status; it holds its own as one of the better small private liberal arts colleges.

Founded as the Rice Institute in 1912 by wealthy merchant William Marsh Rice, the university was originally conceived as a technical school. Now occupying some 300 live-oak-shaded acres on South Main Street, Rice can point with particular pride to its architecture, computer science, and engineering departments. Rice's endowment is among the largest of any private American university.

HOUSTON'S EDUCATIONAL institutions have earned a national reputation for providing excellent scholastic opportunities.

Houston Community College (CENTER LEFT) serves more than 33,000 students with two-year programs on multiple campuses; its imposing Central Campus is in the Binz neighborhood a few miles from downtown. Houston Baptist University (CENTER RIGHT), founded in 1960, is known for small classes and personal attention. The Catholic-affiliated University of St. Thomas (BOTTOM LEFT) was rated one of America's best liberal arts values by *Money* magazine. The student body at Texas Southern University (TSU), near the Third Ward and the University of Houston, is primarily African-American (BOTTOM RIGHT). TSU gets high marks for its Graduate School of Pharmacy, top-ranked debate team, and Thurgood Marshall School of Law.

RICE UNIVERSITY'S BREEZE-catching passageways and Gothic arches (LEFT) were planned by architect Ralph Adams Cram. In 1912 he hired an Austrian stonecutter to carve intricate column capitals (OPPOSITE, TOP) at the Administration Building, now called Lovett Hall.

MORE THAN 450 BIRD SPECIES migrate through the Houston area, and more than 100 species are year-round residents. Houston routinely ranks first or second in the number of species counted during the Audubon Society's annual bird census. A quarter-million snow geese winter west of town on the Katy Prairie (TOP LEFT). Resident black skimmers nest and raise their chicks on oyster-shell reefs in Galveston Bay (TOP AND BOTTOM RIGHT). Cormorants are skilled fishers; the ones shown here are watching for prey on Lake Conroe (BOTTOM LEFT).

ONE OF THE BEST REASONS TO live near the Texas Gulf Coast: You never know when you'll catch sight of roseate spoonbills lifting off in unison over a tidal flat. This flock is cruising Christmas Bay, just south of Galveston Island.

THE MAGNIFICENTLY RESTORED square-rigger *Elissa* docks at Galveston's Pier 21 and is open for tours when she's not on one of her two or three annual voyages in the Gulf of Mexico. The *Elissa* is the oldest ship in Lloyd's Register, and one of the oldest merchant vessels still afloat.

THE GULF OF MEXICO, approximately 50 miles away, inexorably draws Houstonians to it. The city of Clear Lake, besides being home to the Johnson Space Center, is Houston's sailboat central—more than 2,500 vessels are docked in the area. Galveston's 32 miles of beaches are relatively undeveloped toward the western end of the island, and intensely civilized toward the east. Stewart Beach (BOTTOM), in the middle of town, is toward the east.

Line dance: A graceful cowboy practices his lariat routine, while a surf fisherman practices his own routine at sunset on the Texas Gulf Coast.

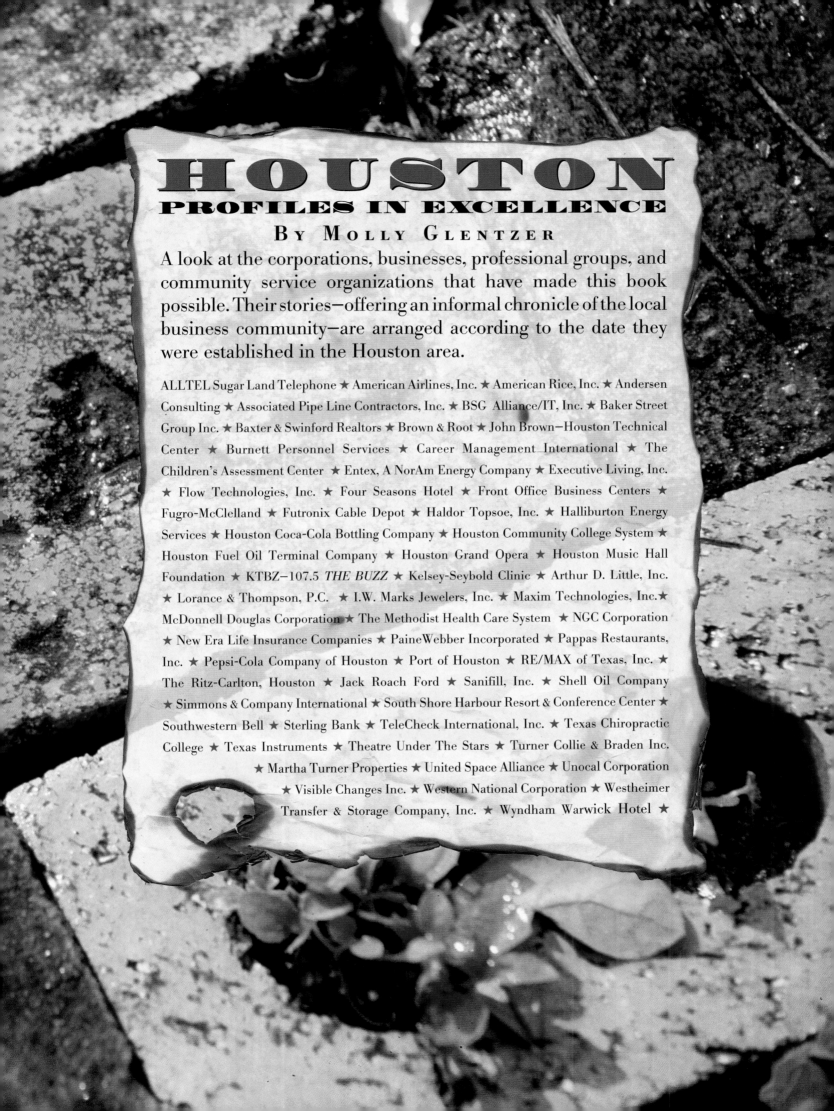

HOUSTON
PROFILES IN EXCELLENCE
By Molly Glentzer

A look at the corporations, businesses, professional groups, and community service organizations that have made this book possible. Their stories—offering an informal chronicle of the local business community—are arranged according to the date they were established in the Houston area.

ALLTEL Sugar Land Telephone ★ American Airlines, Inc. ★ American Rice, Inc. ★ Andersen Consulting ★ Associated Pipe Line Contractors, Inc. ★ BSG Alliance/IT, Inc. ★ Baker Street Group Inc. ★ Baxter & Swinford Realtors ★ Brown & Root ★ John Brown—Houston Technical Center ★ Burnett Personnel Services ★ Career Management International ★ The Children's Assessment Center ★ Entex, A NorAm Energy Company ★ Executive Living, Inc. ★ Flow Technologies, Inc. ★ Four Seasons Hotel ★ Front Office Business Centers ★ Fugro-McClelland ★ Futronix Cable Depot ★ Haldor Topsoe, Inc. ★ Halliburton Energy Services ★ Houston Coca-Cola Bottling Company ★ Houston Community College System ★ Houston Fuel Oil Terminal Company ★ Houston Grand Opera ★ Houston Music Hall Foundation ★ KTBZ—107.5 *THE BUZZ* ★ Kelsey-Seybold Clinic ★ Arthur D. Little, Inc. ★ Lorance & Thompson, P.C. ★ I.W. Marks Jewelers, Inc. ★ Maxim Technologies, Inc.★ McDonnell Douglas Corporation ★ The Methodist Health Care System ★ NGC Corporation ★ New Era Life Insurance Companies ★ PaineWebber Incorporated ★ Pappas Restaurants, Inc. ★ Pepsi-Cola Company of Houston ★ Port of Houston ★ RE/MAX of Texas, Inc. ★ The Ritz-Carlton, Houston ★ Jack Roach Ford ★ Sanifill, Inc. ★ Shell Oil Company ★ Simmons & Company International ★ South Shore Harbour Resort & Conference Center ★ Southwestern Bell ★ Sterling Bank ★ TeleCheck International, Inc. ★ Texas Chiropractic College ★ Texas Instruments ★ Theatre Under The Stars ★ Turner Collie & Braden Inc. ★ Martha Turner Properties ★ United Space Alliance ★ Unocal Corporation ★ Visible Changes Inc. ★ Western National Corporation ★ Westheimer Transfer & Storage Company, Inc. ★ Wyndham Warwick Hotel ★

1866★1963

Entex, A NorAm Energy Company

Westheimer Transfer & Storage Company, Inc.

Houston Coca-Cola Bottling Company

Port of Houston

Maxim Technologies, Inc.

The Methodist Health Care System

Southwestern Bell

Shell Oil Company

Brown & Root
Halliburton Energy Services

Wyndham Warwick Hotel

American Airlines, Inc.

Jack Roach Ford

ALLTEL Sugar Land Telephone

Andersen Consulting

Pepsi-Cola Company of Houston

Unocal Corporation

Associated Pipe Line Contractors, Inc.

Fugro-McClelland

Turner Collie & Braden Inc.

Kelsey-Seybold Clinic

Texas Instruments

Houston Grand Opera

Baxter & Swinford Realtors

McDonnell Douglas Corporation

ENTEX, A NORAM ENERGY COMPANY

IN 1866 A SMALL COMPANY CALLED HOUSTON GAS LIGHT WAS formed to supply gas for the streetlights of a fledgling coastal prairie town in Texas. Since then the town, Houston, has grown to become the fourth-largest metropolitan area in the United States, and the company—later named Entex—has grown to become one of the nation's largest distributors of natural gas. ★ In 1912 Houston Gas Light

was succeeded by Houston Gas & Fuel (HG&F). In 1930 HG&F became one of 40 separate companies in Texas, Louisiana, and Mississippi that joined together to form the original United Gas Corporation. Through this venture, the participating companies also created a consolidated distribution system for natural gas. United Gas merged with Pennzoil in 1968, and, two years later, the distribution unit was spun off as United Gas, Inc. In 1974 the name was changed to Entex, Inc.

RAPID GROWTH

Entex grew rapidly and, within two years, significantly increased its customer base by acquiring the gas distribution properties of Houston Natural Gas Corporation. By 1988 Entex had divested its remaining nondistribution assets and—to solidify its position as a

major player in this industry—merged with NorAm Energy Corporation.

Parent company NorAm Energy Corp. is under the leadership of T. Milton Honea, chairman, president, and CEO. NorAm's three distribution companies—Entex, Arkla, and Minnegasco—serve more communities than any other natural gas distributor in the United States. NorAm is the third-largest distribution company in terms of customers and throughput. As one of the largest pipeline companies in the United States, NorAm delivers gas from mid-continent to markets throughout North America and provides distribution services to communities stretching from the border of Canada to the border of Mexico.

Like its parent corporation, Entex has remained at the top. Today Entex ranks eighth among the nation's 300 largest gas dis-

tribution concerns. As a public utility engaged in the distribution and sale of natural gas, Entex serves 502 communities across Texas, Louisiana, and Mississippi, including more than 1.4 million residential, commercial, and industrial gas customers.

In Houston alone, the company serves nearly 690,000 customers and employs more than 1,400 people. Houston is a key market for Entex, accounting for approximately 44 percent of the company's distribution revenues. And, as a result of the merger, Houston became the largest single market for NorAm.

One reason for Entex's success is its tradition of commitment to both customer service and the community. Putting the needs of its customers first is the company's top priority. To maintain and increase market share, Entex's strategy is simple: provide quality, dependable, and courteous gas service while also giving something back to Houston.

CUSTOMER-DRIVEN SERVICE

Entex employees realize that the company is linked to its customers not only through the gas lines that run to homes and businesses, but through its participation in community life as well. As such, Entex places a high priority on individual community involvement and overall corporate citizenship through civic organizations and a series of customer assistance programs. As the company motto states: "Natural gas is our product, but service is our business."

As an extension of the company's dedication to customer service, Entex has created

ENTEX CONTINUES TO WORK VERY CLOSELY WITH ITS INDUSTRIAL CUSTOMERS.

an innovative employee program called Operation Breakthrough. Under the program, employee teams resolve specific issues affecting Entex's efficiency and profitability. Through direct employee involvement—from the executive offices all the way to the frontline level—Entex employees have a say in how they do their work. The company has empowered its employees to influence decisions made concerning their particular areas of expertise.

An important aspect of Operation Breakthrough is its emphasis on real implementable results, not just on reports and activities. As a result of Entex employees' direct participation in the improvement of their work processes, the company's staff has pulled together to meet the challenges and opportunities of a rapidly changing energy industry. They are discovering new ways to improve the quality of Entex's product and service

offerings as well as to improve internal policies, procedures, and systems.

In its constant pursuit of customer satisfaction, the company solicits suggestions from its clients through surveys. Entex is committed to providing its customers with energy that is efficient, environmentally sensitive, safe, and affordable.

An Industry Leader

Entex takes an active leadership role in environmental issues. Although natural gas is hailed as a clean, environmentally friendly energy source, the company still pursues ways to improve its product in these areas. For example, the company has been fueling its vehicles with compressed natural gas (CNG) for more than a decade.

Entex has also used new technology to enhance the quality of customer service and to increase operating efficiency.

In doing so, the company has earned a reputation as a pacesetter in its field and has gained nationwide recognition for implementing an impressive array of high-tech applications, such as computer-aided dispatching of service trucks, handheld electronic meter reading devices, automated mapping systems, solar-powered remote pipeline measurement facilities, radio telemetry, and other innovations.

At the helm of Entex is President and Chief Operating Officer Robert N. Jones. A strong and experienced leader, Jones assumed his current role in 1994 after serving Entex in positions of increasing responsibility over the preceding 14 years. Under his direction and with the support of employee teamwork and ingenuity, Entex looks forward to continued growth for the company while providing the best possible service to its customers at the lowest price possible.

ENTEX HAS ALWAYS ENCOURAGED STRONG EMPLOYEE INVOLVEMENT.

FOR MORE THAN A CENTURY, HOUSTONIANS ON THE MOVE have relied on Westheimer Transfer & Storage Company, Inc. to help them get where they were going. How appropriate then that one of the most heavily traveled thoroughfares in the city, Westheimer Road, is named for the company founder's family. ★ When S.J. Westheimer immigrated to Houston from Baden, Germany, in 1881, he

was only 17 years old. He opened his business two years later, assisted by a team of horses and a wagon. Westheimer worked long hours to lend a caring hand to both the people and the companies he served. That same tradition lives on today through the descendants of his successor, Ben Hurwitz, a young Russian immigrant who joined the company as office boy in 1902.

EARLY HISTORY

Westheimer's early growth was swift. By 1905 the firm employed nine drivers and as many teams of horses, and by 1906 the company was incorporated. In 1911 the company opened its first storage warehouse on Commerce Street—one of many to be built over the ensuing years. The addition of motorized trucks soon followed.

Working alongside S.J. Westheimer in every facet of the business, Hurwitz bought the company when his mentor retired in 1923. Greatly loved and respected by his employees, Hurwitz was described in Westheimer's 50th anniversary newsletter as "one of the only too few

executives who temper their orders with consideration for the hirelings."

Many of Westheimer's early jobs were integral to Houston's growth from a small town into a bustling metropolis. The company lived up to the motto "We

move anything," which appeared on all its moving trucks. Construction materials for the building of the old Southern Pacific Grand Central Station, boilers for many of the city's first office buildings, and even Houston Lighting & Power Co.'s first

WHEN S.J. WESTHEIMER (SECOND FROM LEFT) EMIGRATED TO HOUSTON FROM BADEN, GERMANY, IN 1881, HE WAS ONLY 17 YEARS OLD. HE OPENED HIS BUSINESS TWO YEARS LATER, AND BY 1905 THE FIRM EMPLOYED NINE DRIVERS AND AS MANY TEAMS OF HORSES (BELOW RIGHT).

THE COMPANY LIVED UP TO THE MOTTO "WE MOVE ANYTHING," WHICH APPEARED ON ALL ITS MOVING TRUCKS (BELOW LEFT).

transformers were transported by the company.

While Westheimer Transfer & Storage would agree to move almost any type of cargo, the company specialized in local and long-distance handling of household goods. When the company became an official agent of Allied Van Lines in 1929, it had already established its reputation as the firm to call when national or international moving services were needed. Westheimer was also the first company in Houston to offer its customers individual locked rooms for the storage of their household goods and personal effects.

The original Westheimer Transfer was located on the banks of Buffalo Bayou. By the 1930s the company operated a main office on Commerce Street, two downtown branches, and numerous warehouses. During Westheimer's tenure at its current offices and 100,000-square-foot warehouse at 4700 Kirby, a generation of Houstonians has come of age. Today Westheimer Transfer & Storage employs 70 people, including administrative and sales staff, drivers, packers, and warehouse workers. In addition, the firm contracts with additional independent drivers who own trucks.

SAME FAMILY, SAME VALUES

Westheimer Transfer & Storage is still owned by the Hurwitz family. Ben Hurwitz's sons, Julian and Jay, ran the company for many years, and Julian's son Ben—who joined Westheimer in 1979—is at the helm as president today.

What does it take to keep a company—and a family—in business for more than 100 years? "Old-fashioned values and honesty in dealing with customers, employees, and vendors," suggests the younger Ben Hurwitz. "My father and uncle were old-time Houstonians who were very active and well known in the community. Like

my grandfather, they believed that if you treat people fairly, you'll succeed."

Hurwitz also notes that today's business environment has many challenges. "The competition is tougher than it used to be," he says. "Customers are more demanding and discriminating. As a result, we've become even more service oriented, bending over backwards to serve customers." Hurwitz ends each day by asking his staff, "Are all of our customers happy today?"

Computers have enabled the company to keep close tabs on drivers and loads. But in many ways the moving business is still a matter of proper packing and careful loading and unloading.

"Moving is one of the most stressful events a person can experience," says Hurwitz, "so we try to please customers at a difficult time in their lives. We try to make the experience as stress free as possible." Westheimer's drivers attend a training program at Allied University near Chicago to master the basics not only of loading, unloading, and paperwork, but also of customer service. Participation in an Allied program called At Your Service also builds a healthy attitude among all of Westheimer's employees.

The company has a long history of supporting community activities and charities through the Westheimer Foundation. Among the organizations that have benefited from the firm's benevolence are the United Way and Junior Achievement.

To lead Westheimer Transfer & Storage into the next century, Hurwitz is exploring ways to take advantage of the global economy and to expand the company's international capabilities. Although it is important to keep moving with the times, Hurwitz also knows that good old-fashioned service remains as timeless as the foundation upon which his family's company has grown and prospered.

COMPANY FOUNDER S.J. WESTHEIMER (SEVENTH FROM LEFT) WORKED LONG HOURS TO LEND A CARING HAND TO BOTH THE PEOPLE AND THE COMPANIES HE SERVED. THAT SAME TRADITION LIVES ON TODAY THROUGH THE DESCENDANTS OF HIS SUCCESSOR, BEN HURWITZ (10TH FROM LEFT), A YOUNG RUSSIAN IMMIGRANT WHO JOINED THE COMPANY AS OFFICE BOY IN 1902 (TOP).

EMPLOYEES OF WESTHEIMER TRANSFER & STORAGE, CIRCA 1920 (BOTTOM)

Houston Coca-Cola Bottling Company

IT'S THE WORLD'S MOST SOUGHT-AFTER SOFT DRINK, REQUESTED more than 300 million times daily in at least 155 countries. Its classic bottle ranks among the most recognized trademarks in history. Over the past century, its name has become synonymous with superior quality and taste. Yet when Dr. John Pemberton, an Atlanta pharmacist, created Coca-Cola, he didn't have a beverage in mind. He

promoted the syrup as a medicine. Then a fountain operator accidentally mixed it with carbonated water, and the world's first soft drink was born.

Coca-Cola Enterprises Inc.

Coca-Cola's popularity grew after 1899, when Joseph B. Whitehead and Benjamin F. Thomas of Chattanooga, Tennessee, acquired exclusive rights to bottle and sell the soft drink. With another Chattanooga businessman, John T. Lupton, they began building a nationwide bottling network by granting franchise rights to other entrepreneurs. Consolidation of these operations began in the late 1970s. One of the most prominent mergers resulted in the formation of Coca-Cola Enterprises Inc. in 1986.

Coca-Cola Enterprises continued to consolidate America's soft drink business. After merging with Johnson Coca-Cola Bottling Group, Inc. in 1991, Coca-Cola Enterprises began a $152 million restructuring and decentralization program to enhance its responsiveness to customers and consumers.

Today Coca-Cola Enterprises operates in 38 states, the District of Columbia, the U.S. Virgin Islands, the Netherlands, and the West Indies. The world's largest bottler of Coca-Cola products, the company collaborates closely with its co-owner and business partner, the Coca-Cola Company, which develops products, sells concentrates, and creates advertising campaigns.

A Houston Heritage

Like Coca-Cola, its parent company, the local Coca-Cola Bottler

has a rich heritage. After opening in 1902, deliveries were made on mule-drawn wagons from its plant northwest of downtown Houston. A decade later, the growing organization relocated to larger quarters.

Rationing of sugar—a key ingredient in Coca-Cola—put a damper on production during World War I. However, the drink's postwar popularity prompted a move to even larger facilities in 1929. Demand increased again in the 1930s, when the invention of electric ice coolers and coin-operated vending machines made Coca-Cola more accessible to consumers.

During World War II, Coca-Cola again was in short supply, and long lines formed at stores hours before Coca-Cola shipments arrived. To meet the demand, the local Coca-Cola Bottler relocated in 1950 to its present home on Bissonnet, which, at that time, was the world's most modern bottling facility.

The Houston facility introduced and became the first company to market Sprite. Through the 1950s and 1960s, its product line expanded further to include Tab, Fresca, Mello Yello, Diet Coke, Cherry Coke, and Minute Maid products. In 1977 the bottler began producing soft drinks other than those of the Coca-Cola Company, including Welch's Grape and Strawberry, Barq's Root Beer, Sunkist Orange, and White Rock and Schwepps mixers. Today the local Coca-Cola Bottler employs more than 1,200 people at its main plant and offices, eight sales warehouses, and canning plant.

"We have a loyal following in this city," reports David French, division vice president, general manager. "In response to that loyalty, we're active in and support numerous community causes. We're continuing the tradition of quality products, service, and corporate citizenship that has become synonymous with Houston Coca-Cola Bottling Company."

TODAY HOUSTON COCA-COLA BOTTLING COMPANY EMPLOYS MORE THAN 1,200 PEOPLE AT ITS MAIN PLANT AND OFFICES, EIGHT SALES WAREHOUSES, AND CANNING PLANT.

Maxim Technologies, Inc.

T HE HISTORY OF MAXIM TECHNOLOGIES, INC. REFLECTS THE history of the many industries the company serves. Founded in Fort Worth in 1912 as Southwestern Laboratories (SWL), the firm has played a pivotal role in the growth of Texas' petroleum industry. Having established its Houston presence in 1917, Maxim participated in major construction projects that include a majority

of the high-rise buildings that make up the Houston skyline, development of D/FW International Airport, and expansion of Texas A&M University. Maxim provides engineering and consulting services in the environmental, analytical, metallurgical, construction materials testing, and geotechnical testing fields.

Today Maxim is the largest independent single-source engineering and testing laboratory in the Southwest. With more than 1,200 employees located throughout 53 offices, Maxim is also ranked among the largest engineering firms in the United States. The company's growth has continued nonstop, from the first operation through the acquisition and merger with Maxim Engineers in 1995, which formed Maxim Technologies, Inc.

"Our labs are fully equipped and staffed with experienced technicians, scientists, and engineers," says Pete Donaldson, district vice president in Houston. "We offer quality work and rapid response times, both of which are critically important to our clients."

During the 1950s SWL became one of the first labs in the Southwest to evaluate critical welds with radiographic techniques. It also introduced geotechnical engineering services and had a fleet of soil drilling rigs in place by the decade's end. The Houston office expanded regularly, and in the early 1960s became an acknowledged leader in the development of nondestructive evaluation (NDE) services.

The Houston office doubled its space in the 1970s with the addition of an environmental division, which soon became one of the most sought after service

areas. The company also expanded its exploratory programs by acquiring Geo-Electric Logging, a drilling and logging company. Today the Houston office, with approximately 150 employees, provides geotechnical engineering, construction materials testing, NDE, analytical laboratory services, environmental consulting, air emissions, asbestos, industrial hygiene, and metallurgical services throughout the Golden Triangle area.

Today, as part of Maxim Technologies, the southwestern offices are benefiting from the emphasis the company is placing on excellence of service. These "Programs for Employee Success" are an integral part of the company's plan to continue the history of service established over the last 80 years.

Maxim Technologies has developed a set of programs that effectively mirror the changes within the industry. These programs include an Account Management Program, a Project Management Program, and a Quality Assurance Program.

The Account Management Program focuses on developing stronger longer-term client relationships by assigning an account manager (or in some cases several account managers) to each client. Maxim's account managers provide a single point of contact for the client and ensure the highest level of customer service.

Maxim's Project Management Program is designed to give project managers the tools and training necessary to deliver projects within scope, budget, and time constraints. These are essential elements to establishing

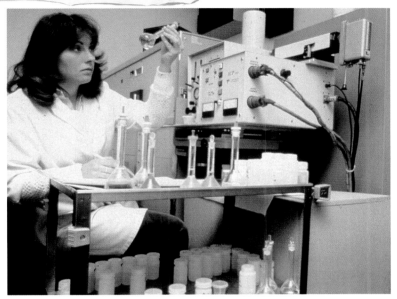

client satisfaction and loyalty, and are at the very core of Maxim's philosophy.

The Quality Assurance Program establishes a policy that focuses on continuous improvement through self-assessment to assure that services exceed client expectations. The quality control process incorporates documentation of conformance to written standards and procedures through a system of internal audits. Maxim believes that quality is the responsibility of every employee, not just the quality assurance/quality control staff.

MAXIM TECHNOLOGIES' LABS ARE FULLY EQUIPPED AND STAFFED WITH EXPERIENCED TECHNICIANS, SCIENTISTS, AND ENGINEERS, WHO OFFER QUALITY WORK AND RAPID RESPONSE TIMES (TOP).

MAXIM TECHNOLOGIES PROVIDES ENGINEERING AND CONSULTING SERVICES IN THE ENVIRONMENTAL, ANALYTICAL, METALLURGICAL, CONSTRUCTION MATERIALS TESTING, AND GEOTECHNICAL TESTING FIELDS (BOTTOM).

PORT OF HOUSTON

HOUSTON'S STATUS AS ONE OF THE WORLD'S FOREMOST international trade and energy centers is tied closely to the Port of Houston. The 25-mile-long complex of diversified public and private facilities is among the nation's top-ranked ports in foreign tonnage. For total tonnage, it is ranked second in the United States and seventh in the world. The city's economic lifeline, the

CLOCKWISE FROM TOP RIGHT:
THE PORT OF HOUSTON AUTHORITY'S
TURNING BASIN TERMINAL LIES AT THE
NAVIGATIONAL HEAD OF THE SECOND-
LARGEST U.S. PORT. THE TERMINAL,
WHICH IS LOCATED 50 MILES FROM THE
GULF OF MEXICO, OFFERS WELL-MAIN-
TAINED WHARVES, WAREHOUSES, AND
OTHER FACILITIES.

THE PORT OF HOUSTON AUTHORITY'S
FENTRESS BRACEWELL BARBOURS
CUT TERMINAL IS THE MOST MODERN
INTERMODAL FACILITY ON THE GULF
COAST. THE TERMINAL FEATURES FIVE
1,000-FOOT-LONG BERTHS, AND CON-
STRUCTION OF ADDITIONAL BERTHS IS
UNDER WAY.

THE HOUSTON PUBLIC GRAIN ELEVA-
TOR NO.2, OPERATED BY THE PORT OF
HOUSTON AUTHORITY, IS LOCATED AT
WOODHOUSE TERMINAL. EXPERIENCED
STAFF AND RELIABLE SERVICE ENABLE
THE ELEVATOR TO ENSURE SHIPPERS
OF THE GRAIN QUALITY THEY NEED.

Port is a gateway to some 250 other ports worldwide.

What is now the Houston Ship Channel was merely a shallow stream in 1836, when founding brothers Augustus and John Kirby Allen envisioned Houston as a great port. They were undaunted by barely passable waterways clogged with overgrown brush and numerous sandbars. While Galveston was sitting on the Gulf of Mexico 50 miles to the south and seemed a more suitable candidate, the Allen brothers were convinced that Houston's link to world commerce was contingent on the development of its own seaport.

The Allen brothers proved their dream was possible when the 85-foot steamship *Laura* called at their Main Street docks in 1837. Skepticism persisted, but as the city's commerce grew, other ships followed *Laura*'s lead. As humorist Will Rogers would note years later, "Houston dared to dig a ditch and bring the sea to its door."

A DREAM FULFILLED

Shortly after the Great Storm of 1900 flattened most of Galveston, Con-gress appropriated $1 million for the first dredging of a ship channel across Galveston Bay toward the confluence of Buffalo Bayou, and Houston's future as a deepwater port was secured. With the 1901 oil gusher at nearby Spindletop, the area's petroleum industry boomed, and the deepwater channel became a catalyst to its success.

The Harris County Houston Ship Channel Navigation District (now the Port of Houston Authority) was approved by voters in 1909. The channel was officially opened in 1914. More than

50 businesses were established along the Ship Channel in the 1920s. The economic boom was fueled by grain elevators, refineries, cotton compresses, fertilizer plants, and other businesses that were dependent on water transportation. Industrial development continued to increase as refineries responded to the nation's needs during World War II.

GATEWAY TO THE WORLD

Today the Houston Ship Channel winds 52 miles inland from the Gulf of Mexico through the world's

second-largest petrochemical complex (after Rotterdam). Led by a board of seven appointed commissioners, the Port of Houston Authority owns and operates public facilities and manages the Malcolm Baldrige Foreign Trade Zone. As the channel's official sponsor, it has been a prime force behind the growth of private industry all along the channel.

More than 5,400 vessels, 50,000 barges, and 200 steamship lines travel to the Port of Houston annually. The list of top foreign trade partners includes Mexico, Venezuela, Saudi Arabia, Algeria, Kuwait, the Federal Republic of Germany, the United Kingdom, Japan, Taiwan, Singapore, Egypt, Spain, Belgium, the Netherlands, Brazil, and numerous other nations.

Petroleum, petroleum products, and organic chemicals are among the top import and export commodities traveling to and from the port. Other major import commodities include iron and steel, crude fertilizers and minerals, and nonmetallic mineral manufactures. Top export commodities also include cereals and cereal preparation products, primary form plastics, and animal oils and fats.

Since 1986 annual tonnage figures have risen by 43 million—an exceptional increase that signifies Houston's leadership role in world trade. An ideal gateway to inland points, the Port is strategically served by four major railroads, about 130 motor carriers, and an extensive network of highways that provide distribution throughout the United States, Mexico, and Canada.

SUPERB PUBLIC FACILITIES

The Port of Houston Authority's public facilities include the Turning Basin Terminal, Fentress Bracewell Barbours Cut Terminal, Bulk Materials Handling Plant, Jacintoport Terminal, Woodhouse Terminal, and Care Terminal.

The navigational head of the Ship Channel, the Turning Basin Terminal is a complex of wharves, transit sheds, and warehouses stretching nearly eight miles. Fentress Bracewell Barbours Cut Terminal at the head of Galveston Bay is the most modern intermodal facility on the Gulf of Mexico. Quick turnaround makes it popular with shippers because drivers

can deliver containers, pick up new loads, and be on their way in less than an hour.

The Bulk Materials Handling Plant accommodates all types of bulk commodities with a $4.7 million ship-loading system. At Jacintoport Terminal, traders make use of three general cargo wharves. Woodhouse Terminal is a $15.25 million facility equipped to handle project cargo and bulk grain shipments. It is also home to Houston Public Elevator No. 2.

The Authority's new $4.5 million Care Terminal is a 35-acre general cargo facility that has a 35,000-square-foot wharf in addition to 45,000 square feet of warehousing; 3,000 feet of rail trackage; and a 916-acre paved marshaling area. In the Malcolm Baldrige Foreign Trade Zone, international goods are exempt from formal customs entry, restrictions, and taxes. The zone's multiple sites offer refrigerated storage for foods, bulk liquid storage, warehouses, and an end-finishing facility for steel pipes.

Economic impact studies confirm the critical role the Port of Houston plays both locally and regionally. The latest figures show the Port's public

and regional marine terminals generate $5.5 billion in business revenues each year. In addition, Port activity creates 196,000 direct and indirect jobs. Of the 53,000 direct jobs affiliated with the Port, approximately 80 percent are held by Houston and Harris County residents. The Port also generates $213 million annually in state and local taxes.

To ensure the Port's competitive edge, Port officials are working with local, state, and federal agencies and environmental groups to widen and deepen the Houston Ship Channel. The project will enlarge a 53-mile stretch of the channel from 400 to 530 feet and deepen it from 40 to 45 feet. By increasing the channel dimensions, safety is increased, the environment is preserved, and the Port will remain competitive and maintain its ability to serve Houston and the world.

CLOCKWISE FROM TOP RIGHT: WHARF 32, LOCATED AT THE TURNING BASIN TERMINAL, IS DESIGNED TO HANDLE HEAVY-LIFT AND PROJECT CARGO.

STEEL IS A COMMON CARGO AT PORT AUTHORITY WHARVES. IT COMES IN MANY FORMS, SUCH AS BEAMS, WIRE, AND NAILS.

THE PORT OF HOUSTON AUTHORITY'S BULK MATERIALS HANDLING PLANT IS LOCATED AT THE JUNCTURE OF GREENS BAYOU AND THE HOUSTON SHIP CHANNEL. THE PLANT IS OPERATED BY ECONO-RAIL CORP. AS A PUBLIC FACILITY.

THE METHODIST HEALTH CARE SYSTEM

F ROM THE STOCK MARKET CRASH OF THE 1920S TO THE initiation of organ transplant services in the 1960s to the rise of health maintenance organizations in the 1990s, The Methodist Hospital has maintained its place not only as one of the largest private nonprofit hospitals in the country, but also as one of the best. In 1995, after successfully adapting to both changing technologies and

harsh industry economics, the institution was one of only four Texas hospitals listed in *The Best Hospitals in America*.

Methodist's focus has recently moved beyond the walls of The Methodist Hospital with the provision of more preventive, primary, and home care services. The formation of The Methodist Health Care System—a network of area hospitals, health and medical centers, a primary care physician group, a secondary health maintenance organization, and a home health care agency—has allowed Methodist to take its high quality of care into communities outside Houston.

THE FOUNDING FAMILIES

T he Methodist Hospital was founded on December 31, 1919, when Dr. Oscar L. Norsworthy transferred his 90-bed Norsworthy Hospital to the trustees of the Methodist Episcopal Church. Norsworthy eventually sold the facility to the church organization for less than half its appraised value, thus beginning a generous philanthropic tradition that has continued through the present at The Methodist Hospital.

The Great Depression years were difficult ones for the hospital, but by the 1940s generous Houstonians saw to it that The Methodist Hospital remained debt free. Over the years, many of the city's prominent families have contributed substantially not only through monetary endowments, but also in land and volunteerism. The institution was offered property in the Texas Medical Center, and soon after, Hugh Roy and Lillie Cullen donated $1 million for the construction of a new hospital, which opened its doors in 1951.

The dedication and commitment of other donors is reflected in the hospital's numerous buildings. The Fondren/Brown buildings opened in 1968 to house cardiovascular and orthopedic services and research. The Fondren portion was dedicated to Ella and Walter Fondren, and the Brown portion was dedicated to the memory of Herman Brown. The Cullens' grandson, Corbin Robertson Jr., was largely responsible for the creation of the Neurosensory Center, which was completed in 1977.

The Scurlock and Smith towers took a prominent place in the Texas Medical Center skyline in 1980 and 1989, respectively,

a tribute to two families who have served for several generations on the hospital's board of directors. Also dedicated in 1989 was the John S. Dunn Tower, named in memory of the man who established the John S. Dunn Research Foundation in Houston to support biomedical, educational, and research activities.

QUALITY CARE AND AFFILIATIONS

A pproximately 40,000 inpatients and 1 million outpatients check into The Methodist Hospital each year, not only from the Houston area but also from all 50 states and

THE METHODIST HOSPITAL, TEXAS MEDICAL CENTER, HOUSTON (RIGHT)

THROUGH AN AFFILIATION WITH BAYLOR COLLEGE OF MEDICINE, MILLIONS OF RESEARCH DOLLARS ARE DIRECTED INTO PATIENT CARE AT METHODIST (BELOW).

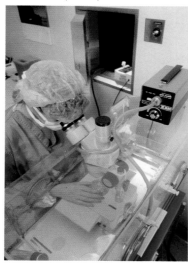

some 88 countries. Those who use the hospital's services have the benefit of both state-of-the-art technology and one of the most impressive medical staffs in the nation. The Methodist Hospital employs more than 4,000 personnel, and 58 of its physicians were cited for excellence in their fields in 1994 by the publication *The Best Doctors in America*.

As the primary adult teaching hospital for Baylor College of Medicine, The Methodist Hospital also has more than 900 staff physicians who hold concurrent faculty appointments. Directing millions of research dollars into patient care, the hospital has established a reputation for research and innovation in many medical fields. Among them are cardiovascular surgery, diagnostic and surgical treatments for aneurysms and cancer, epilepsy and treatment of children with epilepsy, bone and joint surgery, neurosurgery for the brain and spinal cord, and endoscopic surgery. Additionally, the hospital has collaborated with Baylor to develop one of the largest transplant centers in the nation.

The hospital also continues to be the practice home of famed heart surgeon Dr. Michael E. DeBakey. A pioneer in the field of cardiovascular surgery, DeBakey has practiced at The Methodist Hospital for 45 years. His many successes include the development of a series of Dacron artificial arteries, the first treatment of an aneurysm of the thoracic aorta, and the first successful coronary artery bypass. DeBakey also directed the first multiple organ transplant as well as the first successful partial artificial heart implant. Known to patients throughout the world, DeBakey has treated 60,000 people in Houston alone.

Throughout its history The Methodist Hospital has continued to promote the spiritual aspect of health and healing through its connection with the United Methodist Church. The hospital's pastoral staff serves as a resource for both patients and families who struggle with the difficult issues associated with illness. The hospital's clinical pastoral education program continually trains clergy for pastoral care ministry in the church.

FIRST IN HEALTH CARE

In order to remain current with the trends and evolving philosophies of patient care, The Methodist Health Care System continually seeks new and cost-effective ways to serve the community's needs. Through its contracts with managed care providers, The Methodist Hospital serves more than 1.6 million people in the greater Houston area.

The hospital also provides community care through direct patient care programs at many area health care clinics and agencies. The institution's health care capabilities also extend far beyond the neighborhoods of Houston through The Methodist Health Care System's network of affiliated hospitals. These include affiliates throughout Houston and Texas, Louisiana, Mexico, El Salvador, Greece, Guatemala, Honduras, Italy, Panama, Peru, Turkey, and Venezuela.

FROM HOME CARE PROVIDED THROUGH ITS VISITING NURSE ASSOCIATION, TO NONDENOMINATIONAL WORSHIP SERVICES IN ITS WIESS CHAPEL, TO THE LATEST IN HIGH-TECHNOLOGY DIAGNOSTIC AND TREATMENT TECHNIQUES, METHODIST STRIVES TO PROVIDE THE BEST CARE AND SERVICE IN A SPIRITUAL ENVIRONMENT OF CARING.

▶ JIM RANKIN PHOTOGRAPHY

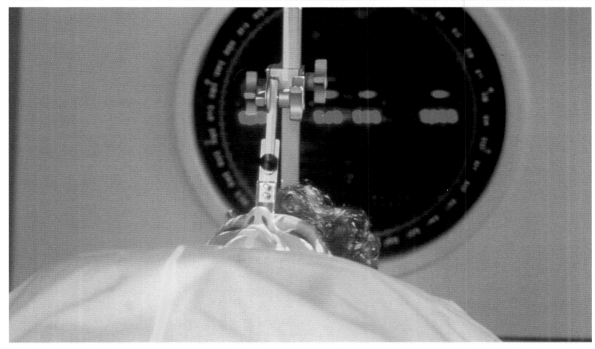

SOUTHWESTERN BELL

WHETHER HOUSTON CUSTOMERS NEED TRADITIONAL telephone service, lightning-quick data transmission, or the latest technology to make their businesses more efficient, they can count on Southwestern Bell—as always—for the best in telecommunications. ★ As Houston's leading communications provider, Southwestern Bell operates a reliable, modern network featuring the city's most extensive fiber-optic facilities and digital switching systems. Southwestern Bell provides a full range of services to help businesses work faster and smarter.

SOUTHWESTERN BELL'S DIGILINE^{SM} ISDN SERVICE MAKES IT POSSIBLE TO BRING IMPORTANT PLAYERS TOGETHER FOR KEY MEETINGS, NO MATTER WHERE THEY ARE LOCATED. ROOM-TO-ROOM VIDEOCONFERENCES INVOLVING GROUPS OF PEOPLE ARE AS SIMPLE AS DIALING UP ORDINARY VOICE CONFERENCE CALLS (RIGHT).

For example, integrated services digital network (ISDN) technology facilitates high-speed transmission of voice, data, and video services over a single telephone line. Using Southwestern Bell's DigiLine^{SM} Service, an employee at home or at the office can talk to a supervisor, send a fax, and transmit data to another computer—all over the same phone line and at the same time. Other DigiLine applications include videoconferencing and high-speed access to the Internet.

Southwestern Bell also offers SmartTrunk^{SM}, an ISDN service for large businesses as well as medical, financial, and educational institutions. With SelectVideo Plus^{SM}, customers can use—and pay for—only the bandwidth they need for video and data transmissions.

Advanced intelligent network (AIN) technology enables Southwestern Bell to customize new services to individual business needs. IntelliNumber^{SM} is ideal for businesses with several sites because all locations can be linked by a single telephone number. Customer calls can be picked up at the right location, making the business easy to reach and providing a competitive edge.

AIN technology gives businesses an effective response to disasters or outages. Disaster Routing Service can forward critical after-hours calls to workers at telecommuting locations or

SOUTHWESTERN BELL'S COMMUNICATIONS TECHNOLOGY CENTER (CTC) IS DESIGNED TO SHOWCASE THE COMPANY'S LEADERSHIP IN INTEGRATING TECHNOLOGY AND PROVIDING USEFUL APPLICATIONS THAT HELP BUSINESSES OPERATE MORE EFFICIENTLY. HIGH-TECH HANDS-ON DEMONSTRATIONS INCLUDE WORK-AT-HOME ARRANGEMENTS, DESKTOP VIDEOCONFERENCING, INTERNET ACCESS, AND REMOTE LOCAL AREA NETWORK (LAN) ACCESS (ABOVE).

elsewhere. Businesses can also respond to heavy call volumes during holidays and other peak periods.

Caller IntelliData^{SM}, another AIN service, arms businesses with valuable information about the patterns of calls they receive. Businesses can better evaluate advertising strategies, target certain customer segments, make more informed staffing and location decisions, and save money on market research.

AreaWide Networking^{SM} can economically link multiple business locations into a single communications network. This software-based AIN service supports future add-ons and eliminates the need for expensive equipment and maintenance.

Asynchronous transfer mode (ATM) technology allows voice, data, and multimedia information to be sent simultaneously over fiber-optic, copper, or coax lines. Through ATM, Cell Relay Service (CRS) provides high bandwidth for businesses that transmit data, video, audio, or imaging over a single broadband facility.

Useful though it may be, sophisticated technology is only as good as the people who support it. Southwestern Bell's greatest resource in serving Houston customers for more than 75 years is highly skilled, highly trained employees who have extensive experience in providing quality telecommunications.

To give customers the advantage of "one-stop shopping," Southwestern Bell operates retail outlets in the Houston area. Customers can purchase a wide range of telecommunications products and services at the retail stores or through kiosks in high-traffic locations.

While communications are constantly changing, Southwestern Bell believes one thing—the company's spirit of service must never change. It was Southwestern Bell's guiding principle when it formally began operating in Houston in 1920, and it's the core value that guides the company today.

The future of telecommunications in Houston looks exciting and promising. Southwestern Bell pledges its full commitment to be the customers' best choice for all their communications needs.

Jack Roach Ford

IN 1921 WHEN JACK ROACH SR. OPENED HIS AUTOMOBILE business in North Little Rock, Arkansas, Warren Harding was president of the United States and the Model T Ford was the hottest selling car in America. Business was still booming in 1929 when Roach moved his company to Houston—and ever since, the names Jack Roach and Ford have been synonymous in the Bayou City. ★ While

literally hundreds of other dealerships have come and gone in Houston, Jack Roach Ford prospered through three major wars and even a national depression. Celebrating its 75th year in 1996, the company remains a solid symbol of integrity and stability in the automobile business. And it's still family owned and operated.

"We're here for the long haul, not the quick buck," explains Jack Roach III, president. "We'd rather sell one person 15 cars in his lifetime than sell 15 people one car."

Jack Roach Ford was incorporated in 1947, the year Jack Roach Jr. became president at the age of 27. The company's first dealership was located in Harrisburg near the Houston Ship Channel, then the hub of the city. As Houston moved westward, so did Jack Roach Ford. In 1954 the company relocated to 3200 Bissonnet. That facility still serves as the company's parts and service department; and its current showroom and sales offices opened nearby on Southwest Freeway in 1978.

By then Jack "Bubba" Roach III had become president—like his father—at the age of 27. His brother Thad is also part of the operation, and his son, Jack Roach IV ("Quad"), and his daughter, Kimberly, are in training. Roach attributes the company's longevity to a philosophy that's simple, but strong. "Our people are the key," he says. Jack Roach Ford hires selectively, then keeps its 135 employees, including 25 sales associates, happy. "We don't make promises to our

people and not follow through," says Roach. As a result, he adds, "We've got salesmen who have been here longer than some other people have been in business."

GREAT OLD-FASHIONED SERVICE

Although Jack Roach Ford historically exceeds its assigned percentage of sales, "Being the number one volume store is not one of our priorities," says Roach. The company doesn't spend big money on advertising, preferring instead to put its energies into good old-fashioned customer service. This strategy has not only kept several generations of Roaches in business,

but brought multiple generations of some Houston families back for their cars.

The customer-oriented approach comes from the top. Roach personally thanks every customer who purchases a car. "There was a time when certain products were substantially better," he explains. "But in today's automobile market, there are so many good products, the difference is strictly the service and the dealership. We're not the best because we're the oldest," he adds. "We're the oldest because we're the best. And I hope we're here for another 75 years."

CELEBRATING ITS 75TH YEAR IN 1996, JACK ROACH FORD REMAINS A SOLID SYMBOL OF INTEGRITY AND STABILITY IN THE AUTOMOBILE BUSINESS.

SHELL OIL COMPANY

A S LONG AS AMERICANS HAVE OWNED CARS, THEY HAVE LOOKED to Shell Oil Company for gasoline and lubricants. The familiar scalloped logo has been fixed in the American consciousness since 1912—when the Royal Dutch/Shell Group in Europe sent a tanker filled with 1 million gallons of Shell Motor Spirit gasoline from its Sumatra refinery to Seattle—and established Roxana Petroleum

Corporation in Oklahoma with a mission to find and process U.S. crude oil. In the nearly 85 years since, Shell's growth has echoed the nation's progress.

Today FormulaShell® gasolines and other automotive products are marketed through nearly 8,600 retail outlets in 40 states and the District of Columbia. The company also produces petrochemicals that are used in a wide array of products including disposable diapers, laundry detergent, adhesive tapes, beverage bottles, and computer chips.

Shell's operations are divided into four primary businesses. Shell Oil Products

Company is a leading U.S. marketer of gasoline and an important supplier of aviation fuel, lubricants, and asphalt. Shell Chemical Company is a leading producer of base and downstream chemicals—primarily ethylene, propylene, and butadiene—used in packaging, coatings, detergents, footwear, pharmaceuticals, and appliances. Shell Exploration and Production Company is a leader in domestic oil and gas exploration and production, holding nearly one-third of the industry's deepwater acreage in the Gulf of Mexico. Shell Services Company's primary

purpose is to support the business needs of Shell Oil—such as computing operations, real estate management, supply chain management, and a wide range of accounting services—and to offer services to outside customers.

HOUSTON HISTORY

Shell's progress also echoes Houston's. The company opened a regional offshore exploration and production office in the Bayou City in 1924, and its presence grew with construction of the Deer Park Refinery in 1929. The Houston Chemical Plant, added in 1941, was the first in America to produce commercial butadiene, the critical building block of synthetic rubber.

These operations gave Harris County the largest concentration of Shell employees for years. In 1971 the company moved its corporate headquarters from Rockefeller Center in New York to Gerald Hines' One Shell Plaza, which faces Houston City Hall. At the time, the 50-story complex was the tallest building west of the Mississippi. The 1970s also brought the opening of the Westhollow Technological Center in west Houston, Shell's research center for gasolines, lubricants, detergents, elastomers, resins, and catalysts.

Roughly one-fourth of the company's 21,000 employees are based in Houston, and the company is an active participant in the community. Its sponsorship of the Shell Houston Open golf tournament raises some $2 million annually for local charities, and its employees and retirees serve as volunteers in dozens of area organizations.

SHELL OIL AND ITS EMPLOYEES, DEALERS, AND JOBBERS HAVE A LONG TRADITION OF INVOLVEMENT IN THE COMMUNITY, WITH ACTIVE PROGRAMS OF VOLUNTEERISM AND FINANCIAL SUPPORT THROUGHOUT THE HOUSTON AREA. WHEN MASSIVE FLOODS STRUCK SOUTHEAST TEXAS IN OCTOBER 1994, HUNDREDS OF SHELL OIL VOLUNTEERS RALLIED TO THE NEEDS OF THE COMMUNITY BY STAFFING SHELL RELIEF TENTS IN THE MOST AFFECTED AREAS (RIGHT).

SHELL OIL IS THE LEADING GASOLINE RETAILER IN THE UNITED STATES. ITS FORMULASHELL® GASOLINES ARE MARKETED THROUGH 8,600 RETAIL OUTLETS IN 40 STATES AND THE DISTRICT OF COLUMBIA (BELOW).

SHELL AND THE AMERICAN LANDSCAPE

Shell's contributions to American business and culture are the subject of a 5,500-square-foot public exhibit at the company's headquarters in Houston, titled *Shell and the American Landscape*. Celebrating the people, technology, and events that helped make Shell one of the nation's most successful companies, the exhibit's features include a five-foot-tall model of a turn-of-the-century cable tool drilling rig, a horse-drawn tank wagon, and a service station vignette featuring gasoline pumps that date from 1912. Other informative displays and interactive videos highlight Shell's technology, products, marketing, and commitment to the environment and the communities it serves.

Shell and its people have always had a zeal for discovery. During the 1930s and 1940s, Shell scientists synthesized 100-octane aviation fuel for military planes, created butadiene for synthetic rubber, produced high-quality toluene for explosives, and found a method of purifying penicillin. After World War II, Shell created new fuels and lubricants for increasingly sophisticated automobiles and airplanes.

By the mid-1960s Shell operated eight refineries across the nation. With dramatic growth in the 1970s and 1980s, the company led the industry not only in fuels development, but also in exploration sciences, offshore drilling and production technology, enhanced oil recovery, marketing networks, and proprietary chemical products.

Many consumers are familiar with Shell's FormulaShell® gasolines, but the company's chemical achievements are no less impressive. Shell became the largest manufacturer of epoxy resins, which are widely used for coatings and adhesives. Its agricultural chemicals have helped farmers increase their yields. Its KRATON® elastomers have applications in a wide variety of adhesives and polymer modifications. And its NEODOL® alcohols have helped make detergents environmentally safe.

Shell also has a long history of major field discoveries, and its leadership work in oil and gas production technologies has set numerous records for water depth and platform size. The company's most recent offshore achievements include the landmark tension leg platforms Auger and Mars. Mars was installed in 1996 in a water depth of 2,940 feet, a record depth in the Gulf of Mexico. Developed at a cost of $1.2 billion, it boasts a hull section that weighs 15,650 tons and a deck the size of two football fields. Mars is expected to produce 100,000 barrels of oil daily and 110,000 cubic feet of natural gas per day. Shell's next generation of gulf rigs is being designed to produce oil and gas from greater depths.

VISION FOR THE NEXT CENTURY

Shell faces a challenging landscape as the next millennium approaches. Since 1993 the company has been defining and living its mission, vision, and core values as it nears the next century. Shell's employees have set the bar high, envisioning Shell as not just a top-tier U.S. company, but the premier U.S. company. The firm's historic ability to adapt to change offers great inspiration for the next generation of company innovators.

HALLIBURTON ENERGY SERVICES

I N A CITY OF GIANT CORPORATIONS, HALLIBURTON COMPANY, parent of Halliburton Energy Services and Brown & Root, stands out as the largest private employer in Houston. The company and its nearly 14,000 local employees contribute more than $1.5 million and thousands of volunteer hours each year to local United Way charities alone. The combined capabilities of Brown & Root and Halliburton

Energy Services form the world's largest provider of energy products and services, and constitute a major player in other key industries.

The success of Halliburton Energy Services is based on its integrated approach and innovative technological solutions. Headquartered in Houston, the firm employs nearly 20,000 people worldwide and maintains major offices in Beijing, Buenos Aires, Caracas, Dubai, London, Moscow, and Kuala Lumpur. The company serves thousands of customers in more than 100 countries, including independent oil and gas companies, multinational companies, and national oil companies owned by foreign governments.

For decades, Halliburton Energy Services has been distinguished by research and development efforts that have resulted in

breakthrough technology for the energy industry. With an annual investment of more than $100 million in research and development, the company is committed to maintaining its role as a technology leader.

TECHNOLOGY SOLUTIONS

Halliburton Energy Services works with its clients to design unique solutions to meet customers' needs. Since pioneering the use of hydraulic fracturing, which has provided tremendous increases in the production of oil and gas, Halliburton has continued to lead this important area. The company's advanced technology gave rise to its FracPac services, which combine the use of specially designed fracturing and completion techniques to optimize completion and production in highly permeable formations. This service is particularly popular in the Gulf of Mexico where several Halliburton stimulation vessels are deployed.

Previously, it was only possible to detect certain features of a geological formation in a well. Now, using borehole imaging, it is possible to get a direct visual description of complex borehole features. Halliburton has devel-

oped an impressive borehole imaging tool and what is considered by many to be the most accurate visualization software in the industry. The circumferential acoustic scanning tool (CAST) and electrical micro imaging (EMI) systems allow oil and gas operators to visualize detailed and complex features of the well bore with a new degree of reality.

As the energy industry continues to advance in the development of environmentally sound exploration, drilling, and production practices, Halliburton Energy Services is also committing significant resources to solutions that are sensitive to the environment. As a result the company has developed the Sea Emerald Clean Burner, a special technology that nearly eliminates pollution generated by well testing.

INTEGRATED SOLUTIONS

Along with the latest technology, Halliburton provides an integrated solutions approach to its customers' projects. As a single integrated organization, Halliburton Energy Services provides a strategic advantage for its customers in an industry where adaptability, efficiency, technology, and economy are critical. The company incorporates performance incentives into many of its integrated projects, helping oil and gas companies achieve maximum efficiency and productivity.

As a global organization with an integrated approach to doing business, Halliburton Energy Services responds to customers' needs by offering them the best of both worlds—global solutions from a locally responsive company.

THE FIRM'S GLOBAL HEADQUARTERS IS LOCATED IN HALLIBURTON CENTER IN UPTOWN HOUSTON (BOTTOM LEFT).

A HALLIBURTON SPECIALIST COMPLETES A UNIQUE OPERATION THAT REQUIRES THE SIMULTANEOUS USE OF TWO COILED TUBING UNITS (BOTTOM RIGHT).

BROWN & ROOT

BROWN & ROOT HAS BEEN A VITAL PART OF THE HOUSTON economy since the day in 1926 when George Brown opened an office that became the center of the company's operations. Since then, Brown & Root has expanded to become one of the world's largest engineering, construction, and diversified services companies, offering its expertise to a broad range of industries through offices on six continents.

The company's global capability means that Brown & Root can handle the most complex geographical logistics. For instance, for a single demercaptanization project in Kazakhstan, Brown & Root performed engineering in London, completed fabrication in Houston, and involved suppliers from 12 countries spanning 20 time zones. Over the years Brown & Root has worked on projects as diverse as paper mills in the United States, ammonia plants in the Netherlands and China, offshore production platforms in the North Sea, and refineries in the Middle East.

TOTAL SOLUTIONS

Brown & Root's success can be found in the company's ability to provide clients with the gamut of services required to develop, renovate, operate, or maintain a facility—including engineering, environmental and financial consulting, procurement, project management, construction, and start-up. The company provides these integrated services for a variety of industries, including oil and gas, petroleum and chemicals, pulp and paper, and manufacturing. It also provides services to governments to support development and operation of public buildings, transportation, and water resources facilities.

The result of Brown & Root's total solutions approach in each market is that the job is done thoroughly, cost effectively, and on time. In just one example, use of an integrated team comprising owner and contractor personnel enabled one oil company to reduce the number of managers it assigned to a $600 million project by 80 percent. This ap-

proach eliminated duplication of effort and created an economical way to develop a subsea field that had gone untapped for 20 years.

COMMITMENT TO SERVICE

Regardless of whether Brown & Root provides one service or many for a customer, the company has proved that it can help lower capital and operating costs by providing solutions that are designed specifically for the job at hand.

For Brown & Root, a job done right means a job that has been designed to place special emphasis on life cycle costs, including the operability and maintainability of facilities. The goal is to provide customers with facilities that are productive and cost-effective not only during their development, but throughout their life cycle. In working with one customer, Brown & Root replaced the traditional hierarchical approach to maintenance management with self-directed work teams. The results included more than a smaller workforce. The firm completed

67 percent more work while improving employee satisfaction.

Although the diversity and technological sophistication of Brown & Root's services have skyrocketed since the early years, the company's commitment to clients remains the same. In the words of George Brown, "When we are working for somebody, we go all out. [The client] wouldn't ask us to do something yesterday unless he meant it. We try our best to do it. You don't get this sort of reputation unless your people have a lot of loyalty, pride, and drive."

UTILIZING THREE-DIMENSIONAL COMPUTER-AIDED-DESIGN CAPABILITIES, BROWN & ROOT DESIGNED A MULTI-LEVEL INTERCHANGE TO RELIEVE MASSIVE TRAFFIC CONGESTION ON THE SAM HOUSTON TOLLWAY AND INTERSTATE 10 (TOP LEFT).

BROWN & ROOT'S GREENS BAYOU FABRICATION YARD ON THE HOUSTON SHIP CHANNEL FABRICATED AND SHIPPED 14 PROCESS MODULES DESTINED FOR KAZAKHSTAN. FOR THIS SINGLE OIL PROCESSING PROJECT, THE FIRM PERFORMED ENGINEERING IN LONDON, COMPLETED FABRICATION IN HOUSTON, AND INVOLVED SUPPLIERS FROM 12 COUNTRIES SPANNING 20 TIME ZONES (BOTTOM LEFT).

WYNDHAM WARWICK HOTEL

TELEVISION TALK SHOW HOST PHIL DONAHUE ONCE ASKED Bob Hope, one of America's most widely traveled entertainers, "What is the prettiest place you have visited?" Without hesitation, the comedian replied, "In Houston, the view from the Presidential Suite of the Warwick Hotel." ★ The reflecting pond at Hermann Park, the red-tiled roofs of Rice University, live-oak-lined

Main Street, the sculptures on the Museum of Fine Arts' lawn, and the sparkling Mecom Fountains all create the breathtaking view that can be seen from the top floor of the Wyndham Warwick, Houston's oldest and most historic hotel. It's no surprise that the hotel has drawn such distinguished guests as Lauren Bacall, Frank Sinatra, Helen Hayes, Julia Child, Aristotle Onassis, Jacques Cousteau, royalty from around the world, and every American president who has held office in the last 20 years.

A MECCA IN THE MUSEUM DISTRICT

Built in 1926 as an apartment house, this 12-story Houston landmark was purchased by oilman John Mecom in 1962. The Warwick, he believed, offered an ideal location for guest lodging. While sheltered from the central business district, it is still centrally located just minutes from downtown Houston and the Texas Medical Center. It boasts of having as neighbors such notable

attractions as the Houston Zoo, Museum of Natural Science, Contemporary Arts Museum, Miller Outdoor Theater, and the eclectic boutiques of Rice Village.

"It was the height of the oil boom, and Mecom wanted Houston to have a hotel with European elegance and flair," Warwick General Manager Jeff Wagoner recalls. To achieve that vision, Mecom spent $11 million to enlarge and refurbish the structure. Another $11 million renovation—undertaken in 1989

when the Warwick became part of the Wyndham hotel chain—upgraded its guest rooms and public spaces.

Today a visit to the hotel takes guests back to 18th-century Europe. The paneling that lines the lobby once graced the walls of several elegant chateaus, including the home of Madame Murat, Napoleon's sister. A painting of the famed French emperor—given by his wife, the Empress Eugénie, to her lady-in-waiting—adorns a wall near the Imperial Suite.

THE ELEGANT NORTH AND SOUTH LOBBIES FEATURE TWO 5,000-PIECE CRYSTAL CHANDELIERS, IMPORTED FROM EUROPE (TOP RIGHT).

THE HOTEL'S 308 ROOMS, INCLUDING 48 LUXURY SUITES, OFFER PANORAMIC VISTAS OF THE HOUSTON SKYLINE (BOTTOM LEFT).

THE WYNDHAM WARWICK'S WELL-APPOINTED MEETING AND BANQUET FACILITIES RANGE UP TO 6,750 SQUARE FEET, OCCUPYING MORE THAN 18,000 SQUARE FEET OF THE ROOFTOP AND LOBBY LEVELS (BOTTOM RIGHT).

Above floors laid with Rose Aurora marble from Portugal, a centuries-old Aubusson tapestry depicts Diana, goddess of the moon and the hunt. Two 5,000-piece crystal chandeliers, imported from Europe, hang in the north and south lobbies. And an 8.5-foot-tall white faience stove commissioned for Emperor Francis Joseph of Austria stands in the Cafe Vienna.

Visiting social, professional, and diplomatic leaders who occupy the 2,600-square-foot Presidential Suite on the 12th floor enter through carved oak doors imported from the Coty palace in France. Glittering Baccarat chandeliers, a marble Louis XVI mantelpiece over a wood-burning fireplace, antique French oil lamps, and intricately carved Louis XVI wall paneling add to the apartment's elegance. And, of course, the Presidential Suite offers the imposing view that captivated Hope.

Although the hotel is already among the most beautiful guest sites in Houston, the Wyndham Warwick continues to undergo renovations. As Wagoner explains, "We're constantly infusing capital into the hotel to keep it appealing and fresh."

CATERING TO CLIENTS' NEEDS

The Wyndham Warwick is as functional as it is beautiful. The facility's well-appointed meeting and banquet facilities range up to 6,750 square feet, occupying more than 18,000 square feet of the ground and 12th floors.

The hotel's 308 rooms, including 48 luxury suites, offer panoramic vistas of the Houston skyline. "The fourth-largest city in the United States, Houston is incredibly fast-paced," Wagoner observes. "The views from our rooms help people understand how beautiful and relaxing it can be, too."

Considering its many amenities, it is no wonder that the Wyndham Warwick merited a

four-diamond rating from the American Automobile Association. From coffeemakers, hair dryers, and shower massagers to telephones with data ports and 25-foot cords, amenities in every room cater to guests' business and personal needs. An outdoor swimming pool offers cabana-style accommodations, and a modern, on-premise workout facility features stair climbers, rowing machines, Nautilus equipment, and poolside his-and-hers saunas. Valet parking and complimentary transportation to downtown and the Texas Medical Center are also offered.

The Wyndham Warwick's dining facilities serve food as rich as the surroundings. The highly acclaimed Hunt Room—with its English club setting—serves seafood, beef, and exotic game as well as a champagne Sunday brunch, offered on the 12th floor, while the Cafe Vienna specializes in contemporary Mediterranean cuisine. Light piano music accompanies the hors d'oeuvre and beverage service in the Lobby Lounge.

Wagoner suggests that one of the Wyndham Warwick's chief attributes is the friendliness of its staff. Because the management wants guests to feel at home, employees undergo a comprehensive two-day training program focusing on attentive, courteous, and efficient service. "We want to make sure our employees keep

these qualities in mind in their everyday dealings with our guests," Wagoner says.

"We do everything possible to make sure our accommodations please our clients, and we'll work with corporate representatives to arrange meetings that are consistent with their budgets," he concludes. "We live by our commitment to doing things 'the right way . . . the Wyndham way.' "

THE HIGHLY ACCLAIMED HUNT ROOM—WITH ITS ENGLISH CLUB SETTING—OFFERS A DRAMATIC FINE DINING ATMOSPHERE (LEFT).

THE WYNDHAM WARWICK HAS HOSTED GENERATIONS OF EXQUISITE WEDDINGS AND SOCIAL EVENTS (BOTTOM RIGHT).

AMERICAN AIRLINES, INC.

ON A SINGLE DAY IN 1995, AMERICAN AIRLINES HIT AN all-time record when it flew 377.3 million passenger miles in one 24-hour period—enough for more than 1,500 round-trips to the moon. It was a big day, but it was nothing this company couldn't handle with typical finesse. After all, American and its predecessor companies have been making aviation history in Houston and

around the world since the 1920s.

Among the company's early hallmarks were Charles A. Lindbergh flying mail for a small company that evolved into American Airlines, some of the first U.S. airmail routes, and the development and pioneering use of the DC-3 airplane. Other pioneering developments included Houston's first scheduled passenger flights, the country's first nonstop transcontinental service, the first transcontinental jet service, and the creation of the industry's first travel award program—AAdvantage.

American also led the way in direct services to passengers. The company introduced the world's first flight attendants in 1933, and the concept of airport VIP lounges was born with American's Admirals Clubs in 1939.

Today the company continues to set industry standards. Along with its regional partner, American Eagle, American flies to nearly 300 cities around the world with a combined fleet of more than 900 aircraft. Every day more than 100,000 American and Eagle employees serve more

AMERICAN AIRLINES' CURRENT FLEET INCLUDES EIGHT TYPES OF STATE-OF-THE-ART AIRCRAFT (TOP RIGHT).

ROBERTSON AIRCRAFT, TEXAS AIR TRANSPORT, AND COLONIAL AIRWAYS WERE AMONG THE MORE THAN 80 REGIONAL CARRIERS CONSOLIDATED IN 1929 AND 1930 TO FORM AMERICAN AIRWAYS, WHICH BECAME AMERICAN AIRLINES IN 1934 (BELOW LEFT).

THE REGIONAL AIRLINE TEXAS AIR TRANSPORT BEGAN OPERATIONS IN HOUSTON IN 1928 WHEN THE FEDERAL GOVERNMENT AWARDED IT A MAIL ROUTE BETWEEN HOUSTON, GALVESTON, AND THE DALLAS/FORT WORTH AREA (BELOW RIGHT).

than 220,000 passengers. With 4,000 daily departures, the company also handles about 291,000 pieces of luggage per day. But impressive numbers tell far less about this airline than does its colorful history, which is truly a record of service.

HOUSTON'S FIRST AIRLINE

The regional airline Texas Air Transport began operations in Houston in 1928 when the federal government awarded it a mail route

between Houston, Galveston, and the Dallas/Fort Worth area. After Texas Air pilots proved their acumen with delivering the mail, the airline began scheduled passenger service on the route, making American Houston's oldest and longest-serving airline.

The year before, Robertson Aircraft Corporation of Missouri sent Charles Lindbergh, its chief pilot, off to carry mail between St. Louis and Chicago. Robertson, Texas Air Transport, and Colonial Airways were among the more than 80 regional carri-

ers consolidated in 1929 and 1930 to form American Airways, which became American Airlines in 1934. One of Texas Air's leading executives, C.R. Smith, assumed the position of chairman as well as a leadership role that would guide American for more than 30 years.

A HISTORY OF SERVICE

When the postmaster general canceled and reallocated mail contracts in 1934, American lost its Houston routes temporarily. The airline held its ground by opening a sales office in Houston, while expanding its presence throughout the United States. By the late 1940s American had regained its routes and the airline began building its Houston service into what it is today.

American inaugurated flights between Houston and New York in 1956, and West Coast routes followed in 1961. A year later the company introduced jet service to Houston with its four-engine Boeing 707. By 1969 American was flying from Houston Intercontinental Airport, and service from William P. Hobby Airport was added in 1983. That same year American opened a direct link between Houston and Canada by introducing service to Edmonton and Calgary via Dallas/Fort Worth. American continues to serve Houston Intercontinental today, while its regional airline associate, American Eagle, serves Houston Hobby.

VISIONARY LEADERSHIP

The most recent developments at the airline have been guided by Robert. L. Crandall—chairman and CEO of American Airlines and its parent company, AMR—since 1985. Known as an industry trailblazer, Crandall is associated with numerous innovations that distinguish AMR and the companies it comprises.

The past few years have seen impressive growth in the operations of AMR's Semiautomated

Business Research Environment (SABRE). The world's largest computerized travel reservation and information system, SABRE allows more than 28,000 travel agencies in 74 countries to book everything from airline and theater tickets to hotel reservations and gifts on one system.

Just as SABRE revolutionized the travel agent's world, American's AAdvantage Travel Awards program forever changed air travel for customers. The industry's first frequent-flyer program, it is still the favorite, serving 28 million members. Services like these—along with American's dedication to safety, security, and service—have won the airline awards and honors from an array of magazines, trade publications, newspapers, newsletters, and special interest groups. American Airlines has been cited for excellence in everything from its wine list to its freight and cargo services— *Business Traveler International* and *Decanter* magazines both applauded American's wine list; *Dallas and Fort Worth Child* appreciated its family friendliness; London's *Daily Telegraph* rated its meals the Best Air

Travel Food Ever; and *Air Cargo News* noted American's outstanding freight and cargo services. In addition, Ivor Herbert, travel editor of London's *Daily Mail*, named American Airlines Best World Airline, and the readers of *Executive Travel* and the Zagat series of travel guides have dubbed American Best U.S. Domestic Airline and Best U.S. National Airline, respectively.

"Our continued success in this increasingly competitive marketplace is a daily challenge," says Crandall. "But American Airlines is staying with the things that got us here—excellence, innovation, safety, and quality service."

IN 1946 AMERICAN AIRLINES ACQUIRED MORE THAN 50 DC-4 AIRCRAFT, WHICH WERE CAPABLE OF CARRYING UP TO 50 PASSENGERS (TOP).

A PIONEER AIRMAIL PILOT FOR ST. LOUIS-BASED ROBERTSON AIRCRAFT CORPORATION, A PREDECESSOR OF AMERICAN AIRLINES, WAS CHARLES A. LINDBERGH, SHOWN A YEAR BEFORE HIS TRANSATLANTIC FLIGHT (BOTTOM).

ALLTEL Sugar Land Telephone

ALLTEL Corporation (NYSE:AT) is a leading telecommunications and information services company that is meeting the demands of today's rapidly changing telecommunications environment. ALLTEL subsidiaries provide local telephone service, cellular service, information services, and other related services. ★ The nation's fifth-largest independent telephone

company, ALLTEL operates more than 1.5 million access lines in 14 states. Two ALLTEL subsidiaries have a presence in the Houston area: ALLTEL Sugar Land Telephone (SLT) and Houston Wire and Cable (HWC) Distribution Corp.

ALLTEL Sugar Land Telephone: A Location as Sweet as Its Name

When Sugar Land Telephone was incorporated in 1931, few could have predicted that the rural hamlet of Sugar Land in Fort Bend County would become one of the nation's most dynamic business and residential communities. Located approximately 20 miles southwest of downtown Houston, Sugar Land was known primarily as the home of the Imperial Sugar Company. Until

Sugar Land Telephone was founded, residents in the Sugar Land community were unable to receive telephone service.

Things began to change in 1976, when development began at a huge master-planned community called First Colony. Twenty years later, Fort Bend County consistently ranks among the nation's fastest-growing areas, with a population base of 290,000. More than 17,000 new jobs have been created in this region since 1990, and, as a result, Sugar Land Telephone has experienced phenomenal growth. The company's service area now spans 77 square miles of primarily residential, commercial, and industrial property—including the 9,700-acre First Colony and a 1,000-acre business and industrial park.

The company was acquired by ALLTEL Corporation in 1993

and remains committed to providing customers with high-quality, state-of-the-art technology and equipment as well as first-rate service. ALLTEL Sugar Land Telephone is a dynamic progressive company poised to help customers take advantage of the latest breakthroughs in telecommunications technology, and its staff continually searches for ways to enhance service and help customers meet tomorrow's business telecommunications needs.

On the Cutting Edge

Sugar Land's business clients and residential customers demand the most technologically advanced telephone services available, and ALLTEL SLT delivers. It was the first company locally to use fiber optics to improve the qual-

ALLTEL Sugar Land Telephone's commercial customers can count on the company's competitive pricing to help them stay ahead in today's aggressive business markets. ALLTEL's service contracts for businesses include all materials and labor as well as routine inspection and preventive maintenance (below left).

As a leader in the conversion to digital technology and the first company locally to use fiber optics to improve the quality of voice transmission, ALLTEL Sugar Land Telephone provides quality, state-of-the-art service to its customers (below right).

ity of voice transmission and was a leader in the conversion to digital technology.

ALLTEL SLT remains on the cutting edge by offering the latest telecommunications services—digital transmission, Centrex, and integrated-services digital networks (ISDN)—to all customers in order to meet all types of business and residential needs. The company's computerized digital switching and fiber-optic lines offer unsurpassed transmission.

The company's remote diagnostics capability allows it to run extensive tests from its offices, often solving problems without the time and expense of service calls. At the ALLTEL SLT central office, experienced technicians continually monitor the status of customers' telecommunications services through advanced switching technology.

ALLTEL Network Management Center electronically monitors the network elements in the entire ALLTEL system to ensure seamless delivery of network services to the entire customer base—24 hours per day, 365 days each year.

UNSURPASSED SERVICE

The company's commercial customers count on ALLTEL SLT for competitive pricing to help them stay ahead in today's aggressive business markets. Service contracts for businesses include all materials and labor as well as routine inspection and preventive maintenance, all of which comply with the highest industry standards.

In most cases, preventive maintenance and routine remote diagnostics uncover problems or failures before customers become aware of them. However, if major failures do occur, the company will work around the clock, if necessary, to get systems back on-line as quickly as possible.

The company's employees also work hard to enhance life in the community they serve. They are active in numerous service and civic organizations, including the Rotary, Exchange, Lions, and Optimist clubs; the Chamber of Commerce; and the Economic Development Council. ALLTEL SLT staffers also volunteer as sports coaches, school tutors, and

literacy program aides, and, during the Christmas holidays, they gather gifts for needy families in the Fort Bend County area. At ALLTEL SLT, leadership—in technology, service, and community—is an everyday affair.

ALLTEL's HWC DISTRIBUTION CORP.

ALLTEL's HWC Distribution Corp., headquartered in Houston, is the nation's largest master distributor of specialty wire and cable, selling exclusively through electrical distributors. Founded in 1970 and acquired by ALLTEL in 1979, HWC boasts 25 years of experience in quality service and innovative leadership. HWC's products include shielded and unshielded power cables; flame-resistant cables; and high-temperature, precision-engineered cables, which are sold to the telecommunications, computer, petrochemical, pulp and paper, and steel industries.

HWC operates nine business locations comprised of a combination of eight sales offices and nine warehouses across the United States. Although HWC's primary business comes from the sale of wire and cable, the company also offers a line of rain-tight connectors and has exclusive distribution agreements with Redi-Rollers and Cable-Smart software.

Having built a significant local presence through Sugar Land Telephone and Houston Wire and Cable, ALLTEL is poised to lead Houston area residents into the 21st century with the most complete array of services available for telephone, cellular, and information services.

ALLTEL SUGAR LAND TELEPHONE'S UNSURPASSED SERVICE QUALITY INCLUDES EXPERIENCED, KNOWLEDGEABLE TECHNICIANS DEDICATED TO PROVIDING CUSTOMERS WITH RELIABLE, QUALITY TELECOMMUNICATIONS SERVICE (LEFT).

ALLTEL'S HOUSTON WIRE AND CABLE DISTRIBUTION CORP., HEADQUARTERED IN HOUSTON, IS THE NATION'S LARGEST MASTER DISTRIBUTOR OF SPECIALTY WIRE AND CABLE, SELLING EXCLUSIVELY THROUGH ELECTRICAL DISTRIBUTORS (ABOVE).

ANDERSEN CONSULTING

REPRESENTATIVES OF A MAJOR ENERGY COMPANY SETTLE into comfortable chairs at Oil 20-20 in downtown Houston—part of Andersen Consulting's Houston office. Through in-depth discussions with the center's expert staff on strategy, positioning, and processes, as well as demonstrations of innovative technology solutions, the group begins to envision how dramatic

improvements in their organization's performance can be made and sustained. One of seven business integration centers around the world affiliated with Andersen Consulting, this 4,000-square-foot multimillion-dollar facility with its state-of-the-art computer systems reflects the firm's commitment to helping its clients become more successful.

Oil 20-20 is just one example of the fast-growing capabilities that Andersen Consulting, a Chicago-based management and technology consulting firm, has experienced since 1989, when it became a separate unit of Andersen Worldwide. Several years later, Andersen Consulting has more than 38,000 employees located in 152 offices in 47 countries, and its revenues have risen from $1.43 billion in 1989 to

$4.22 billion in 1995. With 30 partners and more than 600 personnel, Andersen Consulting's Houston office is a key component of this network.

HELPING CLIENTS CHANGE FOR SUCCESS

Our typical clients are major corporations that want to know where they should be 10 years down the road and how they can get there," says Randell Thomas, Houston office managing partner. To assist clients in achieving their goals, Andersen Consulting does more than recommend solutions. It assembles knowledgeable teams of consultants who work closely with companies to make change a reality.

By aligning strategy, people, processes, and technology—a

formula the firm calls "business integration"—client-consultant teams help to position organizations for long-term success. "They help our clients understand where their industries are headed, how their business processes should be structured to support these directions, and how people can be empowered and technology employed to address their business problems and goals," Thomas explains.

Team members are drawn from four competency groups representing core skills required for true change. Consultants from the firm's Strategic Services Competency Group, for example, help clients develop business strategies and align their organization, business processes, and information technologies. These consultants also provide strategic direction for such functions as sales and marketing, supply chain management, logistics, organization structure, and information and technology.

"Our Change Management Competency Group, which helps clients achieve business and organizational transformation, is one of our fastest-growing fields," Thomas says. "It represents the people side of change. Our Process Competency Group helps define processes—or day-to-day workings—that are required to achieve business results." Finally, the Technology Competency Group applies innovative technology solutions to achieve clients' goals.

Thomas adds, "When it comes to change, we practice what we preach. We continue to restructure to meet our clients' needs." In 1994 Andersen Con-

HOUSTON PARTNERS GATHER TO DISCUSS FIRMWIDE ISSUES WITH MANAGING PARTNER GEORGE SHAHEEN, SEATED AT CENTER.

sulting reorganized its services around major industry categories—consumer, industrial, process, energy, and products; government; health care; financial services; telecommunications; and utilities. As a result, the firm's consulting teams have a keen knowledge of their clients' businesses. "This industry/competency focus," Thomas explains, "enables us to provide the best service for our customers."

Another of the firm's fast-growing areas is business process management—Andersen Consulting's term for outsourcing. This new business service—named Senergy—manages key business processes such as customer service, logistics/procurement, finance, and administration for multiple companies. Andersen Consulting believes this innovative service will allow companies to focus on their core business and improve productivity while cutting costs.

KNOWLEDGE CAPITAL IS KEY

Thomas attributes Andersen Consulting's success to its wide range of resources. "Through partnerships with third-party vendors, for example, we're achieving

our objective of becoming a total service provider," he says.

One such alliance is with SAP. One of the world's largest integrated business applications vendors, SAP has developed leading-edge software applications for both industry-specific and general purposes. "The fact that we have received the SAP Award of Excellence for outstanding customer service combined with the fact that we are the company exclusively assigned by SAP to demonstrate IS-Oil—an innovative software solution for the energy industry that we codeveloped with SAP—is testament to the strength of that alliance."

Andersen Consulting's most important resource, however, is its people and the knowledge they develop, share with each other, and transfer to clients. The firm is committed to having employees who are highly competent and who are dedicated to its customers' success. Each professional receives approximately 140 hours of training per year, which means an annual investment of more than $10,000 per professional. In addition, Andersen Consulting uses an extensive informational database called the Knowledge

Xchange. "This Lotus Notes-based system enables our consultants all over the world to share information," Thomas says. "That way, they don't have to reinvent the wheel. If a problem or issue arises, they can see how others in the organization have addressed it."

A recent issue of *Management Consultancy*, an industry publication, says Andersen Consulting "towers above the rest of the field and has distanced itself further from its rivals." The Houston office has played a pivotal role in this success and continues to be essential in helping Andersen Consulting fulfill its vision.

CLOCKWISE FROM TOP LEFT: RECENTLY HIRED ANALYSTS RECEIVE EXTENSIVE TRAINING DURING THE FIRST FEW MONTHS OF EMPLOYMENT AT ANDERSEN CONSULTING.

THE HOUSTON OIL CENTER OF EXPERTISE IS ONE OF ANDERSEN CONSULTING'S SEVEN BUSINESS INTEGRATION CENTERS LOCATED AROUND THE WORLD.

ANDERSEN CONSULTING LAUNCHED ITS NEW BUSINESS SERVICE—NAMED SENERGY—AT THE HOUSTON OIL 20-20 CENTER. SENERGY IS ANOTHER STEP IN THE FIRM'S GLOBAL STRATEGY FOR RESPONDING TO RADICAL CHANGE FACING THE ENERGY INDUSTRY.

Pepsi-Cola Company of Houston

YOUNG NORTH CAROLINA PHARMACIST CALEB BRADHAM could not have imagined the $25 billion soft drink empire he was creating when he mixed together kola nuts, vanilla extracts, rare oils, and soda water during the hot summer of 1898. Bradham created his drink as a cure for dyspepsia—or indigestion—and began marketing it as Pepsi-Cola in 1902. ★ Today Pepsi-Cola is the flagship soft drink of the world-wide conglomerate PepsiCo, Inc., which is the world's second-largest producer of soft drinks, largest snack food company, and largest restaurant system.

The Total Beverage Company

Houston's Pepsi franchise began when the North Carolina-based parent company appointed the Pepsi-Cola Bottling Co. of Houston—which was founded in 1939 by Carl Lockshin and Joe, Julius, and N.H. Darsky—to bottle and distribute the famous beverage. In 1951 Golden Age Beverage Company won the parent company's bottling appointment, opening the first local plant in 1955 at 6626 Gulf Freeway.

The franchise returned to Pepsi-Cola Bottling Co. of Houston in 1963. Union Bottling Works, owned by brothers George and Fred Pothoff, bought the franchise in 1967. The Pothoff brothers built the company's current headquarters on LaPorte Freeway, and some employees still remember the hoopla of its grand opening, which was attended by film star Joan Crawford, who was married at the time to the PepsiCo chairman.

PepsiCo, Inc. took control of

the operation in 1970. Ten years later, the firm added another plant to the Houston operation with the purchase of Conroe Packaging, Inc. In later years, the Houston territory expanded with the addition of Beaumont to its service areas.

Pepsi's Houston Market Unit now encompasses 18 counties in Texas and serves more than 10,000 stores from Huntsville to Galveston (north to south) and Dayton to Katy (east to west). Owned by Pepsi-Cola North America, part of the PepsiCo organization, the company employs 400 people and operates two plants. The Houston and Conroe plants together produce about 20 million cases of products annually. Bottled packages and fountain soft drinks are produced at the 135,000-square-foot Houston facility, while the Conroe plant produces all of the market unit's canned packages.

Pepsi-Cola produces 150 different products, including Pepsi, Diet Pepsi, and Mountain Dew soft drinks; Lipton's Brew Ready to Drink Iced Tea; All Sport Body Quencher; and 12 single-serve varieties of Ocean Spray fruit juices. In 1995 the company introduced Aquafina, a purified water that is the fastest-growing bottled water in Houston.

"The consumer is demanding more choices. We have introduced teas and juices to appeal to a wider variety of customers," says Houston Market Unit Manager Chris Van Horn. Aquafina water is as healthy as it gets. "It's more pure than spring water," Van Horn adds. About the only thing Pepsi doesn't produce is alcoholic beverages, making it very much a "total beverage company."

A LONG HISTORY

Pepsi's road to global success has been tied to food products since the Great Depression, when the company was owned by a candy manufacturer named Loft, Inc. Striving for a marketing advantage, Loft sold 12-ounce bottles—which were twice the size of those used by the competition—for five cents. Pepsi sales immediately jumped and have soared ever since.

Pepsi-Cola became a food industry giant in 1965 when it merged with Frito-Lay, a thriving snack food manufacturer, to form PepsiCo. Snack food sales now account for approximately one-third of PepsiCo's total annual sales. The company mushroomed again in 1977, expanding into food service with the purchase of 2,600 Pizza Hut restaurants (the company now owns more than 10,000) and the acquisition of both the Taco Bell chain in 1978 and the Kentucky Fried Chicken (KFC) chain in 1986. PepsiCo has continued to acquire other food service companies throughout the 1990s.

HOUSTON BOOSTERS

Pepsi-Cola Company of Houston is one of the city's most active charitable benefactors. A major corporate sponsor each year for the March of Dimes Walk America event, Pepsi also sponsors the Children's Festival as well as a summerlong program called Fun Day in the Park. In addition, the company is a major financial contributor to the city's soccer league, which was created by Mayor Bob Lanier.

In addition, many of the company's employees volunteer their time to participate in Junior Achievement programs. "Supporting the community where we do business is simply the right thing to do," says Van Horn.

PEPSI-COLA COMPANY OF HOUSTON'S BOTTLING PLANT OPENED AUGUST 1969.

UNOCAL CORPORATION

ONE OF HOUSTON'S MAJOR INDUSTRIES WAS CREATED WITH THE drilling of the world's first offshore oil well in the Gulf of Mexico in 1937. It was a project of Union Oil Company of California (Unocal), then a nearly 50-year-old firm with a reputation for technological innovation. As the years passed, the company known today as Unocal Corporation also became a pioneer in the development of oil and gas exploration and production in Southeast Asia.

Unocal is a fully integrated high-technology energy resource company and a leader in low-cost energy production. According to Jack Schanck, group vice president for worldwide oil and gas, "We are focusing our investment plans on integrated energy projects. This involves connecting growing energy markets to known resources and optimizing risks and returns through deal structuring, financial innovation, and strong alliances."

LOCAL HISTORY

Unocal was founded in 1890 in Santa Paula, California, by pioneers from Pennsylvania with an oil industry background. The firm opened its first Houston office in 1939 to serve its growing offshore interests in the Gulf of Mexico. As the company's focus expanded globally, its Texas office developed into an important hub.

When potential venture partners and other foreign visitors call on Unocal in the United States, they typically travel to the firm's Sugar Land offices just southwest of Houston, which serve as the management center for the company's worldwide oil and gas operations. This location also serves as headquarters for much of the company's new venture activities to identify new energy resources and develop market-to-resource opportunities.

Unocal's oil and gas production operations stretch across seven countries. In addition to exploring for and producing oil, gas, and geothermal energy, the firm manufactures and markets a wide range of petroleum products, agricultural chemicals, fertilizers, specialty metals, and carbon products.

Although the corporate headquarters remains in the Los Angeles area, the Sugar Land hub employs around 1,000 of Unocal's 12,500 staff—the company's largest concentration worldwide. "The future of our company will be shaped to a large degree by our Sugar Land employees," says Schanck.

HIGH TECH, LOW COST

Unocal's innovative spirit was born early with the introduction of the now-conventional technology of cementing oil well casings in 1905. The same year it drilled the first offshore well near Houston, Unocal also drilled the world's first well deeper than 11,000 feet in Rio Bravo Field, California. In 1953 Unocal built the first floating ocean drill rig and subsea wellhead. In Alaska the company built the world's first single-leg drilling and production platform at Cook Inlet in 1966 and the world's first drilling island on ice at Beaufort Sea.

In 1981 Unocal built and installed the world's largest single-piece platform jacket in the Gulf of Mexico. And in the stormy North Sea, the company drilled the first horizontal well in 1982 and installed the world's first reusable tripod-tower platform in 1986. Unocal also introduced the horizontal redrilling of wells in the North Sea, increasing oil reserves by more

PLATFORM CERVEZA, INSTALLED IN 1981 IN THE GULF OF MEXICO, WAS THE WORLD'S LARGEST SINGLE-PIECE PLATFORM JACKET.

BOB THOMASON

than 1 million metric tons in its offshore Netherlands operation.

Unocal is also a leader in developing technology for geothermal drilling, production, and reservoir management. Since 1974 it has been the world's largest producer of geothermal energy for electricity generation. The company now supplies geothermal energy of approximately 1,870 megawatts of installed capacity worldwide and operates major production facilities in Indonesia, the Philippines, and the United States—including Geysers Field, the world's largest geothermal power project, which has operated for more than 30 years in Northern California.

Unocal's applied technology has contributed to its status as one of the most efficiently operated oil and gas companies in the world. Since 1990 the company has ranked at or near the top of the industry in low-cost oil and gas production. By reducing drilling time in Thailand from more than 60 days per well in 1980 to eight days presently, Unocal has reduced drilling costs by 80 percent.

WORLDWIDE OPERATIONS

In 1890 our founders recognized the need to leave their early oil roots in Pennsylvania to head for the frontier areas of California. We're doing the same thing today, becoming a truly multinational company, as the frontiers have moved overseas," says Schanck.

"Unocal's low cost structure, flexible team-based organization, and strong operating history overseas uniquely position us to benefit from the rapidly growing natural gas demand in southeast and central Asia," says Schanck. Unocal has operated in Asia since 1962, when it was the first oil company to be awarded exploration rights in Thailand. With more than 70 platforms in the Gulf of Thailand, production there is expected to reach 900 cubic feet of gas per day in 1996, accounting for more than 65 percent of its total gas production and generating 35 percent of its electricity.

Unocal and Pertamina, Indonesia's state oil company,

signed one of the world's first production-sharing contracts in 1968. At Attaka, Indonesia's largest offshore oil and gas field, Unocal pioneered seafloor well templates and subsea completions, sophisticated drilling techniques that make it possible to recover oil from locations too distant to be reached from existing platforms.

The future for Unocal looms as bright as its past. Among other significant overseas projects are venture partnerships in a $1 billion natural gas project offshore Myanmar with production expected to begin in 1998, and a development project in the Caspian Sea with estimated oil reserves of 4 billion barrels, and recently signed agreements with Turkmenistan to transport oil and gas to new markets in Pakistan.

Unocal is well positioned for future growth. As Schanck describes, "This company combines the financial and technical strengths of a major international energy company with the speed and agility of a smaller independent one."

ASSOCIATED PIPE LINE CONTRACTORS, INC.

WHEN OIL AND GAS COMPANIES NEED PIPELINES BUILT through nearly impervious or impenetrable terrain, many construction firms are reluctant to attempt such projects. Houston-based Associated Pipe Line Contractors, Inc. is proud of building a reputation for tackling many types of challenging jobs. Now celebrating its 50th year, Associated has proved its mettle in some

of the world's most extreme climates and conditions, including bitterly cold tundra in Alaska, blazing deserts in Saudi Arabia, boggy Louisiana marshes, and treacherous mountain summits in Utah.

"We've always been willing to take on the most difficult jobs, and to make sure they are completed under budget and on time," says chairman and CEO Paul Somerville. Regardless of the challenges, the company's focus is straightforward: to move energy from where it is to where it needs to be. Since its founding in 1946, Associated has constructed more than 16,000 miles of pipeline overland and 5,000 miles of pipeline through shallow water and marshlands.

ONE OF THE WORLD'S MOST RESPECTED PIPELINE CONSTRUCTION FIRMS

Fifty years ago, in the first full year after the end of World War II, the U.S. economy was booming, as was consumer demand for energy, which was cheap, abundant, and readily available. Oil and gas were abundant from the marshlands of Louisiana to the rugged plains of West Texas, and in this environment, several pioneers of the industry founded Associated Pipe Line Contractors, Inc.

The company was innovative from the start, creating installation techniques and utilizing special equipment to improve pipeline productivity over difficult terrain. Near Anchorage, Alaska, the company constructed the first pipelines to be installed across Turnagain Arm—a body of water that records the second-highest tides (up to 38 feet) and currents in North America. Throughout its early years, the company built a reputation for excellence.

As energy exploration expanded worldwide, Associated's international capabilities grew

with the industry. The company was active overseas as early as the 1950s, working with European partners to build the first large-diameter pipelines in France, Germany, the Netherlands, Italy, Syria, and Turkey.

Today Associated Pipe Line Contractors' three divisions provide both international and domestic services. The Land Division offers international experience in constructing pipelines on all types of terrain, ranging from large-diameter cross-country projects to small-diameter projects in both open and congested areas. The Marine Division has built a solid reputation for performance in shallow water—including swamps, marshlands, estuaries, and bays—as well as in offshore waters, to depths up to 35 feet. The Specialties Division contributes additional capabilities in hydrostatic testing, rehabilitation (pipe upgrading) work, and pipe double-joint welding.

Aside from its corporate headquarters in Houston, the company operates a land and marine storage yard and warehouse on 27 acres near Morgan City, Louisiana, and has an office in Saudi Arabia. The company also has representation in more than 25 other countries around the world. Associated has completed projects for many of the world's major oil, gas, and petrochemical companies, as well as the U.S. Department of Energy and NATO.

NO JOB TOO CHALLENGING

Among Associated's other noteworthy projects have been some of the most challenging construction jobs ever undertaken, including

ASSOCIATED PIPE LINE CONTRACTORS, INC. INSTALLING 30-INCH PIPELINE IN OREGON (BELOW).

laying sections of the Alaska Pipeline System and the Kern River Gas Transmission pipeline. "We made the final weld on both," says Somerville. Associated completed a 147-mile section of the 800-mile 48-inch Alaska Pipeline System in 1977. Working at temperatures as low as 90 degrees below zero, the company's crews overcame mountainous terrain, hard rock, and dense forests while still preserving the area's delicate environment. This project was so successful that Associated was selected to perform the final phases of work along the entire length of the Alaskan pipeline.

Associated constructed Section 2 (64 miles) and Section 5 (81 miles) of the 900-mile 36-inch Kern River Gas Transmission pipeline. The route of Section 2 took it over the summit of the rugged Wasatch Mountains in Utah. This land—some of the most treacherous terrain ever faced by a pipeline construction company—is marked by steep ravines, rushing streams, and narrow mountain passages. Associated had to complete the project within one season to avoid winter snows. Stringing trucks hauling joints of pipe had to be towed up and let down the steep slopes by bulldozers and winch cables. In the steepest areas the pipe joints were hauled and strung by large helicopters.

Commitment to Safety and Environmental Protection

Two important commitments that Associated makes on every project that it undertakes are reflected in the company's proven job safety and environment protection records. The company is totally dedicated to safety on and off the job, and this commitment to safety is reinforced by Associated's top management. It is the company's safety policy to conduct all of its operations in a manner that results in the highest protection for its employees and the general public.

Compliance with environmental regulations presents the biggest challenge for pipeline contractors today. For every Associated project, Somerville notes, "We choose the right people and train them to work with local and federal environmental agencies on a cooperative basis. We always go the extra step with the agencies, and with the landowners, whether it's cleaning up mud from the roads, helping to get scared cats out of trees, or planting grass where it's necessary." Associated is very proud of its record of protecting the environment during all of its construction activities. The company has worked successfully in the very sensitive tundra of Alaska and in the wetlands as well as other ecologically sensitive areas of the lower 48 states. During the installation of pipelines through these areas, Associated has maintained a constant awareness of the need to protect the natural habitat and native wildlife of these areas and to restore these areas to their original condition as soon as possible after pipeline installation.

With more than 50 years of experience constructing pipeline in some of the world's most rugged areas, Associated Pipe Line Contractors, Inc. has built a solid foundation. The company is well positioned to tackle future pipeline construction projects that will be needed to serve oil and gas requirements around the world.

CLOCKWISE FROM TOP LEFT: ASSOCIATED PIPE LINE CONTRACTORS' MARINE PIPE-LAYING OPERATIONS FOR U.S. DEPARTMENT OF ENERGY.

THE COMPANY COMPLETED SECTIONS OF THE ALASKA PIPELINE SYSTEM.

WORKERS WELD 36-INCH PIPE IN UTAH.

FUGRO-McCLELLAND

FOUNDED IN HOUSTON IN 1946, McCLELLAND Engineers merged in 1987 with Fugro to become one of the largest international multidisciplinary consulting firms providing geotechnical, environmental, and surveying services. As Houston grew into a large international city, Fugro-McClelland mirrored that growth and developed a small geotechnical firm into a multinational

consulting firm with offices in more than 40 countries.

As home to more than 5,000 energy-related firms, energy has often been called the "Big Wheel" of Houston's economy. As a consultant to most of the area's oil, gas, and pipeline companies, Fugro-McClelland has performed thousands of studies worldwide. When the energy industry begin to flourish, Houston's infrastructure was forced to grow with it. Roads, bridges, airports, buildings, and dams were all required as part of this massive expansion. Although geotechnical engineering was a relatively new discipline, the company became the first geotechnical firm in the Southwest to help Houston companies and city and county governments lay the foundation for the city's infrastructure.

The firm prides itself on performing the geotechnical services for many of Houston's landmark projects, including the Johnson Space Center, the 75-story Texas Commerce Tower, and the George R. Brown Convention Center. Fugro was also involved with the Sam Houston

Toll Road and major runways at both Houston airports.

This groundwork for Houston's onshore energy business preceded the drilling of the world's first offshore wells in the Gulf of Mexico in 1947. That same year, the company performed geotechnical analysis for the first offshore oil and gas platform for Chevron. Since then the company has performed thousands of geotechnical/geoscience studies worldwide. Projects such as Conoco's first deepwater tension-leg platform in the Gulf of Mexico and Shell's first platform—situated in more than 1,000 feet of water—have made Fugro a household name in the marine industry.

As the need for environmental protection increased, Fugro expanded its base of services to include air quality, asbestos abatement, soil and groundwater remediation, and underground storage tanks. Visible projects, such as the remediation of all underground tanks for the city of Houston, established Fugro as a leader among Houston's environmental firms. The firm pioneered deve-

lopment of cone penetration technology (CPT) for environmental studies. This technology has now become the preferred method for conducting subsurface site investigations.

In 1991 Fugro acquired John E. Chance and Associates of Lafayette, Louisiana. Chance was the largest supplier of survey services in the Gulf of Mexico. Several other recent acquisitions have made Fugro the largest supplier of survey positioning services in the world.

Fugro offers several portable Geographic Information System (GIS) tools for data acquisition. TruckMAP™, introduced in 1994, is a device that adopted On-the-Fly software into its mobile mapping/land information data acquisition system. This system combines real-time positioning with high-resolution imaging capacity to identify, position, and record data via a small truck or van. FLI-MAP™ offers these same capabilities by helicopter. This system provides data acquisition for topographic mapping/profiling and is therefore ideal for pipeline mapping and corridor projects. Fugro's Omnistar system, introduced in 1994, is enabled by a Differential Global Positioning System (DGPS) and incorporates a network of 10 DGPS reference stations at permanent locations throughout North America.

Fugro-McClelland is pleased to celebrate its 50th anniversary in 1996 as a Houston company whose success has been tied to the growth of the city's energy and space industries. The company is committed to remaining one of Houston's technological leaders for many years to come.

FUGRO-McCLELLAND PERFORMED THE GEOTECHNICAL STUDIES FOR MANY OF THE SKYSCRAPERS THAT GRACE HOUSTON'S SKYLINE.

BAXTER & SWINFORD REALTORS

WHAT DOES IT TAKE TO SUSTAIN A REAL ESTATE business for more than four decades? "Strict adherence to the highest of ethical principles," says Baxter & Swinford's CEO, Ray Baxter. Founder of the oldest independent real estate company in Houston, Baxter opened his doors for business in 1959. The following year, he incorporated his growing business with

Sam Swinford, creating Baxter & Swinford Realtors.

GROWING WITH A UNIQUE CITY

Baxter moved to Houston from West Texas and, after college, determined that he would become involved with helping people with their biggest lifetime investments. After Swinford's death in 1985, Baxter's daughter, Kelly Baxter Stewart, worked side by side with her father, and today she serves as the company's president. "Although Houston is the fourth-largest city in the nation, it is unique in that its sprawling 250 square miles include countless, yet convenient, self-contained communities and townships," says Stewart.

Ray Baxter once called his Memorial location "a little field office." Today the company's corporate headquarters is an elegant contemporary building located at Memorial and Kirkwood, which houses dozens of offices. "In 1959 this land was nothing more than pasture," he says, "and the average house sold in Memorial for $27,500. Now the same house sells for 10 times that amount."

Baxter & Swinford operates strategically located offices in the Houston area with more than 50 dedicated sales associates. Both Baxter and Stewart are active within the Houston Association of Realtors and have served on numerous committees throughout the years. Baxter served as president of the association in 1983. Each year, he and his daughter support the efforts of the National Real Estate Political Action Committee, of which both are life members.

"My father founded our company on the principles of expertise and integrity, with the belief that one cannot work without the other," says Stewart, "and his reputation in the Houston real estate community is revered."

RELOCATION SERVICES

Baxter & Swinford became part of the International Relocation Network (RELO) in 1967, and has been awarded each year as one of its Top 20 Producers. Comprised of 1,000 independent real estate brokers, RELO serves 14,000 communities coast to coast as well as 22 foreign countries. With 40,000 sales associates, the organization's collective knowledge and skill facilitated 1 million transfers and $67 billion in home sales in 1995. Last year Stewart served as RELO's 35th president, the first second-generation president in the organization's history. She proudly followed her father's footsteps, as he was RELO's president in 1977.

Additionally, Baxter & Swinford enjoys a highly acclaimed corporate department, which was recently recognized nationally by the Associates Relocation Management Company, Inc. for excellence in home-finding services. "The list of corporations who place their trust in our ability to meet the needs of their employees is vast. Every transferee is offered total professionalism and guidance by our staff and talented relocation specialists," says Baxter.

The team spirit at Baxter & Swinford goes far beyond the day-to-day business of real estate, and is evident through active participation in charitable and civic organizations. Whether sup-

FOUNDER AND CEO RAY BAXTER AND HIS DAUGHTER, PRESIDENT KELLY BAXTER STEWART, ENJOY WORKING TOGETHER TO ENSURE THE CONTINUING SUCCESS OF THE FIRM (ABOVE).

THE BAXTER & SWINFORD EAGLE HAS BEEN LANDING ON HOUSTON PROPERTIES SINCE 1960 (LEFT).

porting hungry children, abused children, or adult cancer victims, the enthusiasm for each cause is unparalleled by Baxter & Swinford's associates. "We are a family within a family," says Stewart, "and we are truly blessed."

Turner Collie & Braden Inc.

It's nearly impossible to live in Houston without being affected by the work of Turner Collie & Braden Inc. (TC&B). Established locally in 1946, TC&B is one of the city's oldest civil engineering and project management firms. The company has been involved in the planning and design of major projects that touch every aspect of life in the Bayou City: toll roads and highways, Houston Inter-

continental Airport (IAH), master-planned communities, public schools, and water and wastewater treatment plants.

"TC&B grew up with Houston," says TC&B President James R. "Jim" Royer, P.E. "We derived our strength from Houston and the opportunities it presented." Celebrating its 50th anniversary in 1996, TC&B has maintained relationships with blue-ribbon clients throughout changes in the city's political leadership and economy. The firm survived tough times locally by expanding its vision worldwide. A 1996 merger with one of the largest public infrastructure consulting organizations in the nation further ensures TC&B's stability for the next 50 years and beyond.

Multidisciplinary

TC&B's comprehensive engineering and project management services are offered through its four divisions: aviation, transportation,

public works, and land development. The firm's clients are located throughout the United States, Latin America, the Middle East, and the Pacific Rim.

The Aviation Services Division provides innovative planning, design, and construction oversight of airport and airfield

◄ T.C.B. / MCNAIR

facilities. TC&B's list of aviation projects stretches from Texas to Taipei, Taiwan. Closer to home, the firm developed the master plan for expansion phases of IAH, designed taxiway and service bridges, and currently is involved in planning passenger terminals there. TC&B also provided master planning and other services at Dallas/Fort Worth International Airport. At Denver International Airport, the firm played a major role in site development and engineering.

TC&B's Transportation Division earned its reputation for fast-track design and management of major highway projects such as Grand Parkway and Hardy Toll Road. When completed, the Grand Parkway will provide Houston's third highway loop, traversing 170 miles through seven southeast Texas counties. TC&B transportation engineers designed portions of Hardy Toll Road while coordinating work on that project by 21 other firms. Hardy Toll Road was delivered two months early and 10 percent under budget.

The Public Works Division

At the Southland Paper Mill near Houston, TC&B initially designed a 10 million-gallon-per-day (MGD) surface water treatment facility. Subsequently, the firm prepared plans and specifications for an additional 10-MGD train (top right).

One of the main plazas of the Hardy Toll Road makes an impressive display under a full Texas moon. TC&B served as general engineering consultant on the toll road, managing the work of 21 other design firms (below).

established a strong practice from the firm's earliest days, and has provided engineering services for the planning, design, and construction of major infrastructure projects for the City of Houston and surrounding counties. Those projects include wastewater and water treatment facilities, drainage and storm systems, environmental services, and water resource planning for a wide range of clients, both foreign and domestic. Locally, the division recently participated in Project Renewal, a $371 million improvement program for the Houston Independent School District.

For more than three decades, TC&B's Land Development Division has helped clients comply with the many jurisdictional controls and regulations involved in site development: water, sewage, drainage, dry utilities, and environmental. "We've worked with all of the state's premier land developers including Friendswood Development, American General, and Del Webb," Royer recalls. TC&B also provides site development services for smaller projects such as restaurants, small office buildings, factory outlet centers, and mixed-use facilities.

EXPERT STAFF

Of approximately 350 permanent TC&B employees, 100 are professional engineers who practice in the disciplines of civil, chemical, mechanical, structural, electrical, and sanitary engineering. TC&B also maintains a full complement of professional support personnel, including economists, technical editors, certified environmental planners, biologists, hydrologists, and information processing specialists.

The ethnic and gender makeup of TC&B's staff embraces the diversity of the urban areas in which the firm operates. More than 45 percent of TC&B's employees are minorities; 22 percent of TC&B's engineers are minorities, compared with

17 percent industrywide.

In addition to its personnel, TC&B is truly distinguished by its clients. Annually more than 75 percent of the firm's new projects originate from existing customers. Client satisfaction is a cornerstone of the firm's operating philosophy, and that emphasis is reflected in the high percentage of repeat business. Royer acknowledges that, in a service industry, one of the critical factors separating winners and losers is how quickly, how well, and how sincerely a firm responds to its clients.

The firm's founders had the foresight to transfer ownership to help the company grow. Original partners Nat Turner and Bob Collie added Bob Braden as an owner in 1965.

Subsequently, additional employee shareholders were added. Today TC&B is a wholly owned subsidiary of the Los Angeles-based AECOM Technology Corporation, also an employee-owned firm. With the merger, TC&B joined a family of nationally known companies in the civil engineering and architectural design industries.

"Now we not only have access to new technologies but, through our sister companies, to experienced people who have applied those technologies successfully," Royer comments. "The merger enhances the capabilities TC&B developed during its first 50 years, giving us expanded potential for growth into the 21st century."

CLOCKWISE FROM TOP:
AT HOUSTON INTERCONTINENTAL AIRPORT, A PLANE CROSSES ONE OF THE SIX TAXIWAY BRIDGES DESIGNED BY TC&B ENGINEERS.

MOTORISTS CROSS ONE OF TWO PARALLEL WEST LAKE HOUSTON PARKWAY BRIDGES DESIGNED BY THE FIRM'S TRANSPORTATION ENGINEERS.

A NEW ECOSYSTEM DEVELOPS AT THE LARGEST DEMONSTRATION MARSH SITE EVER DESIGNED IN THE UNITED STATES. TC&B ENVIRONMENTAL SCIENTISTS PARTICIPATED IN THE CREATION OF THIS BENEFICIAL USE OF DREDGE MATERIAL, A BY-PRODUCT OF THE DEEPENING OF THE PORT OF HOUSTON.

WHEN DR. MAVIS P. KELSEY FOUNDED HOUSTON'S first multispecialty group practice in 1949, the concept of prepaid medical care may have seemed unthinkable to most people. But his enlightened leadership gave Kelsey-Seybold Clinic a definite edge in today's dynamic health care marketplace. ★ Embracing change as a means of providing better value

to health care buyers—be they individuals, employers, or insurers—Kelsey-Seybold focuses on quality seamless health care with a good balance of primary care physicians, specialists, and other necessary medical services. "Whether people come here for routine care or a complicated problem, we have the resources to get them to the right place," says J. Michael Condit, M.D., F.A.C.P., chairman of the Board of Directors.

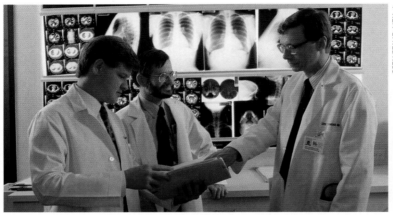

▼ KEN CHILDRESS

KELSEY-SEYBOLD'S TEXAS MEDICAL CENTER LOCATION AND ITS 27 OTHER NEIGHBORHOOD CLINICS THROUGHOUT THE HOUSTON AND BEAUMONT AREAS SERVE MORE THAN 300,000 PATIENTS EACH YEAR (ABOVE RIGHT).

KELSEY-SEYBOLD HAS INVESTED IN STATE-OF-THE-ART IMAGING SERVICES TO AID IN THE DIAGNOSIS AND TREATMENT OF INJURIES AND DISEASE. ALL TESTS ARE PERFORMED BY REGISTERED AND LICENSED TECHNOLOGISTS AND ARE INTERPRETED BY BOARD-CERTIFIED RADIOLOGISTS (ABOVE LEFT).

VALUE DYNAMICS

The original Kelsey-Seybold Clinic was located on Fannin Street, not far from the organization's current Texas Medical Center headquarters. Far ahead of today's managed care trend, Kelsey-Seybold became the first contract medical service provider for NASA in 1966. In fact the organization still serves four NASA locations across the United States.

Although Kelsey-Seybold operated two outpatient clinics in Houston even before the advent of managed care in 1983, explosive growth began soon after that. Today the clinic serves more than 300,000 patients at 28 locations across Houston and Beaumont, about 8 percent of the population. And 65 percent of those patients are pre-

paid, resulting in healthy annual revenues of $170 million.

Kelsey-Seybold's 270-member medical staff have the support of 1,400 other employees, and active contracts with 500 physicians not in the group also add value to the service.

A major factor in Kelsey-Seybold's strength is the ready availability of its specialists. "We want to make sure the linkage between hospitals, purchasers, and physician/providers is strong," says Managing Director Mike Fitzgerald. "We provide it all, like a purchasing agent, guiding you through the whole system of opportunities."

Yet primary care has become increasingly important as a value factor and now represents 60 percent of Kelsey-Seybold's business. "We're trying to be good stewards of the health care dollars being spent," says Fitzgerald. "In everything we do, we have to ask the patients, 'How are we doing?' It's not just about cutting costs, but whether a patient sees the service as the same or better each time he or she visits."

With studies funded through the Kelsey-Seybold Foundation, the organization is also focusing substantial research on ways to improve outcomes for chronic diseases such as diabetes and hypertension. "Every time you can improve a patient's outcome, it costs less. You're reducing the number of visits to specialists, with more emphasis on primary care," says Fitzgerald.

A Healthy Work Environment

Kelsey-Seybold's patients are happy, Condit suggests, because its medical professionals are also happy. "We encourage diversification," he says, "and we provide upward mobility for people who want it." Many of Kelsey-Seybold's medical staff hold appointments at the universities of the Texas Medical Center, and within the organization, there are myriad opportunities for researchers, administrators, and practicing physicians.

"Kelsey-Seybold's physician-led focus fosters a three-way partnership between payers, hospitals, and physicians," adds Fitzgerald. "The key to our success is organized collaborative care—a formal process where physicians and administrative staff support each other."

Changes in the market have meant major changes in the way physicians do business. "It's been a cottage industry, with broad autonomy. These days, there's no such thing as an autonomous physician," explains Condit. "You've got to interact and you have to be able to compete for big blocks of patients. Our multispecialty group focus gives us enough manpower to get the job done clinically as well as administratively."

Kelsey-Seybold allows physicians to focus on good practice, while the collaborative leadership watches the business. "Our doctors can practice medicine the way they think it should be done. We don't have to make 800 calls for approvals," Condit adds.

Kelsey-Seybold does most of its own insurance approvals, whereas a freestanding physician may have to deal with 40 different companies, says Fitzgerald. "In a collective environment, we can remove hurdles, so it feels like the old fee-for-service days.

"There's not much difference, from the physician's perspective, in how medicine is practiced here versus 20 years ago," he adds. "As a matter of fact, the fourth doctor to sign on with Kelsey-Seybold in the very beginning is still practicing here."

Future Vision

Kelsey-Seybold's top 150 physicians and administrators recently drafted mission, vision, and value statements to take the organization into its next 50 years. In addition to delivering comprehensive quality medical services and providing exceptional personal and professional growth opportunities for staff, the clinic has set its sights even further than Houston with the goal of creating a nationally recognized, integrated managed care delivery system.

Fitzgerald suggests that the medical industry is undergoing the same kinds of changes the oil, gas, and banking industries did in the 1980s and Kelsey-Seybold is positioned to take advantage of it. Condit concurs. "If something is going to succeed in today's health care market," he says, "this is it."

▶ KEN CHILDRESS

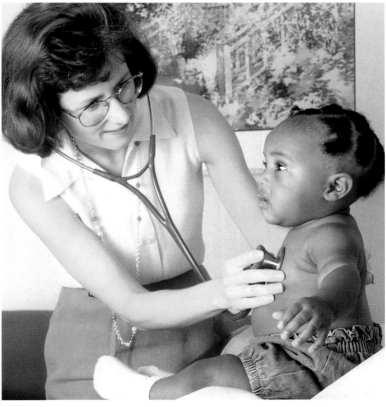

▶ KEN CHILDRESS

SENIOR PATIENTS RECEIVE ONE-ON-ONE ATTENTION AND PERSONALIZED CARE AT KELSEY-SEYBOLD CLINIC. WHAT'S MORE, THE CLINIC PROVIDES A FULL SPECTRUM OF SERVICES DESIGNED TO CARE FOR THEIR SPECIAL NEEDS (LEFT).

GOING TO THE DOCTOR DOESN'T HAVE TO BE A FRIGHTENING EXPERIENCE. KELSEY-SEYBOLD'S PEDIATRICIANS ARE TRAINED TO WORK WITH CHILDREN TO MAKE THEM FEEL AT EASE DURING THEIR VISITS WITH THE DOCTOR (LEFT).

COMPACT DISCS. CELLULAR TELEPHONES. HOME SHOPPING networks. Electronic auto alarms. As recently as 20 years ago, they were science fiction. Today digital technology is everywhere, and much of it originates from a Lone Star company that got its start in the oil industry: Texas Instruments (TI). ★ For more than 45 years TI has been a leading provider of the products, systems, and

technologies driving the information revolution. These technologies have already vastly changed the way people live, learn, work, and play. And as the global network continues to expand, TI's next generation of innovations will no doubt enable consumers to do even more with products that—at this point—most people can only imagine.

OVER THE YEARS, TI HAS HELPED PIONEER SOME OF THE 20TH CENTURY'S MOST IMPORTANT DEVICES, AND THE HOUSTON SITE IS BUILDING SOME OF THE DEVICES THAT WILL REVOLUTIONIZE OUR WORLD WELL INTO THE NEXT CENTURY (RIGHT).

LEADING THE DIGITAL REVOLUTION

TI's tradition of advanced ideas was born in Dallas in 1930 when Doc Karcher and Eugene McDermott chartered Geophysical Services, Inc. (GSI) to utilize Karcher's formula for reflective seismology in oil exploration. By 1951 GSI's capabilities had evolved beyond the oil patch, and TI was launched.

Still headquartered in Dallas, TI employs 60,000 persons, with sales and manufacturing facilities across 30 countries. A Fortune 500 company, its annual revenues topped $13 billion in 1995.

Over the years, TI has

▼ CHRIS KUHLMAN

TI'S HOUSTON SITE MAKES SOME OF THE WORLD'S FASTEST COMPUTER CHIPS—THE ENABLERS BEHIND SOME OF TODAY'S HOTTEST TECHNOLOGIES (BELOW).

helped pioneer some of the 20th century's most important devices, including the silicon transistor; the transistor radio; integrated circuit digital seismic technology; the infrared imager; the electronic handheld calculator; the single-chip microprocessor, microcomputer, and digital signal processor; and the multiport video random-access-memory chip.

Among the company's vast array of products are semiconductors, defense electronics systems, software productivity tools, electrical controls, and metallurgical materials. Products marketed directly to consumers include notebook computers, printers, and calculators.

TI is the acknowledged leader in digital signal processing semiconductors (DSPs), which comprise the heart of multimedia and digital communications. DSPs are single-chip microprocessors designed to perform mathematically intensive operations much more rapidly than traditional processors. The result is a faster, more powerful use of resources.

"From the beginning TI has been a leader in signal processing. We began using it in oil ex-

ploration and have evolved that technology into its major role in the information revolution," says one of Houston's TI Fellows, Gene Frantz. "Today's digital signal processors are the vital components of a large number of current technologies, including cellular phones, video compression, digital cameras, telecommunications, and computer networking."

EXPANDING WITH THE INDUSTRY

TI's Houston history began in 1953 when it purchased Houston Technical Laboratories, a manufacturer of industrial products. Serving initially as TI's industrial products division, the company purchased the land for the Houston site in the 1960s about 40 miles west of downtown in Stafford. By the mid-1980s other operations had been moved to the site from Dallas, including the Semiconductor Group, the Digital Systems Group, GSI, World Wide Supply, and the U.S. Consumer Products Group.

Work at the Houston site includes design and manufacture of leading-edge technologies, such as DSPs, memory, and microcontroller products. The Houston location also houses one of TI's larger wafer fabrication plants for manufacturing some of the company's leading-edge computer chips. With the cost of building one of these plants reaching the $1 billion mark, Houston represents a major investment for the semiconductor manufacturer.

TI's investment in Houston is not limited to concrete and steel. With a growing population of engineers, technicians, and support staff, the Houston location bustles with some of the company's top talent. "We have more talented people at TI than at any other company I've encountered," says WW Automotive MCU Manager Gregg Lowe. "Their focus and dedication give us a tremendous competitive edge in the marketplace."

BUILDING THE FUTURE

TI has always stressed the practical application of advanced research and continues to invest heavily in research and development. In the last 10 years alone, TI has received more than 4,265 patents worldwide. Through strategic relationships with other global companies, TI is applying its innovative technologies to dozens of future opportunities.

Many of these technologies originate from Houston. The company has announced plans for a DSP that can process 100 million instructions per second (MIPS). This type of speed from a DSP is critical for performing a variety of functions on a single chip, an achievement that will drive down the cost of devices while increasing their power and performance. Although this is leading-edge technology today, the Houston site is constantly looking ahead to the time when today's fastest chips won't meet the need of tomorrow's powerful applications. With foresight and creativity, the Houston site is working on solutions that will strengthen TI's leadership in digital signal processing solutions.

The Houston location also contributes to TI's strides in the critical areas of valuing individuals and safety. The Houston site was recently named the winner of TI's U.S. Corporate Safety Excellence Award for the third straight year and remains a benchmark for safety performance throughout the corporation. Diversity initiatives provide valuable workshops, community involvement opportunities, and site events for the Houston population. These initiatives were key contributors to TI's gaining national recognition in 1996 as a winner of the Catalyst Award, an annual award that honors firms for creative initiatives to recruit, retain, and develop women employees.

In a city known for leadership, innovation, talented people, and change, Houston plays a key role in TI's strategy for winning in the digital society. As the next century approaches, there seems to be no end to the TI universe. "Our vision for the company is world leadership in digital solutions for the networked society. This means that we will be the company that wins in the marketplace created by the information revolution," says Ramesh Gidwani, Stafford site manager. "At TI, we believe in the future."

TI's HOUSTON SITE IS THE HOME OF THE DSP GROUP. TI IS THE MARKET LEADER IN DSP TECHNOLOGY, ONE OF THE KEY FACILITATORS OF THE NETWORKED SOCIETY (BELOW LEFT).

SOME OF THE MAJOR TECHNOLOGIES OF THE NEXT CENTURY WILL BE A RESULT OF THE WORK DONE BY TI EMPLOYEES IN HOUSTON (BELOW RIGHT).

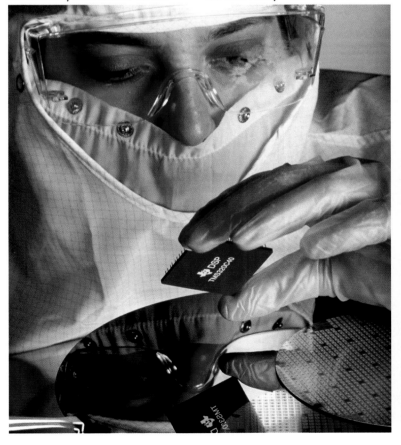

ONE NIGHT IN THE FALL OF 1995, SEVERAL THOUSAND people gathered on the plaza outside Houston's Wortham Theater Center to see contemporary diva Cecilia Bartoli perform in Rossini's *La Cenerentola*. They weren't waiting in line to buy tickets to the sold-out performance; they were making history as the first American audience ever to watch a free outdoor live opera telecast. ★ The

ALVY POWELL (PORGY) AND MARQUITA LISTER (BESS) STAR IN HOUSTON GRAND OPERA'S (HGO) 1995 PRODUCTION OF *Porgy and Bess*, WHICH TOURED 10 CITIES IN THE UNITED STATES, JAPAN, ITALY, AND FRANCE (TOP).

THOUSANDS FILLED THE OPERA HOUSE PLAZA TO SEE HGO'S "LIVE" PUBLIC BROADCAST OF ROSSINI'S *La Cenerentola* (BOTTOM).

JIM CALDWELL

event brought opera right out to the streets with the help of a 30-by-22-foot screen with stereo loudspeakers placed outside the theater. It was the kind of spectacle that has made Houston Grand Opera one of the most daring—and exciting—companies in the United States for more than 40 years.

WINNING AUDIENCES AND MORE

Houston Grand Opera was founded in 1955 through the combined efforts of Maestro Walter Herbert and Houston cultural leader Mrs. Louis G. Lobit. Since 1972 the company has flourished under the leadership of General Director David Gockley.

Known internationally as one of the six major opera companies in the United States, Houston Grand Opera's innovative programs, trend-setting events, and record-breaking performances attract a growing and diverse audience of more than 145,000 persons annually. Houston Grand Opera has greatly expanded since its first season of three performances, and now produces six to eight works per season, with an annual budget of $15 million.

Houston Grand Opera is unique in its commitment to performing and creating works that reflect American culture. "Until we have a repertoire of American operas and develop an American musical style," Gockley says,

"people will always consider opera an import. The Americanization of opera is a long process. We are part of a crusade to set an example of what American opera must be in order to be a community-supported resource that can survive into the next century."

A PREMIER COMPANY

It is a testament to the cultural community of Houston that in a state that ranks 54th (behind Guam) in state funding for the arts—and in a climate of harsh economic times—Houston Grand Opera raised $72 million to build its home entirely from private funds.

The Wortham Theater Center opened in October 1987 with three productions chosen by Gockley. One of those works was the world premiere of John Adams and Alice Goodman's *Nixon in China*, directed by Peter Sellars, which subsequently won both Grammy and Emmy awards. Critics from around the world were present for this awesome event, which included a life-size construction of Air Force One.

Dramatic flair has become the company's hallmark. In addition to standard repertory productions of the operatic classics, the company's 20 world premieres have included Stewart Wallace and Michael Korie's *Harvey Milk*, based on the life and murder of San Francisco's first openly homosexual city supervisor (1995); Noa Ain's *The Outcast* (1994); Robert Moran and Michael John LaChiusa's *Desert of Roses* (1992); the revised version of Carlisle Floyd's *The Passion of Jonathan Wade* (1991); Meredith Monk's *ATLAS: An Opera in Three Parts* (1991); Sir Michael Tippett's *New Year*

BRUCE BENNETT

(1989); Philip Glass and Doris Lessing's *The Making of the Representative for Planet 8* (1988); Leonard Bernstein's *A Quiet Place* (1983); Floyd's *Willie Stark* (1981); the revised edition of Gioacchino Rossini's *Tancredi* (1977); Floyd's *Bilby's Doll* (1976); and Thomas Pasatieri's *The Seagull* (1974).

Houston Grand Opera has also hosted several American premieres, including Philip Glass' *Akhnaten* (1984); a new edition of Rossini's *La Donna del Lago* (1981); the stage premiere of George Frideric Handel's *Rinaldo* (1974); and Ralph Vaughan Williams' *Hugh the Drover* (1973).

BUILDING OPERA'S FUTURE

Houston Grand Opera's touring company, Texas Opera Theater, was founded in 1974 and given the task of bringing opera out of the theater and into the community. Texas Opera Theater has since staged three world premieres and one American premiere, including Craig Bohmler and Mary Carol Warwick's *The Achilles Heel* (1993), and Wallace and Korie's *Where's Dick?* (1989). Now collaborating with a local professional touring company under the auspices of Opera to Go!, the company presents fully staged operas to more than 40,000 school-children per year.

The Houston Opera Studio, cofounded in 1977 by Gockley and composer Carlisle Floyd, is an acclaimed training and performance program for talented young artists who have the potential for major careers. "We want to involve young Americans and train them to be total performers, not big voices," says Gockley. Successful alumni of the Opera Studio include Bruce Ford, Denyce Graves, Jan Grissom, Susanne Mentzer, Herbert Perry, and Stella Zambalis. The Houston Opera Studio performed the

PAT (CAROLANN PAGE) AND RICHARD NIXON (JAMES MADDALENA) ARRIVE ON AIR FORCE ONE IN HGO'S WORLD PREMIERE OF JOHN ADAMS' *Nixon in China* (TOP).

VERDI'S *Aida*, STARRING PLACIDO DOMINGO AND MIRELLA FRENI, OPENED THE WORTHAM THEATER CENTER IN 1987 (LEFT).

world premiere of Robert Moran and James Skofield's *The Dracula Diary* (1994), Ricky Ian Gordon's *The Tibetan Book of the Dead, a liberation through hearing* (1996), and the American premiere of Philip Glass' *The Panther* (1981).

In 1990 Gockley founded Opera New World to expand the company's commitment to contemporary music theater. The program received a $1 million grant from the National Endowment for the Arts and produced 14 opera/music theater works in its first five years.

"In this climate, it is very easy to become redundant," says Gockley. "If we aren't consistently extraordinary, we will be cut adrift." Much of Houston Grand Opera's success has been attributed to Gockley's extraordinary energy and vision.

"Houston's wildcatter mentality offers a positive atmosphere for new ideas, where the opera is able to try a cutting-edge performance, even if it must absorb a few failures along the way," says Gockley. "People who want to get ahead can make a mark in Houston, where there are no artificial barriers, where the community is generous and proud, and where the talent can do something important. With fewer traditions to buck, good ideas get done."

HALDOR TOPSOE, INC.

CATALYSTS. THEY'RE SUBSTANCES THAT INCREASE THE SPEED of chemical reactions. From gasolines that fuel automobiles to fertilizers that enrich the soil, the multitude of materials created through catalytic processes play a pivotal role in improving the quality of life in countries around the globe. Because they also can be used to remove noxious compounds in industrial gas emissions, catalysts are

critical to meeting America's increasingly stringent environmental control standards.

Haldor Topsoe A/S of Denmark and its subsidiaries are involved in almost every aspect of the catalyst industry, from developing, producing, and marketing superior-quality catalysts to designing chemical processing units for plants in which catalysts are used. The company's average annual growth rate of about 20 percent over the last two decades attests to its success in creating effective energy-efficient catalysts that work under a variety of operating conditions to obtain the purest possible products.

COMING TO AMERICA

The company was founded in 1940 by Dr. Haldor Topsoe, a chemical engineer whose humanitarian efforts on behalf of Third World nations recently earned him the Hoover Medal, the highest honor awarded by America's engineering societies.

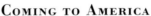

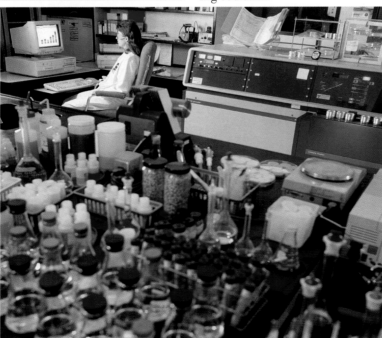

In the mid-1960s the company expanded its operations into Houston to take advantage of the Bayou City's extensive transportation infrastructure and the proliferation of petroleum refineries and petrochemical plants along the Texas Gulf Coast that employ catalytic processes.

Since building its first plant in Bayport near the Houston Ship Channel in 1965, Haldor Topsoe, Inc. has steadily expanded its local facilities. Today about 12 percent of the firm's 1,400 employees worldwide are based at the Bayport plant and at Haldor Topsoe's Clear Lake City offices, serving clients in the United States, Canada, and Latin America.

Haldor Topsoe's major clients include heavy chemical and petrochemical plants, oil and gas refineries, and companies involved in mining and electricity generation. Known for its achievements in synthesis gas technologies, the company also

is a world leader in technologies and catalysts for producing ammonia for fertilizer, methanol, and other heavy chemicals.

Haldor Topsoe's catalysts account for more than half the ammonia produced worldwide, and in the last 15 years, the firm has designed more ammonia plants internationally than any other company. Committed to remaining at the forefront of the catalyst industry, Haldor Topsoe dedicates substantial resources to ongoing research and development of catalysts and chemical processes. As Erik Vohtz, P.E., executive vice president and general manager of Haldor Topsoe's Houston operations, maintains, "Our heavy involvement in research and development represents one of our strengths. We cover the gamut from basic research to applied research to pilot plant testing."

About 20 percent of Haldor Topsoe's worldwide revenues and one-fourth of its personnel are allocated to research and development. Pilot plants at the company's facilities enable Haldor Topsoe researchers to test new and improved catalysts and catalytic processes on a semi-industrial scale. The company also maintains close relationships with its clients' research and development staffs and operating groups in order to direct research and development efforts toward clients' future needs.

As a result of these efforts, Haldor Topsoe produces an array of catalysts for processing, including hydrogen and synthesis gases, ammonia, methanol, formaldehyde, sulfuric acids, and catalysts for hydroprocessing and environmental control. Catalysts manufactured in Houston and imported from the parent company in Denmark are marketed not only through the Houston and Denmark offices, but also through branch offices in Moscow, New Delhi, Tokyo, and Beijing.

COMMITTED TO SERVICE

When we sell a catalyst, we also sell service throughout the life of the catalyst. We assist our clients in using our catalysts, in operating their plants optimally, in troubleshooting if problems arise," Vohtz explains. Tapping more than 50 years of experience in the catalyst field, the company provides catalyst users with general consultation, advice on catalyst selection and use, development of customized operating instructions, and start-up supervision, as well as evaluation of catalyst performance and recommendations for optimizing and timing catalyst replacement.

In 1980 Haldor Topsoe's Houston operations followed the lead of the parent company by forming an engineering division to design catalytic units for processing plants. The division's services include conducting feasibility studies; handling licensing; and providing process and detailed engineering, site supervision, and start-up assistance.

Already successful in environmental control activities in Europe, Haldor Topsoe is concentrating on developing catalytic processes that remove sulfur compounds, nitrogen oxides, carbon monoxide, and other noxious substances from waste gases at refineries and power plants in the United States. In a development that offers promise for improving air quality, Haldor Topsoe researchers recently discovered a catalytic process that can be used to produce a cleaner-burning alternative to diesel fuel used in trucks and buses. "Because the fuel can be produced by capturing methane gas from landfills," Vohtz explains, "it addresses two urban environmental issues at once."

Vohtz believes Haldor Topsoe's commitment to developing and producing high-quality catalysts and catalytic processes reflects its commitment to society overall. "By enabling our clients to make better, less costly products and by developing catalysts that remove pollutants from the air," he says, "we're improving the quality of life for us all."

COMPUTER-AIDED-DESIGN FACILITIES ARE USED EXTENSIVELY IN SERVICING TOPSOE ENGINEERING CLIENTS (LEFT).

HIGHLY SKILLED ENGINEERS AND TECHNICIANS PROVIDE TOPSOE TECHNOLOGIES AND ENGINEERING SERVICES WORLDWIDE (LEFT).

TOPSOE CATALYSTS ARE PRODUCED IN WELL-MAINTAINED MODERN FACILITIES (BELOW).

PAINEWEBBER INCORPORATED

IT WAS ONLY FITTING THAT HOUSTON WOULD BE CHOSEN TO become the site for PaineWebber Incorporated more than 30 years ago. The Bayou City serves as the center of finance and commerce for the Southwest, and PaineWebber ranks among America's leading full-service securities firms. ★ As Houston has grown, so has PaineWebber's presence. Today the company is the city's second-largest

brokerage firm. Its 419 employees, including 263 investment executives, account for about 5 percent of the company's brokerage force nationwide. PaineWebber's seven Houston-area offices control assets valued at approximately $7.8 billion and generate gross revenues of about $75 million annually.

STRONG AND INDEPENDENT

Established locally in 1965, Houston is the Southwest regional headquarters for PaineWebber Incorporated, the largest subsidiary of the PaineWebber Group, Inc., a New York-based securities firm. Among the parent company's key businesses are private client brokerage, investment banking, municipal securities, real estate, institutional equity, and fixed income sales. The firm is also involved in trading, research, international, asset management, and transaction services.

The PaineWebber Group—which was founded in Boston in 1879—is one of the last independently owned firms on Wall Street. Its assets approach $40

billion, and its 6,000 investment executives and approximately 10,000 other employees serve more than 2 million clients from 310 offices worldwide. The PaineWebber Group has the international network and financial strength required to compete effectively in today's global business environment.

"In an era that has seen contraction of its industry overall, we not only have survived, but also have experienced phenomenal growth," says Hale Cullom, regional director for PaineWebber Incorporated. A series of strategic acquisitions substantially increased the firm's talent base, the size and quality of its distribution network, and its overall capabilities.

In 1983 PaineWebber expanded its local presence by acquiring the Houston-based Rotan Mosle Financial Corporation, the parent company of Rotan Mosle Inc. The Southwest's premier regional securities firm, Rotan

Mosle Inc. was the first New York Stock Exchange firm in Texas. The acquisition added more than $90 million to PaineWebber's revenues and strengthened the company's growing foothold in the Lone Star State.

Founded in 1907, Rotan Mosle had provided financing for some of Houston's best-known organizations and corporations. Rotan Mosle also had financed many of the state's schools and highways, and the company was linked closely with the energy business—the lifeblood of Texas' economy.

Continuing to implement its growth strategy, PaineWebber acquired the Kidder, Peabody Group in October 1994. This transaction, which added 1,100 brokers to the workforce, made PaineWebber the nation's fourth-largest securities firm in terms of the number of brokers, and ranked it fifth among publicly traded brokerages in equity capital.

INVESTMENT EXECUTIVES AT PAINEWEBBER OFTEN FORM SPECIAL TEAMS TO TARGET A PARTICULAR PRODUCT AREA. THIS GROUP SPECIALIZES IN STOCK OPTION FINANCING AND OTHER CORPORATE SERVICES (RIGHT).

IN A TYPICAL PAINEWEBBER OPERATIONS DEPARTMENT, THOSE ORDERS THAT MUST BE ENTERED BY WIRE ARE TRANSMITTED TO THE VARIOUS STOCK EXCHANGES BY THE COMPANY'S STATE-OF-THE-ART COMPUTER SYSTEM (BELOW).

UNMATCHED SERVICE

PaineWebber's success is also attributed to its continuing commitment to high-quality personalized service. The firm's clients include individual investors as well as institutions, corporations, state and local governments, and public agencies in the United States and abroad.

PaineWebber's brokers are knowledgeable responsive investment executives who advise and tailor each client's plans to meet their individual needs. In addition, these individuals undergo continual training to expand their technological knowledge and service capabilities.

"We're willing to go the extra mile to provide value-added service for our clients," says Cullom. For example, PaineWebber works closely with a network of retirement and estate planning attorneys who assist the firm's clients with financial planning. Clients receive free advice on structuring their plans with legal and tax issues in mind. They are not charged until a plan is executed.

PaineWebber also continues to upgrade its technical capabilities. "Over a three-year period, we spent more than $100 million to establish ourselves on the cut-

ting edge of new technology," Cullom says. In 1994 the company began using state-of-the-art customized software that allowed PaineWebber's investment executives to have access to vast information resources through their workstations. A trade monitoring system was also implemented, allowing branch managers to supervise their offices' trading activities electronically.

In 1994 alone, PaineWebber spent $50 million on research. "That's just one reason why we have dramatically outperformed the market over time," says Cullom.

Growth has also enabled the firm to expand the options

it offers to clients. "Because of our size," explains Cullom, "we have the capital base needed to build a large inventory of products and services. We also can continue to bring new issues to the public."

Cullom continues, "Our strategy for the future is not to become the biggest brokerage firm, but to become better at what we're already doing well—providing unmatched service and innovative, quality investment solutions for our clients. We don't want to institutionalize what we do. We want to remain small enough to provide the personal touch as we continue to address our clients' capital and investment needs."

CLOCKWISE FROM TOP LEFT: THIS SMALL GROUP OF EMPLOYEES FROM PAINEWEBBER'S DOWNTOWN OFFICE COLLECTIVELY REPRESENTS 115 YEARS OF SERVICE.

A GROUP OF PAINEWEBBER'S RETIREMENT PLAN SPECIALISTS GATHERS IN THE CONFERENCE ROOM FOR A SHORT BRIEFING.

INVESTMENT EXECUTIVES MUST COMMUNICATE WITH THEIR ASSISTANTS TO ACCOMMODATE THE NEEDS AND DESIRES OF CLIENTS. THIS TOP PRODUCER WORKS CLOSELY WITH HIS ASSISTANTS, WHICH ENABLES HIM TO SERVE HIS CLIENTS.

WHEN THE SPACE SHUTTLE *Columbia* TOUCHED DOWN on the runway at Edwards Air Force Base, California, on April 12, 1981, it marked a major milestone in America's conquest of space. ★ The successful maiden voyage of the world's first reusable spacecraft meant the National Aeronautics and Space Administration (NASA) could propel people and payloads into orbit

A FORMER ASTRONAUT AND LOCKHEED MARTIN EXECUTIVE, JIM ADAMSON (LEFT) IS COO OF USA. KENT BLACK, FORMER COO OF ROCKWELL INTERNATIONAL, IS USA'S CURRENT CEO (TOP LEFT).

ASTRONAUT ANDREW S.W. THOMAS, MISSION SPECIALIST, IS ASSISTED BY TWO SCUBA-EQUIPPED DIVERS DURING A FAMILIARIZATION DIVE IN THE 25-FOOT POOL IN THE JOHNSON SPACE CENTER (JSC) WEIGHTLESS ENVIRONMENT TRAINING FACILITY (WETF) (BOTTOM LEFT).

in a craft that could be brought back to earth. Since then, experiments conducted aboard NASA's space shuttles have led to major discoveries that have advanced America's knowledge of other worlds while enhancing the quality of life on this planet.

In November 1995 NASA placed overall responsibility for space shuttle launch, mission, and landing operations under the management of one prime contractor: the United Space Alliance (USA). Headquartered in Houston, USA is a Rockwell/Lockheed Martin joint venture formed specifically to conduct the Space Flight Operations Contract for NASA.

USA was created in August 1995 in response to NASA's desire to consolidate all shuttle contracts and operations under a single management team. Rockwell and Lockheed Martin,

NASA's two largest shuttle contractors, realized that the best solution was to form a joint effort since Rockwell's Space Operations Contract (SOC) in Houston for flight operations in support of the Johnson Space Center (JSC) and Lockheed Martin's Shuttle Processing Contract (SPC) in Florida for launch and landing activities at the Kennedy Space Center (KSC) accounted for 80 percent of all shuttle operations contracts on the program. Also the two companies accounted for approximately 70 percent of the total contract value on the shuttle program, including hardware and operations.

On April 12, 1996, NASA and USA signed agreements that passed on authority for these two prime contracts previously held by Rockwell in Houston and Lockheed Martin in Florida, thereby establishing USA as the

single prime contractor for shuttle operations. USA unites under one management team all former Rockwell SOC employees and all former Lockheed Martin SPC personnel. In addition to the 1,800 Rockwell personnel in Houston, USA will also include approximately 2,200 subcontractor employees in Houston, primarily those working for Unisys, AlliedSignal, Hernandez Engineering, and Barrios Technology. Additionally, members of Rockwell's Florida shuttle logistics operations have also been folded into USA.

REACHING FOR THE STARS

USA blends the rich histories and talents of two aerospace giants, Rockwell and Lockheed Martin, companies that have played major roles in America's space program since its inception. Rockwell's relationship with NASA dates back to the 1960s, when the space agency began its historic Apollo missions to the moon.

"Our predecessor, North American Aviation, was in the aircraft-building business in California for many years," recalls Glynn S. Lunney, vice president and program manager of United Space Alliance. "Out of that heritage came the people and the organization that became major players in the Apollo program."

Rockwell's Houston involvement in the space program during the Apollo era was limited primarily to hardware construction, and only a few hundred people were employed at its offices near JSC. The company's Houston contingent grew substantially in 1985, when NASA consolidated about 20 separate

SOUTH

contracts for its shuttle systems and operations into a single contract, which subsequently was awarded to Rockwell and performed by its newly formed subsidiary in Houston, Rockwell Space Operations Company (RSOC).

Since then, RSOC has been immersed in almost every aspect of NASA's human space program (shuttle and station), including planning and scheduling missions, training the ground controllers and flight crews, supporting missions, and analyzing data gathered in orbit. Responsibilities also include strategic planning, project management, reporting, and maintaining NASA facilities to ensure that they are constantly in mission-ready condition. The same professionals who have supported a world record number of shuttle missions as members of Rockwell Space Operations Company will continue to do so as members of United Space Alliance.

Rockwell Space Operations Company became USA in June 1996. Through Rockwell Space Systems Division-Houston, the company continues to provide engineering and integration support for NASA and the JSC, including orbiter operations support as well as systems and payload integration. The division also conducts product design and light manufacturing, orbiter systems analysis, mission evaluation management, and integration analysis. Its Houston Design and

▶ NASA

Fabrication Facility designs and manufactures orbiter and crew-related hardware.

While Rockwell has a long history in human space flight, Lockheed Martin has a vast background primarily in unmanned space programs. The company has major interests in space and strategic missiles, aeronautics, electronics, information and technology services, energy, and the environment. Today the company is the world's largest defense, Department of Energy, and NASA contractor.

For the past 13 years, Lockheed Martin, in conjunction with other contractors and NASA civil service counterparts, has served as NASA's launch and landing team at KSC. These former Lockheed Martin SPC employees will continue to perform these activities as members of USA.

Looking Ahead

The Clear Lake-based United Space Alliance is the major corporate partner in NASA's space shuttle program. By late 1996 USA will manage approximately one-third of NASA's $3.2 billion annual shuttle budget.

A NEW MISSION CONTROL CENTER (MCC) BEGAN OPERATIONS IN 1995, FEATURING A WORKSTATION-BASED OPERATING SYSTEM AND AN UNPRECEDENTED FLEXIBILITY IN FLIGHT CONTROL OPERATIONS (ABOVE).

THE SPACE SHUTTLE *Discovery* LAUNCHES FROM KENNEDY SPACE CENTER IN FLORIDA (BOTTOM LEFT).

UNITED SPACE ALLIANCE'S HEADQUARTERS BUILDING IS LOCATED IN THE CLEAR LAKE AREA OF HOUSTON (BOTTOM RIGHT).

▶ NASA

▶ SKY CAM AERIAL PHOTOGRAPHY, INC.

TEXAS CHIROPRACTIC COLLEGE

CELEBRATING 100 YEARS OF THE CHIROPRACTIC PROFESSION, Texas Chiropractic College (TCC) is part of a legacy of excellence that spans nine decades. Founded by pioneer chiropractor Dr. J.N. Stone in 1908 in San Antonio, and now under the leadership of President Shelby M. Elliott, D.C., TCC operates as a nonprofit institution. In 1955, the TCC Foundation, Inc. established the Board of Regents to have full governing power over the college's policies and programs. Out of 20 accredited chiropractic colleges, TCC is the third-oldest institution in the nation. In 1965 the college moved to a location 25 miles from downtown Houston in Pasadena, Texas. Today the college carries on its tradition of preparing future doctors of chiropractic by providing them with the knowledge, skills, and experience to diagnose and treat patients and to work in consultation with other health care professionals.

HIGH ACADEMIC STANDARDS

The prestige of TCC is documented by its list of accreditations. The college is accredited by the Commission on Accreditation of the Council on Chiropractic Education (approved by the U.S. Department of Education) and by the Commission of Colleges of the Southern Association of Colleges and Schools. It is also recognized by the Federation of Chiropractic Licensing Boards and has been approved by the Texas Education Agency for veterans' training.

Today more than 500 students are enrolled in the college from 30 states and 10 foreign countries. TCC is proud of the great ethnic diversity among its students, having 63.6 percent Caucasian, 16.9 percent Asian, 8.3 percent Hispanic, 7.2 percent African-American, 2 percent Native American Indian, and 2 percent from other ethnic groups. With more women entering the chiropractic field, the college is pleased that 26.8 percent of its student body is comprised of women.

The current requirements for admission are of the highest academic standard. All applicants must have completed 60 semester hours or 90 quarter hours at an accredited institution, with minimum requirements that include successful completion of biological science, general inorganic chemistry, organic chemistry, general physics, and general psychology. "I'm impressed daily by the fine quality of highly educated students the Admissions Department brings to my office," says Dr. S.M. Elliott, president. Once accepted, students tackle a rigorous curriculum that spans five academic calendar years and is geared to prepare them for their future as top chiropractic health care professionals.

The TCC faculty has a wide range of specializations, such as physical therapy, nutrition, radiology, biology, and anatomy, among others. With this array of expertise, the students are well prepared and can continue the

WITH AN 11-TO-ONE STUDENT/TEACHER RATIO, STUDENTS GET INDIVIDUALIZED ATTENTION FROM FACULTY WITH A RANGE OF EXPERTISE IN MEDICINE, CHIROPRACTIC, PHYSICAL THERAPY, RADIOLOGY, AND ANATOMY, AMONG OTHER AREAS.

works of chiropractic—the healing art.

STATE-OF-THE-ART FACILITIES

The TCC campus spreads across 18 landscaped acres, which enhances its modern facilities and provides a friendly, yet professional atmosphere. Newly remodeled classrooms include auditorium-style seating and audiovisual and videotape resources, as well as laboratories outfitted for X-ray, pathology, histology, and dissection. Off campus, students participate in specialty rotations within the Texas Medical Center.

State-of-the-art scientific equipment includes the innovative Animated Dissection of Anatomy for Medicine (ADAM) software, which is housed in TCC's multimedia library. This CD-ROM program provides students with detailed, four-dimensional views from the back, front, side, or cross-section, as well as descriptions of human anatomy. Additionally, video microscopes are available that allow students to inspect and record biological and chemical components.

In addition to the classroom environment, TCC operates the W.D. Harper Chiropractic Health and Research Center, which offers students a practical culmination to their training by allowing interns to treat patients in need of chiropractic care. Interns work under the direction of licensed attending physicians who offer guidance throughout the clinical training process.

The outpatient clinic is equipped with a variety of modern adjusting tables, examination rooms, a diagnostic imaging department, a clinical laboratory, and a department of physical medicine and rehabilitation. Designed to care for more than 450 patients per day, the outpatient clinic is open to the general pub-

lic weekly from Monday through Saturday, offering services such as sports physicals. A student clinic was recently expanded to span an additional 7,560 square feet, completing the health center. "Plans are also under way for interns to work in the University of Houston Health Center," says Dr. Elliott. Dr. Elliott's primary ambition is to be part of the university system and he is currently working toward that end.

Despite TCC's high-tech educational facilities and unique learning opportunities, it's not hard to imagine that the college itself was once the site of a country club. In fact, the lush campus is home to the Student Outdoor Activities Center, a swimming pool, and a volleyball court. Unwilling to cease expansion of the current site, TCC is negotiating for more space. "Presently the college is dealing with the neighboring landowner concerning the possibility of purchasing land or entering into a cooperative development program," says Dr. Elliott.

COMMITMENT TO COMMUNITY

Texas Chiropractic College is highly involved in the local community. Over the years, TCC has sponsored and hosted a variety of community events and charity fund-raisers, including their annual Gala and Homecoming Convention, sponsored by the Texas Chiropractic College Alumni Association. Currently, the college is closely linked with Bridge Over Troubled Waters, Inc., a shelter for battered women and their children. Along with spearheading major fund-raising efforts and treating the children to special holiday outings, TCC provides free services to the women and children at the shelter.

"It's been very exciting to work with Bridge Over Troubled

Waters, Inc.," says Dean of Clinics Dr. Lawrence H. Wyatt. "It's rewarding to see the difference TCC can make in the lives of women and children who need our help."

THE FUTURE

As an extension of its commitment to providing the best academic environment to its students, TCC has plans for further expansion and modernization of its facilities. "We're currently lobbying for state funding," says Dr. Elliott. "We have visions of new buildings that require a great deal of planning. We're meeting weekly with builders, engineers, architects, and government officials as part of our continuing growth."

After nearly nine decades, Texas Chiropractic College's legacy of excellence continues through the school's commitment to provide the best possible education and preparation for future doctors of chiropractic.

FUTURE DOCTORS OF CHIROPRACTIC TACKLE A RIGOROUS CURRICULUM THAT SPANS FIVE ACADEMIC CALENDAR YEARS (TOP).

AS THE 10TH PRESIDENT, DR. S.M. ELLIOTT CONTINUES TO FOCUS ON THE QUALITY OF EDUCATION FOR TCC'S STUDENTS (BOTTOM).

PAPPAS RESTAURANTS, INC.

IT DOESN'T TAKE LONG FOR NEWCOMERS TO NOTICE SOMETHING familiar about the Houston dining landscape. Nearly everywhere you turn, there is a restaurant that, somewhere in its name, contains the letters P a p p a s. There's Pappas Seafood House for fresh Gulf Coast seafood, Pappadeaux Seafood Kitchen for Cajun and Creole seafood, Pappasito's Cantina for Tex-Mex specialties, Pappamia

Italian Kitchen for Italian cuisine, Pappas Barbecue for slow-smoked barbecue, and Pappas Bros. Steakhouse for juicy steaks. In fact, the Pappas name adorns more than 50 restaurants in all. And for those who prefer to serve friends at home, there's also Pappas Catering.

In the years since brothers Pete and Jim Pappas served their first cup of java to Houstonians in 1966, the Pappas family's business has exploded into one of the most successful privately held enterprises in the city, if not the state of Texas. In addition to their Houston shops, the family

owns dozens of popular restaurants in Austin, Dallas, and San Antonio. The key to the Pappas' success has been ensuring that all visitors enjoy a great dining experience with delicious food, good value, friendly service, and a fun atmosphere.

ALL IN THE FAMILY

The Pappas family's American history actually began near Dallas, where Greek immigrant H.D. Pappas opened the first Piccadilly Restaurant in 1941. Two generations of Pappases have been a fixture on Houston's restaurant scene since 1946,

when H.D.'s sons, Pete and Jim, moved to Houston and established Pappas Refrigeration Company. They built iceboxes topped with bar counters, which helped put plenty of corner bars and icehouses into business. They quickly controlled 90 percent of their market. But profit margins in the restaurant business looked even better, so Pete and Jim opened their first establishment, a Dot Coffee Shop, in 1967, which stood downtown on a site now occupied by Texas Commerce Bank. The brothers opened the Brisket House shortly thereafter and had four restaurants in Houston by 1968.

Jim's sons, Harris, Chris, and Gregory Pappas, grew up watching the business flourish and were always expected to participate. The three brothers officially stepped into the business in 1976, when they opened The Strawberry Patch, a restaurant on Westheimer that hit the pulse of the swinging '70s with a bistro-style menu and huge family-style salads served from glass flowerpots. They followed with The Circus, a fun-themed restaurant with a similar menu. Next came the Pappas Seafood Houses in 1981, which marked a real growth point for the company.

With Pappas Seafood Houses, the brothers began to expand the business on a grand scale. By 1988 Pappas Restaurants, Inc. owned 14 restaurants, including Pappas Barbecue, Brisket House, Dot Coffee Shop, and Pappas Seafood. In 1989 the brothers ventured into Austin with a Pappadeaux Seafood Kitchen, and into the town of Richardson—just outside Dallas—with a Pappasito's Cantina. Here, they turned in-house construction and architectural detailing into a marketing tool, transforming the restaurant's decor each week. This changing of the atmosphere soon became the talk of the town. The Austin and Dallas locations quickly multiplied through other Pappas concepts, and the family opened its first San Antonio Pappasito's Cantina in 1993.

How to Spell Success

The brothers' extraordinary relationship is responsible for transforming three different talents into a single solid foundation. Greg, who died in 1995, set the tone for each facility with dynamic design and construction. His influence is evident from the moment customers pull into any Pappas parking lot. Both interiors and exteriors are decorated with authentic old building materials appropriate to the theme.

Harris handles operations. "You start with a great building, then you have to motivate cooks in the kitchen and find great employees to serve the food. People are the magic, the secret ingredient," he says.

Chris, an engineer, contributes both operation and design expertise. His innovations have included custom cooking equipment that contributes to the smooth operation at each facility. When the brothers discovered that most food preparation tables had been designed for people who are six feet tall—and none of their employees were that tall—he created shorter tables for Pappas kitchens. His custom grills allow food to be placed at different distances from the flames, providing greater control than commercial brands. Frozen drink machines didn't suit the Pappas' needs either, so Chris manufactured machines that eliminated the need for frequent lifting and refilling.

The Pappas' philosophy has proved to be a winner many times over. The family's establishments are frequently voted Number One Restaurants in readers service polls for the *Houston Chronicle, D Magazine,* the *Austin Chronicle,* and other publications.

Last year, the venerable Strawberry Patch site was reborn as Pappas Bros. Steakhouse. In a vintage setting that recalls both the food and the ambience of the 1940s, the Pappases have once again excited the public's appetite. The steakhouse features a cigar lounge offering more than 60 types of fine cigars, a private wine cellar offering more than 500 wines, and the only steaks in Houston dry-aged on the premises for 21 days before they're cut. It's the kind of place where grandfather H.D. Pappas would have felt at home.

The family has come full circle, but its story is hardly closed. The Pappases plan expansion to markets in Atlanta and Chicago in the future. With 50 restaurants and counting, the family will be feeding Houstonians for many generations to come.

PAPPAS BROS. STEAKHOUSE OFFERS A PRIVATE WINE CELLAR OFFERING MORE THAN 500 WINES, COGNACS, AND MALT SCOTCHES, AS WELL AS THE ONLY STEAKS IN HOUSTON DRY-AGED ON THE PREMISES FOR 21 DAYS BEFORE THEY'RE CUT (LEFT).

THE PAPPAS BROS. STEAKHOUSE FEATURES A CIGAR LOUNGE OFFERING MORE THAN 60 TYPES OF FINE CIGARS (RIGHT).

McDonnell Douglas Corporation

McDonnell Douglas Corporation operates in a universe somewhat larger than most organizations. Over the course of its history, the company has virtually helped the nation circle the Earth, land on the Moon, and travel among the stars. ★ Playing a pivotal role in America's conquest of space, today's McDonnell Douglas is poised to help take the nation into the 21st century. Not only do they lend their expertise to NASA's space station program, they also tailor new technologies towards other exciting ventures, as space becomes the next commercial frontier.

TODAY McDONNELL DOUGLAS-HOUSTON ENGINEERS PROVIDE TECHNICAL TALENT TO MANY NASA PROJECTS INCLUDING THE INTERNATIONAL SPACE STATION. WHEN IT IS COMPLETED, THE SPACE STATION WILL BECOME A PERMANENT BASE WHERE ASTRONAUTS LIVE AND WORK IN ORBIT FOR LONG PERIODS OF TIME.

LIFTING OFF FROM HOUSTON

The growth of McDonnell Douglas Corporation's operations in the Houston area parallels the growth of the U.S. space program. Shortly after NASA opened Johnson Space Center in the early 1960s, McDonnell Douglas established a presence in the Clear Lake area by providing support for the Gemini and Mercury space vehicles being fabricated in St. Louis. The Houston operation expanded through the years by providing engineering services to various NASA programs.

Today engineers provide technical talent to many NASA projects including the International Space Station. When it is completed, the space station will become a permanent base where astronauts live and work in orbit for long periods of time. Their research will benefit all people on Earth as well as provide knowledge for man to conduct future interplanetary missions.

McDonnell Douglas is responsible for integrated truss segments, distributed systems, and other hardware and software packages critical to the space station. Many other creative and exciting projects are being designed and built for the space station, such as mock-ups for the weightless training facility and a medical research module.

A WEIGHTLESS ENVIRONMENT

In 1995 McDonnell Douglas began construction on a 6.2 million-gallon pool to be used for training NASA astronauts. The NASA training facility will be located next to Houston's Ellington Field and is scheduled for completion in early 1997—in time for space station training. Immersed in the simulated zero-gravity environment of the 40-foot-deep pool, astronaut crews will practice using specially designed space tools. Future space explorers will also use the giant pool to train for space walks outside their spacecraft.

THE FUTURE

From the development of the first DC-3 airplane through more than seven decades of aerospace, McDonnell Douglas has helped to make the world a little smaller. McDonnell Douglas-Houston is proud to have been a contributor to the opening of the frontier of space. With future space-based commercial ventures that are as boundless as space itself, this company's universe just continues to expand.

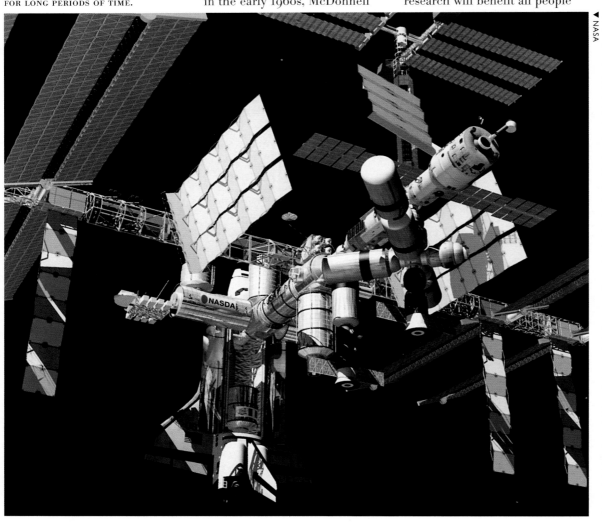

◄ NASA

1964 ★ 1996

Haldor Topsoe, Inc.

PaineWebber Incorporated

Texas Chiropractic College

United Space Alliance

Pappas Restaurants, Inc.

Theatre Under The Stars

John Brown—Houston Technical Center

Lorance & Thompson, P.C.

Houston Community College System

Burnett Personnel Services

Simmons & Company International

Sterling Bank

Career Management International

TeleCheck International, Inc.

RE/MAX of Texas, Inc.

Visible Changes Inc.

I.W. Marks Jewelers, Inc.

Houston Fuel Oil Terminal Company

Martha Turner Properties

Four Seasons Hotel

Arthur D. Little, Inc.

Front Office Business Centers

NGC Corporation

KTBZ—107.5 *THE BUZZ*

American Rice, Inc.

BSG Alliance/IT, Inc.

The Ritz-Carlton, Houston

South Shore Harbour Resort & Conference Center

New Era Life Insurance Companies

Baker Street Group Inc.

Sanifill, Inc.

The Children's Assessment Center

Flow Technologies, Inc.

Futronix Cable Depot

Executive Living, Inc.

Western National Corporation

Houston Music Hall Foundation

FOUNDED DURING GREAT BRITAIN'S INDUSTRIAL REVOLUTION, John Brown Engineers & Constructors has grown from a single entrepreneurial endeavor to become the fourth-largest contractor in the world. The company provides technical expertise to a variety of industries and has international facilities that include John Brown's Houston Technical Center. This international com-

pany was ranked as the number one design firm in 1994 by *Engineering News Record*.

A WORLD OF EXPERIENCE

When the company was established in 1837, founder John Brown outfitted railway pioneers with engineering supplies as they crisscrossed the British landscape. Soon after, his company branched out into shipbuilding and, for almost a century, built the grandest transatlantic ocean liners and state-of-the-art warships.

By 1948 John Brown Engineers & Constructors had entered

JOHN BROWN'S HOUSTON TECHNICAL CENTER HAS EXTENSIVE EXPERIENCE WITH OFFSHORE PLATFORMS; PIPELINES; AND POLYMER, CHEMICAL, AND PETROCHEMICAL PLANTS.

the process engineering and construction business, and soon became the leader in Britain's postwar refinery construction program. The Houston Technical Center was originally established in 1969 by Crawford & Russell, an American chemical engineering company that joined forces with John Brown Engineers & Constructors in 1979.

Since 1986 John Brown Engineers & Constructors has been a part of the engineering division of parent company Trafalgar House Public Limited Company, an international conglomerate with interests ranging from home building to cruise ships.

A LOCAL PRESENCE

In the United States, the company is known simply as John Brown and operates three major centers and four branch offices, including the Houston Technical Center. Employing more than 1,000 people, the Houston Technical Center serves as the corporate headquarters for all projects for John Brown Engineers & Constructors in North and South America. An independently operated, full-service facility, it offers all the necessary tools and support staff for project management, engineering, and construction.

The Houston Technical Center manages government project operations throughout the United States; the Republic of Panama; and Guantánamo, Cuba. It also provides operation and maintenance of facilities at the Department of Defense in Panama; the Department of Energy's Naval Petroleum and Oil Shale Reserves in Colorado,

Utah, and Wyoming; and the U.S. Army's Tropic Test Site.

Thanks to the oil-field-industry expertise that can be found in Houston, John Brown found a natural home for its American operations in the city. Working both onshore and offshore, the firm provides a full range of services from feasibility studies and conceptual engineering through detailed design, project management, construction, and start-up. Among John Brown's clients are the world's major oil and gas companies, including Amoco, Exxon, Mobil, Texaco, Transco, Phillips Petroleum, and Shell Oil.

The Houston Technical Center has extensive experience with offshore platforms; pipelines; and polymer, chemical, and petrochemical plants. The firm is currently designing and building a world-scale methanol facility in Chile, an ethyl vinyl alcohol expansion, and a syngas plant for customers in Houston. Last year, the company's construction safety was recognized as one of the best in the industry. FINA nominated John Brown for the prestigious Houston Business Round Table Safety Award of the Year for the firm's performance on its polypropylene addition. John Brown received second place out of 50 contractors.

From its entrepreneurial beginnings overseas, John Brown Engineers & Constructors has grown to become one of the world's premier construction and design firms. The Houston Technical Center is a fundamental component of this international organization and will continue to offer design and construction expertise well into the next century.

HOUSTON COMMUNITY COLLEGE SYSTEM

HAVING ITS VISION FOCUSED ON THE WORKFORCE OF THE next century, the Houston Community College System (HCCS) prepares individuals to meet the demands of the workplace by anticipating future trends and responding to current needs. This vision—one of the founding principles of Houston Community College System—has continued to strengthen the system through the years.

CONTRIBUTING TO ECONOMIC GROWTH

With an enrollment of more than 55,000 students, HCCS is the largest provider of technical training in Texas, offering career programs designed to meet the needs of the business community. HCCS also serves students who wish to begin their academic degrees at a community college, then transfer to a four-year university. And HCCS offers a broad range of continuing education options, from English as a Second Language to computer training and management seminars.

HCCS also has developed partnerships with major corporations to provide training in areas such as fiber optics, safety and environmental technology, biomedical electronics, and the refinement of "reality" technology for use in technical education programs. These partnerships include companies such as Lyondell Petrochemical, Southwestern Bell Telephone, Browning-Ferris Industries, NASA, Texaco, Cooper Industries, and Shell Oil. To date, HCCS provides educational services to more than 160 companies and more than 6,000 of their employees.

There is a direct link between the economic and social growth of Houston and the Houston Community College System. During the 1993-1994 academic year, HCCS infused the Houston economy with as much as $366 million in business volume, while costing the local economy only half that amount to operate. A total of 20,704 direct and indirect jobs are supported by HCCS. This represents more than $196 million in personal income and more than $59 million annually in business and personal spending, both of which ultimately are recycled back into the Houston economy.

HCCS receives its funding through state appropriations, taxes, and tuition. Additional funding sources include the U.S. Department of Energy, the National Science Foundation, the federal Technology Reinvestment Program, and the U.S. Department of Labor, among many others. These alliances allow HCCS to focus its technical training where it belongs—on the new technology fields that demand highly skilled technicians.

INNOVATIVE PROGRAMS

As part of its commitment to the future, HCCS has found innovative ways to train its students through its mobile computer classroom. This 18-wheel vehicle not only allows HCCS to take training on the road, but also provides students with a vast number of learning experiences that go

beyond typical desktop computer applications. Also, students can take advantage of the HCCS TeleCampus, which was created when the City of Houston awarded HCCS broadcast and operating rights for an educational cable channel. The TeleCampus offers courses on television for students who are unable to attend traditional classes.

The key to HCCS's success is flexibility. While the college system prepares many students for high-tech jobs, there are also other areas of study available, such as peace officer certification, culinary services, real estate certification, paramedic training, and health sciences.

By developing a well-trained workforce for high-demand fields, HCCS contributes to the economic potential of business and industry and increases the earning power of Houstonians. HCCS believes that this formula creates a thriving economy for Houston in a competitive climate of growth and change.

CLOCKWISE FROM TOP RIGHT: HOUSTON COMMUNITY COLLEGE SYSTEM OFFERS EDUCATIONAL PROGRAMS THAT COMPLEMENT THE DIVERSITY OF THE WORKFORCE. FUTURE MEDICAL TECHNICIANS USE THE LATEST IN X-RAY TECHNOLOGY.

AN INSTRUCTOR AND STUDENT EXPLORE THE CUTTING EDGE OF ENGINEERING: COMPUTER-AIDED DRAWING.

A STUDENT APPLIES HIS INDUSTRIAL TRAINING TO A WELDING PROJECT.

LORANCE & THOMPSON, P.C.

FOR MORE THAN 25 YEARS LORANCE & THOMPSON, P.C. has built a reputation as one of Houston's most outstanding civil trial firms. Its reputation stems not only from consistent courthouse victories, but from its dedication to quality service. "It's not enough to win a case for a client. We also have to be there to counsel our clients—big or small—24 hours a day, seven days a week. If a client needs a

lawyer, the problem may not wait until tomorrow," says Larry Thompson, the firm's president and cofounder.

It's that kind of attitude that caused the firm's health care section to establish a rotating call system for its hospital clients. "If a hospital risk manager has a patient crisis at midnight on Saturday night, all she has to do is call our health care beeper and one of our lawyers will respond," adds Frank Stahl, one of the senior members of the health care section.

A BROAD SPECIALTY BASE

In the early years the firm specialized in the broad field of tort and insurance litigation, representing individuals, professionals, self-insured companies, and insurance carriers. But as its reputation grew, so did the diversity of its practice. Now its lawyers can be found defending products as diverse as pacemakers and forklifts; and defending doctors and hospitals from the emergency room to the cardiovascular operating room; defending architects, engineers,

ATTORNEY JOHN CULBERSON, A STATE REPRESENTATIVE, ATTENDS A PRESS CONFERENCE AT THE CAPITOL (RIGHT).

ATTORNEYS DAVID D. CLUCK (LEFT) AND LARRY D. THOMPSON PREPARE FOR A MEDICAL MALPRACTICE TRIAL (BELOW).

insurance brokers, real estate agents, and lawyers, along with any other professional who may be the subject of a malpractice suit. Lorance & Thompson's lawyers are also involved in environmental and toxic tort litigation, insurance coverage disputes, truck and auto litigation, publishing and libel law, and premises cases. Significant clients in these areas include Columbia/HCA, the Texas Medical Liability Trust, Whirlpool Corporation, Jacobs Engineering, the Arthur J. Gallagher Company, Mayflower Transit, Inc., S.C. Johnson and Son, Inc., Dow Consumer Products, Farmers Insurance Group, State Farm, Scottsdale Insurance Company, and Allstate Insurance Company,

On the commercial side the firm has a growing practice in general commercial litigation and employment law, representing clients such as ITT Commercial Finance Corporation, RTC, FDIC, Baker Hughes, and Circle

K. Commercial matters include asset recovery litigation, business contract disputes, state and federal regulatory matters, and oil and gas industry issues.

To preserve its victories at the trial level, the firm has an appellate section headed by Diane Guariglia. Active in the appellate section of the state bar, Guariglia handles appeals in state and federal courts.

As a founding member of the American Law Firm Association (ALFA), Lorance & Thompson is able to call on the individual expertise of more than 100 other firms throughout the United States and a dozen other countries. "That network of really outstanding firms is invaluable in locating experts or obtaining legal opinions in an area where our firm does not have a specialist," says David Webb, of the firm's ALFA contact partners. "All we have to do is send a request over 'ALFA Mail,' the organization's E-mail system,

and we will have a response the same day."

The Cutting Edge of Law Firm Technology

Lorance & Thompson has always been on the cutting edge of law firm technology. Vicki Brann, the firm's first female partner, led the way to the use of computer graphics, video, and multimedia presentations as courtroom tools. "In an age of technical wizardry, you can't expect to win over a juror any longer with just flowery oratory and talking heads. We have to educate them and convince them in every way possible," comments Brann.

In the political arena the firm also leads the fight for its clients' rights. Thompson led the fight to restore balance to the Texas Supreme Court in the 1980s. John Culberson, a senior associate in the firm and a Republican state representative, carried the tort reform package in the Texas House last year. "The result," says Thompson,

"is a level playing field, both in our statutes and at the Texas Supreme Court. Health care providers, professionals, and businesses now have the opportunity to prosper in this state without the once held fear of being put out of business by rampant tort litigation."

As a further service, the firm provides continuing education through regularly scheduled seminars for clients such as doctors, nurses, claims adjusters, and risk managers.

The firm employs 80 persons including members, associates, and support staff. Nearly all of the senior attorneys are board certified in civil trial law or personal injury trial law, with a number of the members certified in both fields. Their broad talents are well suited to the full gamut of legal challenges, from relatively simple personal injury cases, taking only a day or two in trial, to the most complex of commercial litigation that may take weeks or months to conclude.

"Our clients find that they get the same quality of representation that they expect from one of the state's megafirms with better service and at significant bottom-line savings," says Thompson. "That's the reason we've been here for 25 years and know that we will be here next year and next century."

Lorance & Thompson, P.C. is AV-rated by Martindale-Hubbell, the preeminent legal rating service in the country. AV is the highest rating possible.

Attorneys WAYNE LITTLE (LEFT) AND FRANK STAHL VISIT THE SITE OF A TRUCKING CLIENT (LEFT).

LEFT TO RIGHT: "JUDGE" RALPH KEEN, TREY WILLIAMS, LEGAL ASSISTANT POLLY WILSON, AND VICKI BRANN PARTICIPATE IN A MOCK TRIAL (TOP RIGHT).

Attorneys WILLIAM LUYTIES (LEFT) AND MARK FLANAGAN INSPECT A CONSTRUCTION SCENE (BOTTOM RIGHT).

BURNETT PERSONNEL SERVICES

SINCE 1974 BURNETT PERSONNEL SERVICES HAS GROWN TO BE recognized as Houston's largest woman-owned business and its second-largest full-time placement service, as well as the 14th-largest woman-owned business in Texas. Today Burnett Personnel Services employs some 100 full-time staff members and 1,200 temporary/contract employees. Geographical expansion and diversification of services

have seen Burnett grow to eight offices in Houston, two in Austin, and one in El Paso.

CHANGING WITH THE TIMES

Rusty and Sue Burnett have incorporated innovative changes into their company as Houston's economy and market trends have shifted. Two decades ago, the majority of the firm's business involved the full-time placement of professionals in the oil and construction industries. When the recession hit Houston in the 1980s, the need for professionals declined while the need for temporary clerical assistance and secretaries rose. The Burnetts became more focused on temporary placement. Today the company's business is about 90 percent temporary and 10 percent full-time placement.

DIVERSITY OF SERVICES

Recognized for its strong ability to prescreen and test individuals to meet client quality standards, Burnett Personnel hires temporary employees with a wide gamut of skills including administrative, office/clerical, legal, accounting, information technology, electronic and mechanical assembly, and light industrial. High-caliber workers are attracted by the variety of top benefits offered by Burnett and its solid reputation for stability and life-changing employment opportunities.

Computerized dispatch programs designed by Rusty allow Burnett's operations staff to search extensive applicant databases for skilled workers. Clients are notified within 30 minutes of the status of their requests.

The firm also assists companies seeking to hire full-time employees. "Our goal is to make a company's selection process simple and cost efficient," says Sue. "Working closely with companies, we define their exact needs and utilize our extensive network to locate prime candidates."

A leader in testing and training innovation, the company also operates the Burnett PC Learning Center, which offers on- and off-site PC training with instructor-led classes and self-paced labs. Burnett assists companies in keeping their staff members' skills at top proficiency and trains individuals seeking skill expansion and upgrades. Training in electronic and mechanical assembly is also offered in Burnett's Austin Technical Training Center.

COMMUNITY INVOLVEMENT

Burnett takes giving back to the community seriously by playing a very proactive part in charity events and by donating goods and services. Burnett has sponsored and donated countless staff hours to

the Arthritis Foundation's All Star Salute to Secretaries™ luncheons for seven years. Sue serves on the board of the Arthritis Foundation and the advisory board of Goodwill Industries. Rusty serves on the board of the Boy Scouts. An annual sponsor of the Terry Fox 5K Fun Run benefiting the M.D. Anderson Cancer Research Center, Burnett also supports Child Advocates and Soul Patrol educational programs. Burnett has also been recognized as Goodwill Employer of the Year.

A TEAM EFFORT

Rusty and I enjoy working together and complement each other with our abilities and work styles," says Sue. "We share a vision that challenges us and provides a great deal of satisfaction in knowing our efforts benefit so many people." Through their insightful leadership of a very dedicated and well-trained staff, many of whom have been with the company up to 19 years, Texas' business communities' personnel needs will be well met in the next century.

SUE AND RUSTY BURNETT OFFER DAILY HANDS-ON LEADERSHIP TO THEIR AWARD-WINNING COMPANY (RIGHT).

BURNETT'S CORPORATE HEADQUARTERS IS LOCATED AT 9800 RICHMOND AVENUE IN SOUTHWEST HOUSTON.

218

STERLING BANK

SHARES OF ONE OF THE BEST-PERFORMING FINANCIAL institutions in the region—perhaps even in the nation—are traded on the NASDAQ stock exchange under the symbol SBIB. It is Houston's Sterling Bank, a company that has literally grown with the city, carving a unique niche by offering exceptional service to owner-operated businesses for more than 20 years. ★ Sterling Bank was founded

in 1974 by seven men and women who believed in small business. While dozens of Houston banks failed for thinking too big during the 1980s, Sterling put its faith in behind-the-scenes businesses, such as manufacturers, distributors, engineering firms, and other service providers with annual sales between $3 million and $30 million. The institution has grown to become a $690 million-asset banking company with 13 bank offices that provide traditional commercial and retail banking services, investment products, and cash management services, all delivered by Sterling Bankers who truly understand that the bank's success depends upon the success of its customers.

Sterling Bank's overall growth has been the result of strong growth at existing locations, through the opening of profitable new offices, and by select acquisitions. In 1995 Sterling offered the highest return on equity of all publicly traded Texas banking companies, at 19.91 percent. Even more impressive is Sterling's five-year average return on equity of 18.5 percent and five-year average

▶ JIM OLIVE

growth in earnings per share of 22 percent.

SERVING LOCAL BUSINESSES

Owner-operated businesses continue to give Sterling Bank the edge. "Our customers are the kind of local companies that make Houston go, even though they might not grab the headlines," says President Mark Giles. "They're people we have plenty of room to grow with." Sterling recognizes that what customers need most from a bank are relationships, responsiveness, and service. Sterling provides

all three through "supercommunity" banking, which gives small companies ready access to decision makers at every single bank office. The CEO of each bank office is an industry veteran with close ties to his or her community.

Sterling Bank has centralized only those functions that are transparent to the customer, such as statement rendering. "Our goal is to 'out-national' the local banks and 'out-local' the national banks," says Giles. Sterling Bank is able to offer a broader product line and greater convenience than most local banks. At the same time Sterling knows its market and customers better and has less turnover than larger national banks. Indicative of the bank's emphasis on enduring relationships, four of the founding officers—including Chairman of the Board George Martinez—are still with the company.

"Quality service is all about maintaining a balance between the right people and the right systems, working together to really meet customer expectations," says Martinez. "We never take that balance for granted."

CLOCKWISE FROM TOP:
STERLING BANK HAS 13 BANK OFFICES
AND $690 MILLION IN ASSETS.

GEORGE MARTINEZ (LEFT), CHAIRMAN
OF STERLING BANK AND STERLING
BANCSHARES, INC., AND MARK T.
GILES, PRESIDENT OF STERLING BANK
AND STERLING BANCSHARES, INC.

STERLING RECOGNIZES THAT WHAT
CUSTOMERS NEED MOST FROM A BANK
ARE RELATIONSHIPS, RESPONSIVENESS,
AND SERVICE.

▶ BETH LAUNIUS

▶ BETH LAUNIUS

FEW COMPANIES HAVE RIDDEN THE VOLATILE OIL AND GAS waves of recent years as well as Simmons & Company International. Long before the phrase "niche strategy" was coined, this Houston investment banking firm dared to specialize in one of Wall Street's most misunderstood sectors. The premise was definitely on target: Since its inception, Simmons & Company has

executed more than 300 corporate finance transactions worldwide, with a combined value in excess of approximately $20 billion.

UNIQUE FIRM, UNIQUE INDUSTRY

The first and only investment banking company dedicated to the oil service and petroleum equipment industry, Simmons & Company was founded in 1974 on the heels of the world's first oil embargo. "At the firm's foun-

PARTNERS OF THE FIRM DISCUSS LONG-TERM STRATEGY (BELOW).

▼ STEVE BRADY

MATTHEW R. SIMMONS, PRESIDENT (ABOVE)

dation, we set four simple goals: To maintain our specialization, to provide only the highest quality advice to our clientele, to remain a small group of senior professionals, and to have fun," says President Matthew Simmons. "These goals are not only still intact, they're more important than ever."

Simmons & Company intentionally keeps its focus on oil service and equipment firms. The operating heart of the worldwide energy industry, these service firms have become increasingly important now that major energy companies outsource much of their drilling and production work.

Simmons & Company's corporate finance services encompass a wide range of investment

banking advice, including the execution and closing of mergers, divestitures, and acquisitions, as well as debt and equity financings. In 1993 Simmons & Company expanded its scope to include research, sales, and trading services for institutional investors with publicly held oil service and equipment securities.

"By maintaining our distinctive focus, we are building strategically on the knowledge and expertise that has made us the premier source for corporate finance advice for industry clientele," says Simmons. "We intend to gain a similar confidence level with institutions who want accurate and timely advice on which stocks to own and how best to

execute purchases and sales of oil service securities."

INVESTMENT BANKING'S HIGHEST SUCCESS RATE

Simmons & Company has had more success in finishing projects than any other firm in the entire investment banking industry. The negotiation skills, attention to detail, and diplomacy of Simmons & Company's financial professionals also figure into the picture, giving the firm the ability to help clients close an uncommonly high proportion of merger and acquisition projects.

The firm's skill in helping clients raise new capital is rooted in a broad knowledge of capital availability and the cost differences of each capital source. "We maintain a close dialogue with the active providers of all types of funding," says Simmons. "Financial institutions often use us as a sounding board even when we're not involved in a project."

A More Informed Investment Universe

Simmons & Company's securities group concentrates on core institutional investors who are the primary owners of the approximately 150 publicly traded oil service companies.

"We strive not only to supply timely reports on key trends and companies whose stock prices are out of line with their peers, but also to translate this knowledge into specific investment recommendations," Simmons says. "Our research product is backed by more depth and experience in oil service than any Wall Street firm."

Simmons & Company has compiled the industry's most complete database, with specific information on more than 1,500 companies, and market and financial data on every public firm. The company also owns a comprehensive library of petroleum statistics, trade journals, regional directories, government publications, and industry position papers.

By integrating outstanding research with the most focused distribution and execution of trades, Simmons & Company offers institutions better knowledge, more timely insights, an informed perspective on key energy issues, and sound judgment on the management of companies within the industry.

The securities research also benefits Simmons & Company's corporate clients. "By disseminating accurate forecasts of trends, we help create a more informed universe of institutional owners and better liquidity for their stocks," Simmons says. He envisions his company as the comanager of choice for all discerning issuers of oil service securities.

Shared Success

As Simmons & Company has prospered, so have its clients. One offshore support services client, which had annual debt service of more than four times its cash flow in 1985, today enjoys record earnings with almost twice the market capitalization it had in the early 1980s, even though the market has shrunk by more than half. Yet another client, a large diversified company, has monetized two oil service entities into more than $1 billion of added value with guidance from Simmons & Company.

The success stories could be told for pages, with a client list that reads like a who's who of industry, including such major firms as Baker Hughes, Brown & Root International, Dresser Industries, Inc., General Electric Company, Ingersoll-Rand, Panhandle Eastern Corporation, Teledyne, Inc. and TRW, Inc.; and financial institutions including Bank One, Texas; CIGNA Corporation; and World Bank.

"We've enjoyed the successes of the 1970s, worked through the brutal conditions of the 1980s, and helped oil service leaders restructure their companies to meet the industry's demands in the 1990s," says Simmons. "We anticipate providing that same level of unparalleled service for years to come."

The firm's growing securities group actively trades oil service stocks, buying and selling for institutional clients.

TELECHECK INTERNATIONAL, INC.

AMERICANS WILL WRITE MORE THAN 180 MILLION CHECKS this year, and estimates predict that check fraud may represent well over $5 billion in losses to the retail industry. Since checks account for more than half of all noncash retail transaction payments, businesses must rely on innovative methods to combat the risk associated with check acceptance. ★ TeleCheck International, Inc. helps

THE COMPANY'S SOPHISTICATED RISK MANAGEMENT SYSTEMS AND EXTENSIVE DATABASES PROVIDE THE MOST ACCURATE CHECK ACCEPTANCE SOLUTIONS AVAILABLE, WHILE BOASTING THE HIGHEST APPROVAL RATES IN THE INDUSTRY.

AMERICANS WRITE MORE THAN 180 MILLION CHECKS EACH YEAR, REPRESENTING MORE THAN $5 BILLION IN LOSSES TO THE RETAIL INDUSTRY DUE TO CHECK FRAUD.

more than 160,000 subscribers reduce the risk in accepting checks, while increasing sales and maximizing customer service. TeleCheck offers specialized programs to meet the unique needs of businesses in the retail, grocery, automotive, travel, hospitality, gaming, video rental, wholesale, and financial industries. This Houston-based organization boasts the most extensive and accurate check acceptance service in the industry.

TeleCheck, a wholly owned subsidiary of First Data Corporation, processes more than 585 million check inquiries and authorizes over $36 billion worth of checks annually. TeleCheck provides a broad range of services, from check guarantee and verification to check loss and debt recovery as well as point-of-sale authorization equipment and complex data processing.

Founded in Hawaii in 1964, TeleCheck has grown to be the world's largest check acceptance company. Over the years the TeleCheck operation grew to include franchises throughout the country, and in 1976 partners John D. Chaney and Ken Wait opened a franchise in Houston. After rapid growth in subsequent years, the franchises merged to form today's TeleCheck operation, with corporate headquarters in Houston.

The Houston office employs approximately 850 of the company's 1,850 employees, with the remainder located in TeleCheck's sales and service centers in 90 cities throughout the United States and Canada, and in its full-service operating centers in Australia, New Zealand, and Puerto Rico. Corporate headquarters is home to most of the company's operating functions, including one of its two large authorization centers, which is accessible to subscribers worldwide, 24 hours a day, every day of the year.

At the core of the TeleCheck system are the industry's largest and most accurately maintained

positive and negative databases. This data, compiled with TeleCheck's sophisticated risk management systems, assures the most accurate check acceptance solution available, approving more than 98 percent of all check inquiries—the highest approval rate in the industry. These systems consider several relevant variables for each check presented, effectively stopping bad check writers without turning down good ones.

In 1995 TeleCheck introduced the Accelera™ authorization terminal—the fastest, easiest, and most accurate way to accept checks. The terminal brings a total payment solution to the point of sale, combining TeleCheck's check acceptance services with credit card processing through its sister company First Data Merchant Services, as well as debit card processing. With Accelera, check acceptance is faster than ever before, ensuring a response within seconds. Often only a driver's license is required, and since most of the vital information is electronically captured, only a merchant number and approval code must be written on the check—minimizing possible human error and escalating customer service.

In recent years the number of checks written has increased by 21 percent, while at the same time the number of bad checks has grown at a rate of 19 percent. Merchants who face the uncertainty of check acceptance each day can easily achieve peace of mind while protecting themselves from bad check losses. It all adds up to good business sense, not only for TeleCheck, but for any company that cares about reducing risk, increasing sales, and keeping customers coming back.

▲ STEVE CHENN PHOTOGRAPHY

MARTHA TURNER PROPERTIES

I N HOUSTON—AND THROUGHOUT TEXAS—THE NAME MARTHA Turner Properties is synonymous with service. Since 1981 Martha Turner and her team of residential real estate professionals have been dedicated to providing clients assistance in finding the perfect home to fit their individual lifestyles. The company's commitment to excellence was a major factor in Martha Turner Properties

being selected as the exclusive Houston affiliate of the prestigious Christie's Great Estates, a global network of prominent real estate firms authorized to handle the sale of major properties.

Martha Turner's credo, "Excellence Is Never an Extravagance," has never wavered since the company's formation during tough economic times; in 1981 interest rates were above 20 percent and buyers were overly cautious. Turner, positive as always, saw this difficult business climate as an opportunity and jumped in "feet first" with an aggressive marketing and advertising campaign.

"From the beginning, we wanted to present our company, and the homes we represent, at the highest level possible," Turner says.

BUILDING THE BEST

T urner has surrounded herself with highly motivated, educated, and experienced professionals. She provides continuing support for the company's 44 sales associates, not only with more than 36 assistants and office personnel, but also with a team that includes a full-time, in-house business consultant, an information systems specialist, a public relations/ marketing company, a high-rise coordinator, a luxury leasing division, and an executive corporate services director.

The company's state-of-the-art Resource Center provides timely real estate information on Houston's outstanding neighborhoods including River Oaks, Tanglewood, Memorial, the Museum District, Bellaire, Meyerland, and West Houston. This resource enables the agents

to sell their own listings and to cross-sell with other Houston Realtors.

A former schoolteacher, fifth-generation Texan Martha Turner still believes strongly in education and regularly hosts workshops, seminars, and retreats for the company. Top speakers from all over the country are flown in to address the group. And, Turner herself is in great demand as a motivational speaker.

The firm's associates continually have the highest level of production per agent in Houston. "A company is only as strong as its weakest person," Turner explains. "I'm proud that we have created one of the finest groups of real estate agents and brokers in the country."

COMMITTED TO COMMUNITY EXCELLENCE

H ouston, Turner believes, is a terrific city in which to live and work.

"No other city offers the friendliness, openness, can-do spirit, and willingness to embrace newcomers like our hometown," she feels. To support that spirit, Turner volunteers her time and expertise to Houston's civic and charitable institutions. From the Houston Ballet to the Star of Hope Mission, from the Susan G. Komen Foundation to Houston Habitat for Humanity, and from the Texas Business Hall of Fame to Texas Commerce Bank, among countless others, her leadership and dedication have raised awareness and dollars to further important causes.

Turner's commitment to excellence reflects her dedication to the Bayou City and the people who live there. "A real estate broker is involved in one of the largest financial and emotional investments that people make—the purchase of their home," she says. "Every client, and every transaction, deserves nothing less than excellence."

MARTHA TURNER, PRESIDENT OF MARTHA TURNER PROPERTIES, FOUNDED IN 1981 (TOP).

MARTHA TURNER PROPERTIES' HIGHLY MOTIVATED, EDUCATED, AND EXPERIENCED ASSOCIATES (BOTTOM).

SUSAN SILVANO, A PIONEER IN HER PROFESSION, LOOKS AT the future of the American worker from a perspective of 20 years of experience in career counseling. "The single most important professional skill of the next decade will be the ability to repackage yourself at will, to make a new career path when *you* choose." And she leaves no doubt as to her firm's ability to impart this skill.

Founded in Houston in 1976 as a specialized provider of career transition services, Career Management International (CMI) has become a major human resources consulting firm with offices across the United States. Ranked among the 100 fastest-growing Houston companies in 1994, CMI has become a model for swift, decisive adaptation to constantly changing market trends.

"Right now, for example," says Susan Silvano, "corporate human resources departments are very interested in seeing employees take greater control over their own career development, while keeping them under the company roof, if at all possible. One hard lesson of the '80s was that it was very wasteful to terminate valuable experienced em-

ployees, only to have to hire and train others later. Now the trend is to try to keep your people, re-deploying them elsewhere within the company."

But corporate transformation remains a bumpy road for most American companies, and layoffs and downsizing are no less traumatic today than they were a decade ago. CMI's outplacement services provide a sensible, positive, and humane approach to organizational change. Senior CMI consultants work with legal and human resources staffs throughout the downsizing process to arrange staff training, internal and external communication, and a full range of career transition services and support for the outplaced employees.

As the city watched news broadcasts about the closing of the *Houston Post* in April 1995,

for example, CMI was already offering outplacement and counseling services to the 1,900 people who suddenly found themselves unemployed. Within six months, 80 percent had either found new positions or had made a decision to retire permanently. Over a 20-year period, CMI's placement rate has consistently averaged an outstanding 92 percent.

"We don't mess around," says Susan Silvano. "Seriously, it's not about giving people offices to use, or just finding them a job. It's about showing people how to determine exactly who they are and what they have to sell. And *then* showing them how to set their sights on a goal and *go* for it."

CMI's client list includes major corporations in the petrochemical and utility industries as

A SPECIALIZED PROVIDER OF CAREER TRANSITION SERVICES, CAREER MANAGEMENT INTERNATIONAL (CMI) HAS BECOME A MAJOR HUMAN RESOURCES COUNSELING AND CONSULTING FIRM, OFFERING A VARIETY OF WORKSHOPS AND SEMINARS TO ITS CLIENTELE.

▲ MIKE DUHON PRODUCTIONS

RICHARD AND SUSAN SILVANO REVIEW CMI's NEW SCHOOL TO WORK PROGRAM (TOP LEFT).

CAP™, AN INNOVATIVE AND INTERACTIVE CAREER PLANNING PROGRAM DEVELOPED BY CMI, HELPS THE USER DETERMINE THE CAREER PATH TO WHICH HE OR SHE IS BEST SUITED (BOTTOM LEFT).

well as hospitals and health care organizations, educational institutions, publishing companies, and manufacturing businesses. Among the familiar names are Exxon USA, Dow Chemical, Public Service of New Mexico, Lockheed Corporation, Marriott Hotels and Resorts, Kelsey-Seybold Clinics, John Hancock Insurance, North Forest Independent School District, NASA, and the Texas Youth Commission.

Another division of CMI provides customized training seminars, retirement preparation, executive coaching and change management, policies and procedures manuals, and conflict resolution programs. The firm has developed a number of innovative team building tools, such as its Team of One™ program. "With Team of One™, you get to know yourself first. Then you see how you relate to other parts of the group with which you work," says Susan Silvano. "Today teams change constantly, so it's important to know who you are, what you have to contribute, and how you relate to others."

Another of CMI's developments has blossomed into an attraction on the World Wide Web. Kingdomality™, a personality preference profile designed by CMI, attracted 20,000 "hits" in its first week on the Web, and now routinely captures the attention of 800 to 1,000 Internet users each day. Kingdomality™ expresses complex psychological profiles in a very user-friendly way. Based on medieval archetypes, Kingdomality™ helps individuals and team members to see themselves more clearly, better understand the differences among people, and appreciate the importance of personality differences to the success of the team.

Kingdomality™ is included as part of the Career Alignment Profile™ (CAP™), an interactive program that helps the user determine the career path to which he or she is best suited. "CAP™ sorts out real interests, natural abilities, and individual personality traits," says Susan Silvano. "It's a good tool for students designing a course of study, or for a company's employees to work on their own career plan. It also has the great advantage of being adaptable to any company."

CMI's programs have been strongly influenced by the firm's three directors: Susan Silvano; her husband and partner, Richard Silvano; and Dr. John Foreyt, all of whom share backgrounds in psychology and education.

"We don't *give* people anything," says Susan Silvano. "We help them discover what they've already got. There are few things as rewarding as helping people see their own hidden potential, then watching them set goals and achieve them. We just show them how to find and use what's been there all along."

RE/MAX OF TEXAS, INC.

LIKE THE SOARING HOT AIR BALLOON OF ITS LOGO, RE/MAX of Texas, Inc. has taken the business of real estate to new heights. The firm operates more than 112 offices statewide, with more than 2,100 sales associates whose successes add up to a number one market share in Houston, Dallas, Beaumont, Tyler, Wichita Falls, and other Texas communities. ★ In 1995 RE/MAX associates so dominated

the market that they outsold their next four competitors combined, accounting for 26.59 percent of all the homes sold in the Houston area in 1995. The numbers are similar in Dallas, where one-fifth of all homes sold are listed by RE/MAX. Both *Entrepreneur* and *Franchise* magazines have rated RE/MAX franchises number one in growth and franchise opportunities, respectively.

A DEPARTURE FROM THE SPLIT COMMISSION REAL ESTATE COMPANY

RE/MAX of Texas was founded in 1977 by Frank DeCicco, an insightful businessman who had been in business since 1936. DeCicco, his wife Jean, and their five daughters moved to Houston from upstate New York in 1965. They established Sun Aero Real Estate, but after five years the

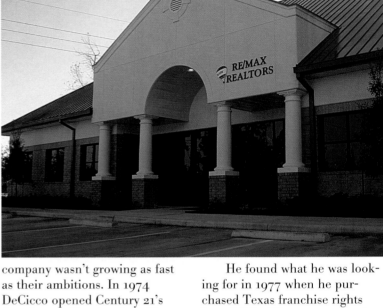

RE/MAX ALL STARS FORT WORTH IS ONE OF NINE OFFICES IN TARRANT COUNTY. WITH THE NUMBER ONE MARKET SHARE IN ARLINGTON, RE/MAX CONTINUES TO GAIN PREMIER MARKET PRESENCE IN TARRANT COUNTY (RIGHT).

THE RE/MAX SYSTEM EXPANDED RAPIDLY FROM HOUSTON TO DALLAS, WHERE THERE ARE PRESENTLY 18 OFFICES IN THE DALLAS AREA. RE/MAX PRESTON ROAD NORTH, SHOWN HERE, IS ONE OF THE DALLAS OFFICES THAT HAS ACHIEVED NUMBER ONE MARKET SHARE (BELOW).

company wasn't growing as fast as their ambitions. In 1974 DeCicco opened Century 21's first Texas office, but he still wasn't quite satisfied. "I knew that something bigger and better was lurking just over the horizon," he says.

He found what he was looking for in 1977 when he purchased Texas franchise rights from RE/MAX, an upstart real estate company based in Denver. RE/MAX, founded in 1973 by a young real estate broker named Dave Liniger, was causing a stir in the market with its unconventional way of doing business—a radical concept in which agents kept 100 percent of their commissions and paid shared overhead expenses plus a small management and promotions fee.

Traditionally, real estate agents pay as much as 50 percent of their commissions to the broker who represents them in exchange for administrative and advertising support. "We allow our agents to establish their own commission," explains DeCicco. "We estimate what it costs us to operate the office and divide the cost by the number of people in it." A similar program had been attempted as early as 1946 in Canada, and companies in the United States had also tried it without lasting success.

"We're the greatest untold story on the face of the earth, because this is a program that

should not have worked," says DeCicco. Old-line brokers and others in the industry tried to discredit RE/MAX, indoctrinating agents against Liniger's plan and even denying RE/MAX sales associates access to the Multiple Listing Service (MLS). Colorado's state real estate commission audited the company's trust accounts weekly, and the state attorney general's office investigated RE/MAX after competitors complained the firm was violating fair trade practices.

Things changed in 1977 when Liniger decided to franchise. RE/MAX wasn't the first real estate franchise business, but it was the first to combine the 100 percent commission concept with franchising—and the combination sparked a revolution. That year the company's growth of sales associates exploded by 274 percent, escalating dramatically each succeeding year.

In Houston DeCicco jumped on the RE/MAX bandwagon quickly, but he admits the first 10 years were tough—even though the late 1970s and early 1980s were boom years in the market. Luckily, he was also selling real estate to survive. "It seems to me, if you're going to be in business where your only compensation is commission, the 100 percent is important," he says. "The key was finding enough sales associates who had the courage to cast themselves as individual contractors and agents instead of splitting their commissions."

THE SKY'S NO LIMIT

Today the RE/MAX concept seems simply more practical than radical. "The same thing that's happening in the retail business is occurring in our industry," says DeCicco. "Mom and Pop operations are going out of business, because they're no longer able to keep up with the technology." RE/MAX has grown so phenomenally, it now offers its sales associates access to a worldwide satellite network system and the referrals of more than 43,000 other sales professionals across the globe.

"We're carrying an average of 15,000 listings across Texas, and also have MLS listings in the hundreds of thousands," says DeCicco. In 1995 RE/MAX of Texas sales associates were involved in more than 44,000 transactions, with sales reaching $5 billion. "In the majority of cities and towns we're in, we're number one by far," says DeCicco.

In Houston alone, nine of the top 25 agents (by total dollar volume) were RE/MAX sales associates, and 16 of the top 25 agents (by listings sold) were RE/MAX sales associates, as ranked by the *Houston Business Journal*. The firm has 45 offices in Houston with more than 900 associates in the local system. "We have the best people, the best system, and the best technology," DeCicco says.

"It took a long time to get the concept across that people could stand on their own two feet," he adds. Yet as thrilled as he is with RE/MAX of Texas' success, DeCicco is still hungry for more. His next goal is to double the company's size. Even after all these years in the business, DeCicco is obviously still a believer in the RE/MAX motto: "The sky's no limit."

CLOCKWISE FROM TOP LEFT: NUMBER ONE MARKET SHARE IS ENJOYED BY RE/MAX ASSOCIATES IN SMALL MARKETS. ABILENE, BEAUMONT, AND TYLER ARE A FEW OF THE CITIES WHERE RE/MAX MAINTAINS DOMINANT MARKET SHARE.

RE/MAX YARD SIGNS DOMINATE MOST COMMUNITIES THROUGHOUT THE HOUSTON AREA. WITH A 26.59 PERCENT MARKET SHARE, HOUSTON-AREA RE/MAX SALES ASSOCIATES OUTSOLD THEIR NEXT FOUR COMPETITORS COMBINED IN 1995.

SAN ANTONIO AND AUSTIN ARE TWO MAJOR GROWTH AREAS FOR RE/MAX OF TEXAS. RE/MAX NORTHEAST OPENED IN 1986, NINE YEARS AFTER FRANK DeCICCO—FOUNDER OF RE/MAX OF TEXAS, INC.—PURCHASED THE FRANCHISE RIGHTS FOR TEXAS.

VISIBLE CHANGES INC.

WHILE MANY PEOPLE SIMPLY DREAM OF BECOMING successful, for the people who come to Visible Changes Inc., dreams really do come true. Visible Changes Precision Haircutters is a hair salon chain based on a revolutionary concept, an idea that worked so well that in 1988 cofounder John McCormack appeared on the cover of *Inc.* magazine as the hottest entrepreneur in America. Today Visible Changes owns 17 salons across Texas as well as the Visible Changes University in Houston.

HUMBLE BEGINNINGS

McCormack was an ex-New York City cop who'd made and lost $1 million on Wall Street. His wife, Maryanne, owned a hair salon on Long Island. But a lot of things changed when the husband-and-wife team came to Houston in the mid-1970s and founded a company based on people, not profits. John had spent nearly a decade studying under immigrant businessmen, learning how people with no working knowledge of America's language, currency, or business practices could become successful. Maryanne honed her haircutting and customer service skills by training under the renowned Paul Mitchell. Together, the McCormack had a dream to build a successful haircutting operation with a "people come first" philosophy.

VISIBLE CHANGES' TOP STAFF MEMBERS PROUDLY DISPLAY THE TOOLS OF THEIR TRADE. HAVING A GOOD TIME WHILE WORKING HARD IS A LARGE PART OF THE COMPANY'S PHILOSOPHY (FAR RIGHT).

VISIBLE CHANGES UNIVERSITY, A 25,000-SQUARE-FOOT EDUCATIONAL FACILITY FOR NEW STYLISTS, PROVIDES COMPLETE COSMETOLOGY TRAINING IN HAIRDRESSING, MAKEUP, NAILS, AND SKIN CARE (BELOW).

PEOPLE BEFORE PROFITS

When the McCormacks opened their first Visible Changes salon in 1977 at Greenspoint Mall in Houston, the industry was largely mom-and-pop oriented and notoriously disorganized. The average hairdresser was paid by the day, earned about $6,000 a year, and received no benefits. John saw a huge potential for building a chain that focused on giving the staff all the advantages of a "legitimate" business and creating an environment where they could earn a rewarding salary. As John says, "If we take care of our people, our people take care of our customers." Haircutters didn't have to answer phones, make appointments, or do shampoos—new stylists shampooed clients in their training phase, and receptionists were hired to run the front desks. "We reassigned all the jobs that were nonproductive to the stylist, and then gave the cutters incentives to service more clients," John explains.

The McCormacks devised a unique layout for the Visible Changes salons with open 50-foot glass fronts to showcase the hairdressers, who stand on platforms under spotlights. "In 1977 there was no such thing as a salon you could see into," recalls Maryanne. "We wanted an exciting atmosphere where our stylists and their clients could be the stars." Bright neon accents, popular music, and state-of-the-art equipment round out the salons' arrangement.

To make the business work, John created a system for servicing the maximum number of customers efficiently—with great haircuts—in a minimum amount of time. "In the beginning, we basically had to give away haircuts until we built up a customer base," says John. Maryanne turned her expertise to the haircutting side and designed a training program that would ensure a quality haircut from any of the company's hairdressers. Even today, every Visible Changes stylist must complete a six-month basic training course, as well as attend quarterly refresher classes. The McCormacks also established the Visible Changes University—an institution that not only trains students to cut hair, but also equips them with life and career survival tools—to achieve the quality factor they wanted.

CREATING A PROFITABLE COMPANY

From the beginning, Visible Changes offered hairdressers much more than a paycheck. The company paid salaries based on the quality and volume of cuts performed. The stylists were among the first in the industry to receive health insurance in addition to generous cash bonuses and company trips to exotic locations. In the late 1970s, 70 percent of the stylists in Houston didn't have high school diplomas, so the McCormacks quickly urged their staff members to get their GED, to remove the notion that hairdressers were uneducated. Today Visible Changes Education Fund provides scholarships for employees' children.

The company didn't turn a profit until 1980, when it made $100,000—which the McCormacks promptly put into a profit-sharing fund for the staff. "People thought we were nuts for putting back everything we made," recalls John. "But we knew it would pay off in the growth and stability of our company." In 1995 Visible Changes' profit-sharing plan amounted to nearly $10 million shared by 650 staff members.

The McCormacks' marketing savvy only strengthened the business. By locating salons in major regional shopping malls, they attracted customers by making haircuts an impulse buy. Customer loyalty remains high, as 85 percent of Visible Changes' business is from regular clients. Early on, John developed a com-

▶ WALTER JIMENEZ

puter system to track and promote client services, sending discount coupons to customers on their birthdays and at Christmas.

John—who is cofounder of the Entrepreneurship Program at the University of Houston and who is also an adjunct professor at Rice University—emphasizes that entrepreneurship only has meaning if it helps other people in their lives. Ninety-six percent of the Visible Changes staff are women, many of whom are the primary source of income. The McCormacks are proud that their company provides the means for these women to earn a salary to support their families. The average Visible Changes stylist earns $35,000 annually.

Fifty percent of the company's profits are dedicated to staff inspiration and education, including lavish trips that encourage employees to strive for even higher goals. Also, Visible Changes frequently sponsors motivational speakers and encourages the staff to share what they've learned with patrons. As a result, John says, "Our clients are blown away by what our hairdressers talk about." The company's internal mentoring program—The Fisherman's Club—nurtures productive employees by teaming experienced stylists with newer ones.

In an industry that typically has a three-month turnover, Visible Changes' employee loyalty is evident in the fact that more than half the staff have been with the company for more than seven years.

Visible Changes encourages its people to give as much as they receive. Throughout the company, the McCormacks have inspired a strong sense of community. Several times a year the entire staff donates their time in "cut-a-thons" to raise money for various charities, primarily the Arbor Preschool, a teaching organization that helps students with a multitude of physical problems.

By 1982 Visible Changes had the number one volume among hair salons in the country and remains first in the nation in volume today. To maintain that ranking, John instills another grain of wisdom in his staff: "I don't believe anybody comes in just for a haircut," he says. "They come in for an experience." In the 17 Visible Changes salons across Houston, San Antonio, Austin, and Dallas, clients of all ages, from children to seniors, sample that experience and leave with the feeling that they've not only received a great haircut, but they've also been a part of someone's dream.

JOHN MCCORMACK, CEO OF VISIBLE CHANGES, INSPIRES AND MOTIVATES PEAK PERFORMANCE FROM HIS STAFF THROUGH QUARTERLY MEETINGS (TOP).

THE FLAGSHIP OF THE COMPANY, VISIBLE CHANGES' HOUSTON GALLERIA SALON BOASTS 60 STYLING STATIONS AND A FULL RANGE OF SERVICES, INCLUDING PERMING, COLORING, NAILS, AND MAKEUP (BOTTOM).

I.W. Marks Jewelers, Inc.

GLITTERING GOLD AND DAZZLING DIAMONDS MAY BE THE stuff some people's dreams are made of, but they're the love and livelihood of Irving W. Marks. His commitment to providing quality jewelry and customer service has enabled him to build his company from a small mom-and-pop store into the largest and most successful independent jewelry retailer in Houston. ★ Marks' career

began when he was a 16-year-old student working as a trainee for a large jeweler in Chicago. "When things got busy, I helped out on the selling floor," he recalls. "Eventually, I began outselling the regular sales staff."

Although he left the company seven years after he completed college and eventually moved to Texas, the experience made a lasting impression. After 15 years in the corporate arena, Marks, an entrepreneur at heart, decided to venture out by opening his own jewelry store on Bellaire Boulevard in 1978.

Marks had acquired considerable capital through wise investing. However, he still had to sell his home and borrow funds to purchase the inventory and equipment required to open a fine full-service jewelry store.

The gamble paid off. Thanks to effective marketing and a rapidly growing reputation for personal service, honesty, and integrity, I.W. Marks Jewelers, Inc. began attracting a steady stream of customers. Within three years it had become the largest independent jewelry store in the city, a benchmark it still holds today.

Even during Houston's economic downturn, when dozens of competitors closed their doors, I.W. Marks Jewelers enjoyed steady growth. It has expanded its floor space from 500 to 7,500 square feet, and its 25 employees now generate diamond sales comparable to those of a major 15-outlet chain.

Superior Service

We're diametrically different from the jewelry stores you see in the malls," Marks explains. "We don't have the high rent and other overhead costs those stores have, so we can keep our prices very competitive. And because we don't have to accommodate mall shoppers, we don't have to stay open every night." Because Marks' staff members are paid on salary rather than commission, they remain focused on serving the customer rather than on making a sale. "Since we don't hire part-time help and we don't lay people off," says Marks, "our customers can expect the kind of consistent service they're not likely to find in other jewelry stores.

"Every sales associate in our store has an average of 25 years experience in this business," Marks adds. "They're honest and professional and they treat the customers like they themselves would want to be treated."

When customers come into I.W. Marks Jewelers, they not only enjoy superior service, but can also choose from one of the most extensive selections of diamonds, as well as 14-karat and 18-karat gold jewelry, in the Southwest. The store boasts watches from such noted name brands as Bertolucci, Breitling, Tag Heuer, Raymond Weil, Concord, Omega, Philippe Charriol, and many others. Custom jewelry design and manufacturing, watch repair, diamond setting, pearl restringing, and appraisals by a certified graduate gemologist are performed on the premises.

A Jewel of a Guy

Marks' commitment to his craft led to his receiving the 1994 Houston Award for Quality presented by the Houston Better Business Bureau Education Foundation and the University of Houston

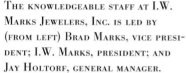

The knowledgeable staff at I.W. Marks Jewelers, Inc. is led by (from left) Brad Marks, vice president; I.W. Marks, president; and Jay Holtorf, general manager.

College of Business Administration. However, Marks is most proud of the awards he has received for community service. Plaques on his wall attest to his leadership role in a variety of nonprofit organizations, including membership on the board of directors for the Houston Livestock Show and Rodeo, Crime Stoppers, the Cancer League of Houston, and the St. Pius X High School Foundation. His humanitarian and philanthropic contributions to the city have prompted two mayors, Kathy Whitmire and Bob Lanier, to proclaim two separate I.W. Marks days in Houston.

A milestone in Marks' career was being named three times as the national recipient of the Business Committee for the Arts' and *Forbes* magazine's coveted Business in the Arts Award—an honor historically bestowed upon heads of major corporations such as Texaco, AT&T, and Boeing. Marks participates on the board and executive committee of the Society for the Performing Arts, serves as vice president of the Houston Grand Opera, and is a member of the board for the Houston Symphony. In addition, he shows his generosity by underwriting opera and symphony productions and special events

for these deserving organizations. In 1996 Marks received the Ovation for Excellence Award from the Houston Symphony, an accolade given to citizens who support the symphony as well as other artistic and charitable causes throughout the community. Marks is also a founder and director of Citizens National Bank of Texas, one of the largest independent banks in Harris County.

Now Marks is grooming his son, Bradley, to follow in his footsteps. Brad Marks began sweeping floors at the store when he was a child and worked there part-time in high school and college. The business graduate of Texas A&M University has joined the store's staff full-time. With his help and that of his father, I.W. Marks Jewelers will continue setting the pace for the jewelry industry in terms of service, selection, quality, and community support.

BRIDAL AND DIAMOND JEWELRY IS A SPECIALTY AT I.W. MARKS JEWELERS.

AN OIL TANKER PULLS AWAY FROM A DOCK AT HOUSTON FUEL Oil Terminal Company, located at the widest point of the Houston Ship Channel that links the city's port with the Gulf of Mexico. Loaded with residual fuel oil, it's destined for the Mediterranean, where its cargo will be burned by utility companies that provide power to another industrialized region of the world. ★ The tanker

CLOCKWISE FROM TOP LEFT: HOUSTON FUEL OIL'S PIPELINES SEND CRUDE OIL TO FOUR AREA REFINERIES AND THE INTERCONNECTING PIPELINES TO THE MIDWEST.

THE TERMINAL COUNTS AMONG ITS CUSTOMERS ALMOST ALL OF THE MAJOR OIL COMPANIES, OIL TRADERS, CARBON BLACK MANUFACTURERS, AND BUNKER SUPPLIERS (COMPANIES THAT PROVIDE FUEL FOR SHIPS).

THE HOUSTON FUEL OIL TERMINAL IS LOCATED ON THE HOUSTON SHIP CHANNEL WITH AN EXCELLENT VIEW OF THE SAN JACINTO MONUMENT.

▲ STEVE HENRY

is just one of about 25 ships—as well as more than 1,000 trucks, 300 railcars, and 350 barges—that arrive at the terminal each month to load or unload residual fuel, crude oil, carbon black, refinery feedstocks, and other specialty oils. Business is brisk at Houston Fuel Oil's 255-acre facility, the largest black oil terminal on the oil-rich Gulf Coast and the fourth largest in the country.

OPERATING AT CAPACITY

The terminal's storage tanks, which hold more than 7 million barrels of product, have been fully utilized since 1990. Houston Fuel Oil's pipelines send crude oil to four area refineries and the interconnecting pipelines to the Midwest. The terminal counts among its customers almost all of the major oil companies, oil traders, carbon black manufacturers, and bunker suppliers (companies that provide fuel for ships). About 80 percent of the company's business is international, compared to only 20 percent in 1990. For instance, crude oil comes from the Mideast and Central America, refinery feedstocks come from Europe and South America, and products are shipped to Asia, Europe, and South Africa.

The original 4.8 million-barrel terminal was built in 1979 by Scallop Petroleum, a former subsidiary of Royal Dutch Shell, and Apex Oil Company, a St. Louis-based enterprise that once

accounted for almost half the residual fuel oil business in the United States. Both firms needed heated storage facilities to satisfy their fuel oil logistical needs, but no significant heated storage facilities existed at that time along the Gulf Coast. As a result, bottlenecks were developing at the companies' refinery sources and in the distribution system, and building the terminal offered a solution to a shared dilemma.

The terminal experienced some difficult days in the mid-1980s when the collapse of the oil business and abundant natural gas drove down the demand for fuel oil. As refineries curtailed production of residual fuel oil, Apex went into Chapter 11 bankruptcy proceedings, and utilization of the terminal dropped to about 30 percent. In 1989 Chartco Terminals, L.P., a private investment group, bought out Apex's share of the business. Meanwhile, Shell restructured its ownership interest under a new subsidiary to replace Scallop. After restructuring, the Houston Fuel Oil Terminal aggressively opened its storage facilities to a broadened list of third-party customers, and business began to improve.

Oil companies and traders eventually booked all the terminal's spare storage capacity. "By 1990 utilization was up to 100 percent, and it has been that way ever since," says Willis K. Rossler Jr., who came on board that year as the terminal's president and chief executive officer.

EXPANSION FOR TODAY AND TOMORROW

To remain responsive to its customers' needs, Houston Fuel Oil Termi-

◄ BOLT PHOTOGRAPHY, INC.

nal Company has spent about $45 million in recent years on two major expansion projects. The first, which took place in 1992, involved constructing a second ship dock, installing a 16-inch crude oil pipeline to connect the terminal with a refinery on the ship channel, adding 1.3 million barrels of storage capacity, and expanding the terminal's product-blending facilities. Another expansion project late in 1994 added a 10.5-mile 24-inch-diameter crude oil pipeline to other refineries as well as additional storage capacity of 650,000 barrels. Four 175,000-barrel tanks were also converted from fuel oil to crude oil. "Without the pipelines, we couldn't diversify in a major way," Rossler recalls.

Today the Houston Fuel Oil Terminal employs 60 people, and the facility boasts 58 storage tanks, 56 of which are heated.

Its two deepwater docks serve the largest vessels that travel the Houston Ship Channel, loading and receiving up to 35,000 barrels an hour. "That speed gives us an advantage over our competitors," Rossler notes, "because it minimizes our customers' dock time and charter expenses."

In addition, the terminal's four barge docks accommodate nine barges simultaneously, loading at a rate of 10,000 barrels hourly. The facility's tank-truck racks can accommodate 11 trucks at a time, and its rail system handles 30 cars simultaneously. The terminal also provides blending services, either in-tank or on-line, that are monitored constantly to ensure customer specifications are met.

"We've continued to expand our facilities to serve crude oil and refinery feedstock customers while maintaining our strong commitment to residual fuels for

the Gulf Coast," Rossler reports. "For example, we've installed state-of-the-art computer systems that enable customers anywhere in the world to dial in by telephone modem at any time to check their inventory."

The company has also enhanced its capability to eventually serve refineries in the Midwest through interconnecting pipelines with its new 24-inch pipeline. Future growth could include a processing plant project and three additional barge docks on the 130 acres of adjacent land the terminal purchased in January 1995.

Its cooperative attitude ensures Houston Fuel Oil Terminal a secure future. "We're willing to build tanks or pipelines or put in special shipping facilities for customers who will be with us for the long term," Rossler says. "We're very progressive and responsive—and we're committed to serving our customers' needs."

EACH MONTH, APPROXIMATELY 25 SHIPS AND MORE THAN 1,000 TRUCKS, 300 RAIL CARS, AND 350 BARGES ARRIVE AT THE HOUSTON FUEL OIL TERMINAL TO LOAD OR UNLOAD RESIDUAL FUEL, CRUDE OIL, CARBON BLACK, REFINERY FEEDSTOCKS, AND OTHER SPECIALTY OILS. BUSINESS IS BRISK AT HOUSTON FUEL OIL'S 255-ACRE FACILITY, THE LARGEST BLACK OIL TERMINAL ON THE OIL-RICH GULF COAST AND THE FOURTH-LARGEST IN THE COUNTRY.

FOUR SEASONS HOTEL

THE LANDSCAPE OF DOWNTOWN HOUSTON CHANGED dramatically in April 1982 when the luxurious Four Seasons Hotel opened its doors. Amid the city's towering skyscrapers, the Four Seasons took its place as an elegant oasis for the Houston corporate community, as well as for visiting dignitaries, business clientele, celebrities, and leisure travelers. ★ As downtown Houston's only AAA Five Diamond Hotel, Four Seasons Hotel Houston is renowned for its impeccable service, outstanding accommodations, and award-winning restaurants. Simply put, this hotel embodies the art of hospitality.

AWARD-WINNING FITNESS CENTER

Adjacent to the Four Seasons' beautiful, climate-controlled outdoor swimming pool and lush, terraced gardens is the hotel's state-of-the-art fitness facility. Recognized by *Travel and Leisure* magazine as one of the top five hotel health clubs in the United States, the fitness center boasts—among other features—Vectra equipment, Lifecycles, Stairmasters, free weights, a 15-foot whirlpool, dry saunas, and a personal trainer who is on hand daily to assist and counsel guests.

Understanding that busy travelers often leave home without their sports attire, the Four Seasons' beautifully appointed locker facilities are stocked with swimming suits, workout gear, and an array of bath amenities. For those guests in need of extra pampering, the Four Seasons also offers Adagio European Spa treatments, such as massage therapy, aromatherapy, loofah salt glow, honey and almond body scrubs, and seaweed body treatments. A full-service unisex salon featuring Erick Mann is also on site.

As an extension of the hotel's fitness services, the Four Seasons offers its guests access privileges to the nearby Houston Center Athletic Club. The club connects to the Four Seasons through a climate-controlled walkway and offers a full range of activities, including aerobic and yoga classes, squash, racquetball, basketball, and an indoor jogging trail.

CULINARY TRENDSETTER

The Four Seasons was the first hotel in Houston to introduce healthy, alternative cuisine. For years, health-conscious guests have been able to order from a range of enticing entrées that are low in calories, cholesterol, and sodium.

Another first was the hotel's initiation of home-style cooking. Restaurant-weary travelers may enjoy comfort food—such as chicken-fried steak, lasagna, fried chicken, and pizza—in the privacy of their rooms. The room service menu also includes the sumptuous dishes served in the Four Seasons' celebrated DeVille restaurant. The DeVille is a culinary landmark that turns dining into an extraordinary experience. The synthesis of stunning decor and warm, hospitable service makes the DeVille an elegant sanctuary.

Behind the scenes, a kitchen

THE FOUR SEASONS HAS BEEN A PART OF THE DYNAMIC HOUSTON COMMUNITY SINCE 1982 (RIGHT).

brigade of 50 staffers at the DeVille create the cuisine from scratch. From the smoked salmon and sausage to the delectable breads and pastries, everything is prepared in the kitchen from start to finish. To complement the artfully executed entrées, diners may choose from any of the 375 vintages on the restaurant's impressive wine list.

The result of the DeVille's commitment to excellence can be witnessed in its roster of prestigious awards, which include the AAA Four Diamond award; the Mobile Four Star award; the DiRONA award; the *Wine Spectator* magazine Award of Excellence; the *Condé Nast Traveler* magazine readers' poll award, Worth the Journey; and the Zagat Restaurant Survey's top winner for Best Hotel Dining, Best Service, Best New American Cuisine, Best Sunday Brunch, and Best Continental Cuisine.

Additionally, the DeVille has become the premier choice for Houstonians to enjoy Sunday brunch. Each week the hotel hosts a champagne jazz brunch, which includes a complimentary glass of champagne and an opulent buffet. To enhance the experience for families over holidays and special events, such as Easter and Mother's Day, the Four Seasons has created the Kids' Castle, where children play in a fanciful castle supervised by bonded sitters who lead their young children in organized activities while their parents continue to savor their meals.

During the holidays, brunch at the DeVille takes on a magical quality and is always celebrated with creative entertainment and festive highlights.

There are also special children's events. One Christmas, the hotel hosted Lunch with Belle. The star from the Broadway production of *Beauty and the Beast* read books to a rapt audience, and then led them in Christmas carols. Another year, children were treated to Brunch with Peter Pan. Actress Cathy Rigby performed before a ballroom full of young admirers, and then orchestrated a pots-and-pans parade to the lobby where a vast gingerbread village awaited them.

Those who want a fine meal in short order may dine in the casual sophistication of the Terrace Cafe. The café specializes in light fare such as pasta, salads, grilled fish, and sandwiches that are served in a relaxed atmosphere.

DEDICATION TO THE ARTS

Over the years, the Four Seasons has underwritten many of the city's most prestigious arts events. Houstonians are still talking about the hotel's world premiere opening night gala for *Beauty and the Beast*. The Four Seasons hosted and sponsored a black-tie gala that saluted the world premiere

CLOCKWISE FROM TOP RIGHT: THE HOTEL'S DEVILLE RESTAURANT IS A CULINARY LANDMARK THAT TURNS DINING INTO AN EXTRAORDINARY EXPERIENCE.

THE FOUR SEASONS OFFERS 103 EXECUTIVE SUITES WITH SEPARATE SITTING AREAS AND BEDROOMS.

THE HOTEL'S 399 GUEST ROOMS REFLECT THE LUXURY AND ATTENTION TO DETAIL THAT ARE HALLMARKS OF THE FOUR SEASONS.

THE FOUR SEASONS LOBBY SETS A TONE OF ELEGANCE THAT GUESTS WILL ENJOY THROUGHOUT THE HOTEL.

ARTHUR D. LITTLE, INC.

THE WAY THE WORLD DOES BUSINESS IS CHANGING. WHILE semanticists debate whether it's evolution or revolution, companies are facing inevitable changes, and they increasingly need consultants to help them manage in more creative and productive ways. ★ Some of the best consultants in Houston are associates of Arthur D. Little, Inc. One of 51 branch locations in 30 countries,

the Houston office opened in 1982 and is among the parent company's largest regional operations.

MIT professor Arthur Dehon Little introduced the world's first business consulting firm in Cambridge, Massachusetts, more than 100 years ago. His original premise—that business could prosper and benefit from the application of scientific thought and methodology—was radical for its day, but time has more than proven Little's hypothesis. The company he founded is as innovative today as it was a century ago.

SUBSTANCE MAKES THE DIFFERENCE

We're quite different from other consulting groups, and the differ-ence is one of substance," says Chris Ross, vice president. Manager of the Houston office since its opening, Ross is also a managing director of the International Energy Directorate, one of the firm's specialty divisions.

Ross points out that his firm employs a collaborative approach in order to establish true partnerships with each of its clients. "We look upon our work together as a shared learning process," he explains, "and the knowledge we generate as a team is valuable permanent capital for our clients. When we're called in—as we have been by more than 75 percent of the Fortune 500 companies—we come with experienced and knowledgeable people who work side by side with our clients to bring about lasting and beneficial change. We don't fix problems—together, we find, plant, and nurture solutions."

Arthur D. Little handles approximately 4,000 assignments each year in 60 countries. Its principal areas of expertise

ARTHUR D. LITTLE EMPLOYS A COL-LABORATIVE APPROACH IN ORDER TO ESTABLISH TRUE PARTNERSHIPS WITH EACH OF ITS CLIENTS. STAFF MEMBERS WORK SIDE BY SIDE WITH CLIENTS IN TEAMS (RIGHT).

ARTHUR D. LITTLE'S HOUSTON OFFICE FOCUSES ON THE OIL AND CHEMICAL INDUSTRIES (BELOW).

are management consulting, environmental, and health and safety consulting, as well as technical and product development.

Houston office projects have historically reflected the company's broad capabilities. Its diverse clients have included NASA (Arthur D. Little was responsible for more Apollo program experiments than any other company) as well as major oil, gas, and chemical companies. Consultants in the Houston office also serve YPF, Argentina's largest single company. Arthur D. Little helped guide YPF through a complicated privatization process. Houston staff associates have recently been very active in a number of other South and Central American projects.

WINDOW ON THE WORLD

Houston is truly a cosmopolitan city, in both the ways and places it does business," says Ross. "Because our company is imbedded in the fabric of key industries worldwide, we have the same world view as our clients, but with a local presence and vision upon which they have come to rely."

The talents and background of the firm's Houston staff match the needs of the local market. Like their associates in the company's offices around the world, Arthur D. Little representatives are distinguished not only by their innate talent and ability, but also by the caliber, breadth, and depth of their experience.

In addition, most Arthur D. Little associates have come to the consulting field after successful early careers in a number of industries served by the firm. Ross' background, for instance, is in the oil industry. Others in the Houston office have had extensive experience in the chemicals, natural gas, engineering and construction, financial, metals and resources, and telecommunications industries. They combine deep understanding of the industries they serve with state-of-the-art expertise in strategy,

HOUSTON CONSULTANTS ARE ABLE TO CALL ON ARTHUR D. LITTLE'S GLOBAL RESOURCES.

organization, supply chain management, information management, and technology.

Most of Arthur D. Little's staff members understand corporate culture because they have experienced it themselves and are able to speak the language of their clients' industries. They also may be aware of a particular industry's tendency to resist change and performance improvement.

"We say here that the right path is not so much discovered as created—tough decision by tough decision," explains Ross. "The courage and tenacity to face and make those tough decisions will greatly enhance the likelihood of a company's ability to prosper." Although many corporations fear the very idea of change, Arthur D. Little is optimistic that its efforts can strengthen the position of its client companies against an uncertain future.

THE RIGHT PATH

Arthur D. Little believes that a company trying to move forward needs to know first where it is, where it wants to go, and finally, how to get there. "We help our clients develop a realistic picture, understanding where they are and developing an exciting vision of where they could be," says Ross. "The dynamic tension between these two positions is the raw material for good strategy development."

Some local associates have used this approach to help area businesses enter international markets. Others have used it to help improve productivity at large chemical companies or to assist oil companies in refining their future visions.

Ross points out that Arthur D. Little has worked with some of the finest, most respected businesses in Houston. "We look forward to continuing these excellent relationships well into the future," says Ross. "In the Houston office of Arthur D. Little, we feel today there's room for pride, but not complacency. Our ambition, after all, is to be the consultant of choice for all clients in the industries we serve."

NGC Corporation

NGC Corporation, based in Houston, has carved out a unique role as a gatherer, processor, transporter, and marketer of energy products and services in North America and the United Kingdom. NGC's customers are not retail consumers: They are local distribution companies, utilities, refineries, chemical plants, and other large industrial end users. The product—energy—is a commodity that can take the form of natural gas, crude oil, natural gas liquids, or electricity. NGC is an "energy superstore," serving both producers and consumers of energy and offering a complete portfolio of products and value-added services.

In a single decade, NGC has grown from a small natural gas marketer to become one of the largest energy commodity marketing companies on the continent. With 700 Houston-based employees, $4 billion in annual revenues, and a listing on the New York Stock Exchange under the symbol NGL, this energy company clearly has emerged as the best of the new breed.

Defying the Odds

By all accounts 1984 was a tough year to enter the natural gas business. Struggling through the early stages of the deregulation of natural gas, the industry endured continual change and uncertainty. Market forces were at odds with remaining price controls and other federal regulations, leading to an oversupply of gas. Adding to these woes were transportation problems caused by pipeline monopolies and inconsistent business practices throughout the industry. But the same conditions that put the gas market into a tailspin also created an opportunity for a group of entrepreneurs who shared a vision for the energy company of the future.

The U.S. Natural Gas Clearinghouse Ltd. (NGC) was formed in July 1984 as an independent marketer of natural gas on the spot market. Rather than simply brokering gas deals as other independent marketers had done, NGC actually bought the gas before selling it. This allowed NGC to aggregate or pool supplies and sell larger volume contracts than most other marketers. As a result, NGC began to build credibility in the marketplace and a reputation for delivering a product no matter how adverse market conditions were at the time.

As deregulation progressed and marketers enjoyed a more level playing field, NGC continued to innovate. While other marketers attempted to make high margins on low volumes in specific areas, NGC built a high-volume low-margin business with geographic diversity. The strategy paid off. By the end of 1988 NGC had become the largest independent marketer of natural gas, with sales representing 3 percent of all gas consumed in the United States.

But NGC was not content with marketing natural gas. In 1989 NGC began acquiring natural gas gathering and processing facilities and expanded the product portfolio to include natural gas liquids and crude oil. NGC's strong nationwide presence and growth potential were augmented by expansion into Canada and the United Kingdom in 1994. With the acquisition of Trident NGL, Inc. in 1995, another brick was added to the foundation of the energy superstore, and NGC became a publicly traded company. Today the company has a

First Interstate Bank Plaza is a 71-story 1.7 million-square-foot building in downtown Houston. NGC will relocate its corporate headquarters from suburban Houston to the upper 10 floors of the First Interstate building in the first quarter of 1997. NGC will occupy 230,000 square feet with approximately 700 employees in its new headquarters.

total asset base of approximately 10,000 miles of natural gas pipelines, 33 natural gas processing plants, three natural gas liquids fractionation facilities, 15.5 million barrels of NGL storage, and an NGL import/export terminal.

NGC has now begun to leverage the experience gained during natural gas deregulation to expand into the newly deregulated electric power marketplace with its Electric Clearinghouse, Inc. (ECI) subsidiary. Since operations began on January 1, 1995, ECI has sold a total of 3.5 million megawatt hours during 1995. Already ECI is ranked as the nation's third-largest independent power marketer.

NGC has built its success on assets, products, services, and entrepreneurial spirit. Just as important, however, is the fact that NGC has positioned itself as the energy superstore of the future. NGC offers customers a custom-tailored package of commodity energy products and the ability to serve as large-scale aggregator, processor, marketer, supplier, asset manager, and financial risk manager.

The evolution of NGC reached yet another high point with the recent proposed merger between NGC and two business units of industry giant Chevron. The newly merged company will combine all of NGC with most of Chevron's Houston natural gas business unit and Tulsa-based Warren Petroleum. Under the agreement, NGC markets virtually all of Chevron's North American production of natural gas, natural gas liquids, and electricity. In turn, the new entity supplies energy and feedstocks to Chevron refineries, chemical plants, and other corporate facilities in North America.

The combined organization links North America's second- and fourth-largest natural gas marketers, with sales of 10 billion cubic feet per day or roughly 14 percent of the total market. It also makes NGC the largest marketer of natural gas liquids and the second-largest

TERRY VINE

TERRY VINE

processor of natural gas in the United States. NGC president and CEO C.L. "Chuck" Watson is quick to point out, however, that size alone does not make a better company: "No matter how large our operations become, it is critical to maintain our entrepreneurial mind-set. At NGC that spirit of hustle is a corporate signature—our most prized intangible asset."

A COMPANY ON THE MOVE

Every growing family needs a larger home. For NGC, home will be a 230,000-square-foot headquarters in Houston. The move from its current space on U.S. 290 in northwest Houston to

the 71-story First Interstate Bank Plaza downtown is expected to take place in early 1997. NGC will occupy 10 floors with options for further expansion.

Throughout the search for new space, NGC was courted by practically every commercial development within a 30-mile radius and lobbied by officials such as Mayor Bob Lanier and the Greater Houston Partnership. But in the end, NGC determined that the best location is one that puts it closest to its customers, the energy companies that densely populate the downtown landscape. That's just what you'd expect from an energy superstore where decisions are always market driven.

NGC's "ENERGY SUPERSTORE" SERVES BOTH PRODUCERS AND CONSUMERS OF NATURAL GAS, NATURAL GAS LIQUIDS, CRUDE OIL, AND ELECTRICITY.

KTBZ-107.5 *THE BUZZ*

ON HALLOWEEN 1994 THE COMPETITIVE LANDSCAPE changed dramatically for Houston's rock radio stations when KTBZ, New Rock 107.5 *THE BUZZ* debuted its Modern Rock format. At last, Houston had joined the list of top 10 radio markets that enjoy their own full-time Modern Rock radio. ★ Modern Rock has become the fastest-growing radio format for the '90s. According

ACCORDING TO GENERAL MANAGER PATRICK FANT, "HOUSTON RADIO WAS NOT SATISFYING THE DEMAND FOR TODAY'S NEW ROCK UNTIL *THE BUZZ* ARRIVED TO PROVIDE A PURE PRODUCT." (TOP)

A UNIQUE ROLLING FLEET, WHICH INCLUDES TWO HUMMERS, CREATES AN UNMATCHED STREET PRESENCE IN HOUSTON (BOTTOM).

to General Manager Patrick Fant, "Houston radio was not satisfying the demand for today's new rock until *THE BUZZ* arrived to provide a pure product—not a hybrid of Modern Rock and some other loosely related music style."

By the end of 1995, *THE BUZZ* had become Houston's fastest-growing radio station among the pivotal 25 to 34 age group.

MODERN ROCK IS MAINSTREAM MUSIC

The Modern Rock style has been developing for nearly 15 years," says Fant. "Time has caught up with this format. Modern Rock now delivers to a mainstream adult audience, along with the younger adults who are naturally passionate about this music because it speaks for their generation.

Artists like The Who, Hendrix, Led Zeppelin—considered cutting edge in the '70s—became mainstream in the '80s. Likewise, Pearl Jam, Stone Temple Pilots, and Smashing Pumpkins have crossed over into the mainstream music from what once seemed extreme. But today, artists develop at an accelerated pace from 'alternative and peculiar' to 'featured performers' on television's high-profile late-night lineup, such as the *Late Show* with David Letterman and the *Tonight Show*.

College students who were listening to The Clash in 1979 are now in their 30s, establishing careers while still listening to the music of their generation.

The qualitative profile for Modern Rock listeners nationwide reflects an audience that is among the better educated and is well above average in income

and technical/computer skills. Fant says, "*THE BUZZ* is a radio station for people with their lights on!"

Listeners who easily embrace new ideas are drawn to *THE BUZZ*. They are forward-thinking individuals who are naturally curious and willing to try new things. *BUZZ* listeners are among the most informed, involved, and aware people in Houston. To further inform listeners, the station has developed a highly refined homepage on the Internet, which provides an interactive path and live broadcasts for listener involvement.

A TOP MANAGEMENT TEAM

When it comes to understanding and interpreting music trends, Fant is a pro. His impressive career in Houston's broadcasting industry spans 30 years. Prior to joining *THE BUZZ* in the spring of 1995, Fant served as vice president and general manager for another local radio station and masterminded its successful evolution into one of Houston's top rock stations.

The news of Fant's move to *THE BUZZ* made national headlines. The idea that an executive would walk away from his highly successful brainchild sent shock waves through the industry. The simple fact was that Fant saw the momentum building for Modern Rock and wanted the challenge of creating a format that reached this fast-growing audience. He states, "We designed the premier rock station for the last generation; now we're building a more refined product for the next one."

Fant also surrounds himself with a team of seasoned veterans.

Bob Livermore was recruited to join *THE BUZZ* as marketing director. A longtime Houstonian and civic leader, Livermore brought his 14 years of experience as a local public relations and advertising executive to the station. Program Director Cruze came on board with a reputation as an innovator willing to challenge traditional limits of programming strategy. Fant also appointed Russell Lindley as general sales manager and Bill Powell as national sales manager because of their winning track record with another local rock station. Music Director David Sadof is the undisputed musicologist in Modern Rock and serves as the final filter in bringing the right new sound to *THE BUZZ*.

In addition, an arsenal of industry-leading consultants, such as Doug Harris and Jeff Pollack, confer to complement the picture. "This is the strongest team that's ever been put together in Houston radio," says Fant. "*THE BUZZ* executives have roots in the community that go very deep. Many of them are native Houstonians who have made their mark in Houston media and gained the respect of our business leaders through years of making things happen."

This all-star team is backed by one of the most well-respected broadcasting corporations in the United States: Ohio-based Nationwide Communications Inc., which operates 13 other radio stations around the country. "*THE BUZZ* may become the template for a Modern Rock network of radio stations," says Fant. "We expect our format and marketing strategies will eventually be duplicated in other markets."

STREET MARKETING

Modern Rock is where music is going, not where it's been. Audiences enjoy the live music experience, and *THE BUZZ* gives it to them all year long. Examples include *THE BUZZ* Festival,

held annually in the spring, which is one of Houston's most anticipated music events. Of course, *BUZZ* cameras capture the event live on the Internet, including interactive Q&A with artists from a backstage website. *THE BUZZ* Labor Day Block Party, Halloween Monster Mosh, and Yuletide Bash are already permanent features of the station's annual calendar. A glitzy event around the holidays called *BUZZ* Style is an art/fashion/dance/technology fair, which celebrates many of the cornerstones of *THE BUZZ* listeners' active lifestyle.

A unique rolling fleet including two Hummers, "Jeeps on Steroids" as Fant calls them, creates a street presence unmatched in the market. Add a "Prize Cannon" to the rear deck of one Hummer and the station appears to cut a "Rat Patrol"-like profile. The Prize Cannon is a nitrogen-powered Buzz-ooka that shoots soft promotional items into the hands of enthusiastic fans more than 50 yards away.

"Radio is the entertainment business. We continuously look for new ways to attract attention," Fant explains. *THE BUZZ* designed and created the radio

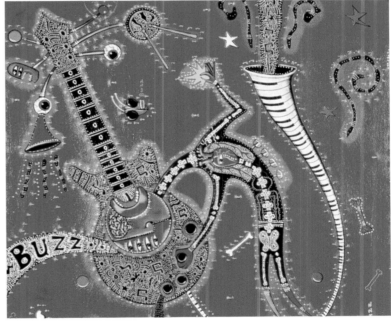

industry's only regulation-size half-pipe skateboarding ramp. The half-pipe brings the spectacle of extreme sports up close and in focus for *BUZZ* clients.

THE BUZZ stands out in Houston's crowded marketplace. High above the street, its market-exclusive freeway billboards tell drivers the name of the band playing on *THE BUZZ* at the moment they pass it.

Advertisers count on *THE BUZZ* to deliver creative marketing strategies, a quality audience and best of all . . . results.

As motorists pass *BUZZ* billboards, a digital data link electronically displays the name of the artist "now playing" (top).

A modern art piece titled "*THE BUZZ*" was designed for KTBZ by nationally known artist Joel Nakamura (bottom).

AMERICAN RICE, INC.

ADOLPHUS®, COMET®, AND BLUE RIBBON® RICE PRODUCTS have become favorite staples on grocery store shelves across Houston, but few shoppers may realize that one locally based company, American Rice, Inc. (ARI), produces each of these brands. ARI has grown from a regional rice milling company to become an international agribusiness firm that is active in all phases of

rice milling, processing, and marketing.

One of the world's leading processors and marketers of branded rice products, ARI controls approximately one-fifth of the total rice processing capacity in the United States and has held an approximate 4 percent share of historic global rice trade. The company's brands hold top positions in many U.S. markets and Puerto Rico, as well as the number one position in Saudi Arabia and Haiti. "We're a value-added company," says Senior Vice President John Poole. "We take the product from the farmer to the final point of sale, be it retail, food service, or export."

A FERTILE BUSINESS

For many years the Texas rice industry was dominated by privately owned mills that set their own quality standards in terms of purchasing crops. In 1969 a small group of farmers founded ARI as a cooperative in order to set uniform grading standards. The cooperative purchased Blue Ribbon Rice Mills, Inc. in 1975. One of the oldest private mills in the area, Blue Ribbon had been operating since 1901.

ARI's business soon expanded into Louisiana and Mississippi. By 1985 the cooperative had outgrown its Blue Ribbon milling facilities and subsequently built the only rice processing plant in the nation adjacent to a deepwater port. The cooperative became a publicly held corporation in 1988, retaining the name American Rice, Inc.

In 1993 ARI's future was secured with the acquisition of Comet Rice, Inc. from the Los Angeles-based ERLY Industries Inc., creating the nation's largest rice miller and marketer. An international agribusiness company, ERLY also has interests in agricultural consulting and forest fire retardant chemicals. ARI employs approximately 800 persons. In addition to its Houston headquarters and the deepwater facility in Freeport,

Texas, the company owns mills in Arkansas, California, Haiti, Jamaica, and Vietnam.

BRANDS OF CHOICE

In 1995 ARI processed and marketed more than 1 million tons of rice. "We are the single largest seller by volume in the United States," says Poole. The company's Adolphus® products have been the number one selling brand in Houston for more than 75 years, accounting now for more than half of all rice sales in the city. Across the United States and Canada, ARI's long grain brands have attained a number one or number two market share in most of the regions in which they compete, including Comet® in North Carolina, Texas, California, and throughout the Southeast; Blue Ribbon® in South Carolina; Adolphus® in Texas; and AA® and Green Peacock® in California.

ARI also markets its many products to restaurants, cafeterias, fast-food chains, and numerous other eating establishments.

The food service division has won gold medal awards for quality from the Chefs In America and the American Tasting Institute for six straight years. Another division—Comet Ventures, Inc.—supplies rice by-products such as broken rice, bran, and hulls to cereal and snack-food processors. ARI recently diversified even further by packaging a full line of durum semolina pasta products under the flagship labels in each of its markets.

Worldwide, ARI products are shipped to as many as 44 countries. The firm's Golden Chopstick brand, known as Abu Bint®, is the top-selling U.S. brand in Saudi Arabia. ARI has also developed a strong relationship with Japan, supplying about 62 percent of that nation's rice imports.

PROCESSING FACILITIES WORLDWIDE

ARI is the only rice marketer in the world with significant sources of rough rice and mills in all of the United States' major producing regions, as well as overseas. Currently ARI obtains rice from every major rice-producing state in the nation.

With an annual milling capacity of more than 600,000 metric tons, ARI's 20-acre integrated complex in Freeport is the industry's largest and most complete facility. It produces parboiled rice, white rice, instant rice, rice flour, rice oil, consumer packages, and export tonnage. The facility also boasts a bulk loading system that is able to service oceangoing vessels, river barges, trucks, and railcars.

ARI also serves growers in the South through its processing facility in Stuttgart, Arkansas, which has a capacity of 200,000 metric tons. The company's two California facilities, in Maxwell and Biggs, have the largest combined milling capacity in that state as well.

ARI's overseas milling capabilities continue to expand. In the Caribbean, an ARI subsidiary operates a 150,000-metric-ton processing and packaging facility on a self-contained deepwater port near Port-au-Prince, Haiti. In Jeddah, Saudi Arabia, the company manages a receiving, processing, storage, and bagging facility. Since 1994 ARI has also participated in the world market for Asian rice through a joint venture in Vietnam called ARI Vinafood. Managed by ARI, the venture's plant in Can Tho province processes 250,000 metric tons of white rice annually.

ARI has enjoyed record financial performance in recent years. In 1995 sales increased 31 percent to $373 million. And with the company's global vision, future prospects have never looked better. Rice consumption continues to rise all over the world, and ARI's foot is firmly in the door in heavily rice-dependent Japan, where acceptance of the General Agreement on Tariffs and Trade (GATT) ensures importation of more than 3 million tons of rice through the year 2000.

BSG Alliance/IT, Inc.

STEPPING INTO THE FUTURISTIC GLASS AND STEEL LOBBY OF BSG Alliance/IT's Greenway Plaza offices feels a bit like entering the next millennium, yet the atmosphere is still somehow welcoming. This dynamic ability to blend the techno-future into a people-friendly culture is the firm's trademark, and part of what makes BSG "the next generation IT (information technology)

services company."

As one of Houston's fastest-growing companies, BSG has enjoyed a growth rate exceeding 50 percent a year, with 1995 revenues in excess of $69.7 million. Founded by Steven G. Papermaster in 1987, the company now employs 650 people at 11 resource centers across the nation. More than half of the staff (including 200 professional consultants) are based in Houston.

The "High Performance IT" Approach

Concentrating solely on client-server networks, BSG maintains a synergistic balance of industry and technical expertise to help customers meet their business objectives. Here, systems integration is not just a technological event that creates business value, but a cultural change that impacts the whole organization.

Thus, the young company dubs its approach for helping companies adapt to changing technology "high performance IT." This approach combines people, business process, and advanced technology capabilities in a comprehensive set of information technology and change process integration services.

"Everything we do with our customers affects the way in which their people do their jobs," explains George Jones, BSG's market segment leader for Houston and south Texas. "The benefit of new technology is that it enables people to do more than ever before, but that also means you inflict change. High performance IT is not just systems and processes; it's also people."

BSG has applied its IT expertise to a diverse range of industries, including energy and petrochemicals, pharmaceuticals, multiunit retail, insurance and financial, entertainment, transportation and distribution, manu-

facturing, and computers and communications. The firm applies the same customer-intensive vision to all of its clients—whether a project involves helping ARA Food Services capture inventory data within the stadiums it serves or moving Exxon's accounts payable department toward paperless offices.

"We don't come in with a we-know-it-all approach," says Jones. In the early days of BSG's ongoing relationship with the Boston Market restaurant chain, that even meant working behind the counters with the public.

A Cool Company

The "Alliance" portion of BSG's name refers to the firm's willingness to partner with clients in applying emerging technologies. "Being a smaller company, we have more capability to be innovative," says Jones. BSG also nurtures alliances that extend its capabilities in strategic consulting, data center management, global telecommunications, process management, and development methodology.

Also unorthodox in its willingness to share ideas, BSG links its offices—and those of its clients—with Lotus Notes, and holds BSG reunion meetings three times each year to keep employees informed. There's no pretense here, and jeans are definitely allowed. It's no wonder BSG recently earned a distinction from *Fortune* magazine as one of 25 Cool Companies.

BSG is a wholly owned subsidiary of Medaphis Corporation (NASDAQ-MEDA), a leading provider of business management and information technology services.

BSG ALLIANCE/IT, INC.'S OFFICES AT GREENWAY PLAZA PROVIDE A WELCOMING ATMOSPHERE THAT COMBINES TECHNOLOGICAL INNOVATION WITH A PEOPLE-FRIENDLY CULTURE.

SOUTH SHORE HARBOUR RESORT & CONFERENCE CENTER

WHETHER THEY ARE INTERNATIONAL CONFERENCE attendees or harried Houstonians in need of a weekend getaway, visitors find good reason to return to South Shore Harbour Resort & Conference Center. A lushly land-scaped tropical paradise within minutes of downtown, it offers a host of recreational amenities. ★ In late 1988, when Houston-area lodging

was considered overbuilt, American National Insurance Company and Gal-Tex Hotel Corporation dared to build a $35 million resort hotel and conference center in the sleepy suburb of League City about 30 minutes south of downtown. The location was no accident: The center was situated in the master-planned waterfront com-munity of South Shore Harbour. And the hotel's management set their sights considerably high.

"Gal-Tex took an entrepre-neurial approach," says General Manager Austin Frame. The company set up three basic mar-keting rules: never to sell the resort for less than its worth, to maintain exceptional cost/value ratios, and to seek businesses that appreciate the difference. "We positioned South Shore Harbour to serve a world market, targeting the international visi-tors to the high-tech industries of the nearby NASA area as well as the region's many petrochemi-cal companies," Frame explains.

The strategy worked: only a month after opening its doors, the 250-room hotel was operat-ing in the black. Within a year, weekending Houstonians had also discovered South Shore Harbour.

SPECTACULAR AMENITIES

The center's superb facilities, on a palm-dotted 12-acre site, rival those of the best resorts anywhere. The resort hotel and conference center rises 11 stories above the water at a 1,000-slip marina on Clear Lake that leads to Galveston Bay. The hotel's de-signer rooms, Jacuzzi suites, and bi-level penthouses all feature waterfront views. Diners at the private elegant Harbour Club

and the informal Paradise Reef Restaurant also enjoy great views, along with fine cuisine by an award-winning chef.

Visitors to international symposia, corporate meetings, seminars, and trade shows at South Shore Harbour enjoy the use of a 1,000-person-capacity ballroom, six flexible executive session rooms, state-of-the-art audiovisual equipment, satellite teleconferencing, and other meeting rooms, all of which comprise a total of 20,000 square feet of meeting space. When meetings are done, the teamwork often moves outdoors to a 27-hole championship golf course that graces the south shoreline of Clear Lake.

Whether here for business or pleasure, few guests can resist the facility's other amenities, in-cluding a 185-foot tropical pool with its swim-up bar and water-fall. Guests are also invited to use the Fitness Center, a 70,000-square-foot facility with indoor/outdoor tennis courts and running tracks, racquetball, aerobics classes, Olympic-sized lap pool, full-court gymnasium, and 5,000-square-foot atrium exercise area. The Fitness Center even offers a Human Performance Lab for on-site fitness testing, massage therapy to augment the whirlpool and saunas, and a nursery and play facilities for youngsters.

While the early marketing helped build South Shore Harbour's reputation, the facility's continued success is a result of superb service. South Shore Harbour's continuing goal is to see that every one of its visi-tors has a memorable and happy experience.

LOCATED ON A PALM-DOTTED 12-ACRE SITE, SOUTH SHORE HARBOUR RESORT & CONFERENCE CENTER'S SUPERB FACILITIES RISE 11 STORIES ABOVE THE WATER AT A 1,000-SLIP MARINA ON CLEAR LAKE, WHICH LEADS TO GALVESTON BAY. THE CENTER FEA-TURES A 27-HOLE CHAMPIONSHIP GOLF COURSE AND 20,000 SQUARE FEET OF MEETING SPACE.

THE RITZ-CARLTON, HOUSTON

"WE ARE LADIES AND GENTLEMEN SERVING LADIES AND gentlemen" is the company credo for The Ritz-Carlton Hotel Company L.L.C. This commitment to excellence was brought to Houston in December 1988 when the company purchased the elegant Remington Hotel on Post Oak Park. Nestled in a wooded park near the city's most prestigious residential and business

district, The Ritz-Carlton, Houston now offers guests a welcome retreat among priceless antiques, fresh floral arrangements, and a collection of art treasures.

AWARD-WINNING SERVICE

As soon as the hotel reopened its doors under new ownership, The Ritz-Carlton credo went into effect. The Ritz-Carlton fulfills this pledge by employing a highly trained workforce that is schooled in the company's "Gold Standards." These standards are dictated by the needs and desires of seasoned travelers and derived from extensive research by the travel industry and the company's customer reaction data, focus groups, and surveys.

The Ritz-Carlton staff is empowered "to move heaven and earth" to satisfy customers. Each line employee is a skilled problem solver with a discretionary fund to draw upon in order to make immediate decisions.

This staff-empowerment philosophy helped The Ritz-Carlton become the first hotel company to win the coveted Malcolm

Baldrige National Quality Award in 1992. This award promotes awareness of quality management and was presented to the company's president and chief operating officer, Horst Schultze, by President Bush. Schultze credits the Ritz-Carlton staff and his total quality management (TQM) program for winning the award. According to Schultze, "With TQM, the employee is made to feel more a part of the organization—a thinking contributor."

Schultze says TQM also allows guests to better express their desires for change and their

idiosyncrasies. For example, The Ritz-Carlton keeps profiles on more than 500,000 customers, listing preferences such as nonallergenic pillows.

In Houston all of the 232 spacious guest rooms, including 24 suites, offer twice-daily maid service, 24-hour room service, same-day laundry and dry-cleaning, and a *Wall Street Journal* and *USA Today* delivered weekday mornings. Each guest room is handsomely appointed with rich brocade fabrics, individually selected artwork, elegant marble baths

FLOOR-TO-CEILING WINDOWS IN EACH GUEST ROOM FRAME VIEWS OF THE DOWNTOWN HOUSTON SKYLINE OR THE NEARBY SHOPPING AND BUSINESS DISTRICT (BOTTOM LEFT).

THE PRIVATE LOUNGE ON THE CLUB OFFERS ADDITIONAL PERSONAL SERVICES (BOTTOM RIGHT).

with oversized tubs, and a selection of imported toiletries.

For guests who desire additional privacy and personal services there is The Ritz-Carlton Club. Located on three floors of the hotel, The Club is accessible only with a special elevator key. The Club provides the services of a private concierge staff and the relaxed atmosphere of a private lounge where complimentary offerings include continental breakfast, afternoon tea, cocktails and hors d'oeuvres, and a selection of cordials with an array of chocolates in the evening.

The hotel's heated outdoor swimming pool is surrounded by a landscaped terrace, which makes it a favorite spot for entertaining. Adjacent to the pool is The Fitness Center, which provides a wide range of exercise equipment and an in-house masseuse. Nearby, there are lighted tennis courts, a golf course, and jogging trails. The Ritz-Carlton is conveniently located near Houston's finest shopping areas, and within the hotel resides one of the world's most exclusive jewelers, Bulgari.

For the business traveler, The Ritz-Carlton provides a full-range support system, which includes conference services managers, conference concierges, a complete business center, and in-house teleconferencing equipment and audiovisual systems. There are boardrooms with wet bars and private entrances for conferences and meetings, and private salons with sophisticated furnishings and original art for social functions. Additionally, every guest room is equipped with three telephones and fax and computer capabilities.

CULINARY EXPERIENCE

Dining is an epicurean treasure at The Ritz-Carlton, Houston. The Grill exudes old-world charm with rich oak paneling, a club-like bar area, and a wood-burning fireplace. Cigar aficionados hold The Grill in high regard with its impressive selection of fine cigars. The extensive menu boasts an array of exotic game and regional favorites. Thanks to the hotel's rooftop garden, the dishes are prepared with freshly picked herbs.

Across the marbled hall from The Grill is The Dining Room, an elegant restaurant decorated with tapestry carpets and antique murals. Along with a delectable selection of Continental cuisine, The Dining Room offers macrobiotic menu items.

For many Houstonians, Sunday brunch at The Ritz-Carlton has become a time-honored tradition with its sumptuous culinary offerings and signature children's buffet table that allows little guests to easily reach for tiny silver chafing dishes that hold their favorite treats. A few steps from the restaurant is a sunny, lower-level conservatory dining area with floor-to-ceiling beveled windows overlooking a walled garden.

Afternoon tea is a daily ritual at The Ritz-Carlton. Served in the gracious Lobby Lounge, tea is accompanied by finger sandwiches, pastries, and the soothing music of a harpist. The hotel also hosts festive afternoon teas for children complete with special entertainment and surprises. From the magnificent ballroom to the intimate salons there is a continual flow of celebrations, from weddings and grand galas to cocktail parties and receptions.

It is little wonder The Ritz-Carlton was ranked number one in Houston in Zagat's prestigious *1995 U.S. Hotel, Resort & Spa Survey* in the categories of "Best Overall Hotel," "Best Rooms," "Best Dining," "Best Service," and "Best Public Facilities." Clearly, the hotel follows the company motto: "We pledge to provide the finest personal service and facilities for our guests who will always enjoy a warm, relaxed, yet refined ambience."

CLOCKWISE FROM TOP LEFT: THE GRILL IS A FOUR-STAR RESTAURANT SERVING DINNER NIGHTLY. LIVE ENTERTAINMENT IS ALSO PROVIDED NIGHTLY WITH DANCING ON FRIDAY AND SATURDAY EVENINGS.

THE SUNNY CONSERVATORY IN THE DINING ROOM IS A PERFECT GATHERING SPOT FOR BREAKFAST, LUNCH, OR SUNDAY BRUNCH.

THE BALLROOM IS A FAVORITE FOR GALA CELEBRATIONS.

FLOURISHING UNDER A CORPORATE CULTURE THAT TAKES its management cues from the East and its marketing savvy from the West, Houston-based New Era Life Insurance Companies grew 80 percent annually during its first five years of business; then a 1996 acquisition doubled the size of the company. ★ "Generally, if an insurance company achieves significant growth shortly after its

formation, it had substantial capitalization compared to our initial capitalization of only $3.1 million," explains Mary Frazier, New Era's vice president and corporate secretary. "Because the industry is subject to strict capital requirements and varying state regulations, it typically takes five years to become profitable." New Era, founded in 1990 by a visionary mathematical genius, was profitable after only seven months in operation.

AN EYE FOR OPPORTUNITY

Dr. Bill Chen, New Era's founder, president, and CEO, immigrated to the United States as a student from Taiwan in the 1960s. He had a singular goal: to apply mathematical knowledge to solve social problems. He earned his doctorate in theoretical statistics from Purdue University in 1970 and spent nearly 25 years as an actuary and insurance company executive, developing new insurance products at several large and small firms. When his for-

mer employer moved to Austin in 1989, he decided it was time to fulfill his dream.

With help from his relative Don J. Wang—who is the chairman of New Era Enterprises, Inc., the parent company of New Era Life Insurance Companies—Chen raised the $3.1 million from family and friends to open the company's doors. Chen created consumer-efficient products, had a sterling reputation, and knew plenty of successful agents. Unexpectedly, however, shortly after New Era opened its doors, several large top-rated insurers failed. Consequently many consumers became wary of the insurance industry and agents were not willing to test their clients' funds on an unproven company.

Luckily Chen had experience in acquisitions and mergers, and, rather than sticking to his original business plan, his flexibility allowed him to turn this obstacle into an opportunity. He tells this Chinese parable to illustrate: "A farmer walks out to till his fields and spots a wild rabbit. He chases it, but the rabbit

escapes, darting down a hole at the base of a tree. All day, the farmer waits by the hole for the rabbit to emerge. The sky grows dark, and the farmer goes home. The next day, he checks the rabbit hole and finally notices that there are two other burrows nearby. The farmer had thought only about the hole near the tree; the rabbit was more flexible."

Instead of selling insurance policies, New Era changed its strategy and bought existing policies from insolvent insurers. Chen began by buying a block of 4,000 policies from an insurer who went bankrupt, thus increasing revenues and providing uninterrupted coverage for those insureds who might otherwise lose benefits. Within seven months, New Era showed a profit.

In 1991 New Era acquired an insurance company with licenses in 10 states. Next Chen bought an Indiana-based insurance company that serviced 14 states. New Era proved so adept at transferring policies smoothly, regulators soon began seeking

CLOCKWISE FROM TOP LEFT:
BILL S. CHEN, PH.D., FSA IS THE FOUNDER, PRESIDENT, AND CEO OF NEW ERA LIFE INSURANCE COMPANIES.

CONCERNED EMPLOYEES PROVIDE SERVICE AND BENEFITS TO POLICYHOLDERS.

CUSTOMER SERVICE IS A TOP PRIORITY. NEW ERA VALUES DIVERSITY IN CULTURES, AND MANY STAFF MEMBERS ARE ABLE TO SPEAK SEVERAL LANGUAGES.

CLIFF ROE PHOTOGRAPHY

CLIFF ROE PHOTOGRAPHY

▲▲ CLIFF ROE PHOTOGRAPHY

Chen out when they had insurance companies to liquidate and needed a reputable company to continue providing benefits and service to the policyholders of those insurers. Within six years New Era had made 21 acquisitions, was licensed to do business in 24 states, and was servicing 65,000 policyholders.

As the rapid growth continued, more and more agents began utilizing the opportunity to offer New Era's products to their clients. Consequently, this allowed New Era to pursue its two-pronged marketing strategy. Now the firm's own products, created primarily as supplements for the burgeoning senior market, were being sold by a vast network of independent agents.

In 1996 New Era made its biggest acquisition yet: the purchase of Philadelphia American Life Insurance Company. Almost overnight, the firm exploded into a major national player. New Era and its subsidiaries now do business in 47 states—with more than 200 employees, a sales force of more than 6,000 agents, and well over 100,000 policyholders.

"In only six years, with such rapid growth, it's difficult to develop a strong management team from scratch; and Philadelphia American's management staff offers some good experience," says Frazier. "It's a real good fit because we are focusing on developing capabilities to perform

in outstanding ways, and we have many young employees from both companies yearning for extra knowledge."

ENLIGHTENED MANAGEMENT

With early success, Chen, with the help of Wang, was able to raise another $14.5 million in three private offerings from the Asian-American community to keep New Era on the fast track. Now Chen would like to take New Era public. Although he's a financial wizard himself, Chen is taking the first steps to going public by committing to the hiring of two additional financial experts in order to help lead New Era through the process.

But Chen—who was named a Houston Entrepreneur of the Year in 1994 by *Inc.* magazine, Ernst & Young, and Merrill Lynch—embraces a vision that doesn't stop with profits. He intends to build a model company for future America and has already established superior standards. For example, the firm often improves many policies it buys by adding benefits such as prescription discount cards—and delighting those policyholders.

"We strive to provide consumer-efficient products that are not just about price, but benefits," says Frazier. "The products and everything we do are based on pure motives

▲ CLIFF ROE PHOTOGRAPHY

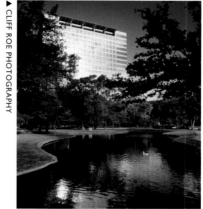

and highly ethical business standards."

Within the company Chen has cultivated an atmosphere where vision, creative ideas, cost efficiency, teamwork, and family concepts are highly valued. "Instead of authority, we use respect and accountability. Instead of delegation, we use self-discipline and teamwork," says Chen. "And teamwork starts from the top." He instills in New Era's staff five principles of success: work hard; work smart; gain knowledge and experience; display a positive and pleasant personality; and remember that luck is not guaranteed.

"There's still a world of opportunity if you are creative and flexible. We haven't even begun to tap the huge Asian-American market," says Frazier. With increased capitalization from a public offering, it looks like Chen will be seeing rabbit holes all over the place.

CLOCKWISE FROM TOP LEFT: NEW ERA LIFE PROVIDES PEACE OF MIND TO SENIOR CITIZENS THROUGH ONE OF ITS PRIMARY PRODUCTS, SUPPLEMENTAL MEDICARE INSURANCE.

NEW ERA LIFE'S NEXT TARGET MARKET IS TO PROVIDE SECURITY FOR ASIAN-AMERICANS.

CORPORATE OFFICES OF NEW ERA LIFE INSURANCE COMPANIES

SANIFILL, INC.

HOUSTON-BASED SANIFILL, INC. IS A YOUNG COMPANY BUT one that has enjoyed robust growth since its inception in 1990. Originally an operator of solid waste landfills in Texas and Georgia, Sanifill has broadly expanded its scope and target markets. Today the company operates in 23 states, the District of Columbia, Mexico, Puerto Rico, and Canada and is widely recognized as a

leader in creative, state-of-the-art waste management. But this is a company with more than good ideas. Sanifill's revenues increased from $12 million to $260 million in the first five years of operations, ranking it among the nation's largest waste management companies.

FROM DISPOSAL-ONLY TO DISPOSAL-BASED

Sanifill's current growth strategy calls for a careful balance between acquisitions and internal development, a stance that has taken the company past the critical five-year milestone.

Founded as a disposal-only company, Sanifill initially received and treated waste collected by others. For the first few years, the company was very successful at operating and building its landfill business. However Sanifill's officers quickly realized that a disposal-based company—one that capitalizes on its landfill operations by adding other services that would be profitable themselves, but would also result in higher revenues and profits at the landfills—would offer far greater opportunity for development. In 1992 the corporate

focus shifted to reflect this new strategy, and Sanifill began acquiring waste collection companies and other related operations.

Today, through fully integrated waste management operations, Sanifill offers collection, recovery, recycling, treatment, landfill disposal, and a variety of special waste disposal options in many markets. Primary locations are in urban areas, where waste volumes are highest and the company has the best long-term opportunities to develop its business.

This integration strategy has put Sanifill in a position to meet an enormous spectrum of business, industry, and community needs in its hometown and in other major cities in North America. But doing business well still means more than simply minding the bottom line.

QUALITY SERVICE WITH INTEGRITY

Sanifill has always followed the corporate credo "Quality Service with Integrity," and the company's commitment to that slogan is

embedded deeply in its culture. Employee, customer, and community relations are all guided by this standard, resulting in an organization with a strong social conscience.

When Sanifill was founded, environmental regulations were just on the horizon. The company has always enjoyed a proactive role in meeting the ecological concerns of Houston and other communities. It is known as an industry pioneer in technological advances that help protect the earth while dealing with the waste its inhabitants generate. This pioneering attitude is evident throughout Sanifill, where employees are encouraged in entrepreneurial thinking and openness.

A true good neighbor in the Houston area, the company is especially active in the communities and neighborhoods where it has operations. Sanifill's goal is to effectively manage the resources that today's children will inherit tomorrow, while also providing attractive returns for its shareholders.

SANIFILL PROVIDES A VARIETY OF WASTE MANAGEMENT SERVICES TO CUSTOMERS IN HOUSTON AND ACROSS NORTH AMERICA (TOP LEFT).

THE COMPANY'S SAM HOUSTON TRANSFER STATION PROVIDES A CONVENIENT DISPOSAL POINT FOR WASTE COLLECTORS IN WEST HOUSTON. WASTE IS EFFICIENTLY TRANSFERRED FROM THE STATION BY TRACTOR-TRAILER TRUCK TO SANIFILL'S BAYTOWN LANDFILL (BOTTOM LEFT).

THE BAYTOWN LANDFILL IS A STATE-OF-THE-ART DISPOSAL FACILITY SERVING THE GREATER HOUSTON MARKET (BOTTOM RIGHT).

▲ TERRY ASKER PHOTOGRAPHY

▲ TERRY ASKER PHOTOGRAPHY

Baker Street Group Inc.

FINDING TALENTED, COMPETENT PROFESSIONALS ISN'T necessarily *elementary* for companies in the highly technical energy and financial services industries. This may explain why Baker Street Group, whose moniker mirrors the address of the fictional detective Sherlock Holmes, found itself among the fastest-growing companies in Houston within its first five years of business. ★ Providing temporary and

contract staffing as well as executive search services, Baker Street Group is a service-driven company in an industry that tends to be sales oriented and intensely competitive. "There are a lot of companies that can generate an initial sale," says Baker Street President Bob Rule. "We like to foster relationships where we can be a service resource—a service partner. We work even harder keeping our clients than we do getting new ones."

Recruiting Is Key

Rule founded Baker Street Group in 1990, combining his experiences in corporate personnel, executive recruiting, and management of a major temporary staffing firm. The company's temporary and contract staffing services offer administrative office support; mortgage banking professionals; information systems technologists; degreed accountants; and technical personnel such as CAD operators, wiremen, and electrical technicians. "Many staffing companies just build their applicant base solely from ad responses," says Rule. "We recruit and screen candidates, rather than just process applicants." Baker Street Group also performs executive recruiting for some of the city's major energy companies, which usually seek experienced professionals in both the engineering/technical and financial/accounting fields.

In recent years, as temporary/contract staffing has become an attractive option for many companies, Baker Street Group has quickly established its reputation. During its first year of operation, the company's revenues topped $250,000; that figure doubled the following

year and skyrocketed to more than $4.6 million by 1993. Now Baker Street Group has achieved annual revenues in excess of $11 million. In addition to its headquarters in west Houston, the company operates satellite hub suites for interviewing candidates. The firm employs 27 full-time staff members and a force of more than 325 highly qualified temporary/contract personnel. According to Rule, the maturity of the staff is what sets Baker Street Group apart from its competition. "We've hired a more seasoned, experienced staff, which has contributed to our philosophy of having longevity with our client relationships," he says.

Still Growing

Twice within its first five years of operation, Baker Street Group was noted among The Houston 100,

a listing of the city's fastest-growing privately held companies. An aggressive acquisition program and plans to expand throughout the Southwest point toward a steadily increasing future profit line.

"We're trying to build a business institution that has momentum beyond any single practitioner," Rule explains. "What distinguishes us is our employees; yet what we're building is bigger than any single employee."

Rule is committed to maintaining Houston as Baker Street Group's headquarters. A former Rice University basketball player, he is active in numerous community activities including the United Way, the Leukemia Society, and charity golf tournaments. With the help of Baker Street Group, Houston companies will continue to fill staffing needs.

▶ DAN HOLMES

THE FIRM TAKES ITS NAME FROM THE ADDRESS OF THE FICTIONAL DETECTIVE SHERLOCK HOLMES (ABOVE).

PROVIDING TEMPORARY AND CONTRACT STAFFING AS WELL AS EXECUTIVE SEARCH SERVICES, BAKER STREET GROUP IS A SERVICE-DRIVEN COMPANY IN AN INDUSTRY THAT TENDS TO BE SALES ORIENTED AND INTENSELY COMPETITIVE (BELOW).

▶ DAN HOLMES

THE CHILDREN'S ASSESSMENT CENTER

HE SOCIAL, EMOTIONAL, PHYSICAL, AND ECONOMIC trauma associated with the discovery of childhood sexual abuse can leave irreparable scars on the life of a victim and his or her family. Events following the discovery of abuse—repetitive interviews, medical examinations, referrals for physical and psychological treatment, investigation, and prosecution—perpetuate the victimization

of children. When not coordinated and processed with a high degree of sensitivity and collaboration, these events often contribute to a systemic breakdown, resulting in failure to protect the child, convict the alleged offender, and stop the abuse.

In a response to the outcry of sexually abused children, The Children's Assessment Center (The Center), a program of the Harris County Commissioners Court, was established in April 1991.

"Our mission is to protect children," says Ellen T. Cokinos, the young, vibrant, and empathetic executive director of The Center. She first recognized the need for a team approach to help these young victims when she was a caseworker for Harris County's Children's Protective Services. She describes some of the heartbreak of victims of sexual abuse: "Typically the child is a girl, between the ages

of eight and 10. Two out of five are boys. The family could be well-to-do, middle class, or poor. Inevitably the child has been molested by someone she knows well: a close family friend, a relative, a stepfather, her mother's boyfriend, or parent.

"We accomplish our mission by providing co-housing, coordination, agency collaboration, and the use of the multidiscipline team approach in prevention, assessment, and treatment of child sexual abuse," says Cokinos.

Located in Houston, The Center is the largest program of its kind in the nation. It is the purest form of a public/private partnership, growing from a need identified by area professionals, corporate leaders, and the community at large.

Agency partners are Baylor College of Medicine, Child Advocates, Inc., Harris County (HC) Children's Protective Services,

HC District Attorney's Office, HC Sheriffs Department, Hermann Hospital, Houston Police Department, Youth Victim/Witness, Texas Department of Protective and Regulatory Services, and University of Texas Health Science Center-Houston.

The Center has served more than 15,000 children in the past five years. Through this work, it has gained the attention of community leaders and philanthropists. One is Houston attorney John M. O'Quinn, whose foundation was created for the support of children, education, and the environment.

"A child doesn't have a chance if he or she is beat on physically, emotionally, or sexually. I think we're losing a lot of kids through child abuse," says O'Quinn, who has built his reputation as one of the top plaintiffs' attorneys in the country.

The John M. O'Quinn Foundation has pledged $1.5 million to a new building for The Children's Assessment Center, which is currently under construction at 2501 Dunstan in the West University area of Houston. As O'Quinn's is the largest single contribution, the facility will be called The John O'Quinn Building, Home of The Children's Assessment Center.

Since 1991 The Center's expansion has been both explosive and consistent. It is located in the third-most-populated county in the nation, for which statistics reflect a 70 percent increase in child sexual abuse referrals since 1989. These statistics emphasize the overwhelming need for specialized services and professional expertise in the prevention, intervention, and treatment of child sexual abuse, says O'Quinn.

The Center—a member of the National Network of Children's Advocacy Centers—offers a child-friendly location, on-site medical and clinical assessments, and joint training for all professionals and volunteers. The center eliminates repetitive interviews of children by offering co-housing of all disciplines and team staffing in all cases. The center also has quality, coordinated assessment and planning by professionals to ensure the success of recovery by children and families.

From the beginning, The Center has shared the crowded offices of Children's Protective Services. In January 1995 The Children's Assessment Center Foundation 501(c)(3) was established in order to support this public/private partnership in raising $10 million to design, construct, and furnish a specially designed facility to meet the program's unique needs.

"Given the crowded conditions, that seems like a long time ago," says Susan P. French, chair of the Capital Campaign and president of the board of directors. "We have raised $7 million, but it took one individual to pledge the gift that moved us to ground breaking on the new building," she adds.

That individual was O'Quinn, the Houstonian who has supported many other children's causes in the past, including Texas Children's Hospital, Be An Angel, Houston Grand Opera's scholarships for young singers, Child Advocates, ESCAPE Center, the Children's Museum of Houston, and the Museum of Natural Science.

"The Children's Assessment Center intervenes on behalf of children every day, providing intervention and healing at no cost to these families," says O'Quinn. "This gift is being pledged on behalf of these defenseless children. We have to help the powerless stand up against the powerful. That's what I stand for as an attorney."

THE CHILDREN'S ASSESSMENT CENTER FOR CHILD VICTIMS OF SEXUAL ABUSE RECEIVED ITS LARGEST PRIVATE DONATION—$1.5 MILLION—FROM HOUSTON ATTORNEY JOHN M. O'QUINN. HE IS SEEN HERE RECEIVING FROM SUSAN P. FRENCH, PRESIDENT OF THE BOARD, A FRAMED RENDERING OF THE NEW FACILITY IN THE WEST UNIVERSITY AREA OF HOUSTON (BELOW).

FLOW TECHNOLOGIES, INC.

CALIFORNIA'S LOSS WAS THE HOUSTON AREA'S GAIN IN 1991 when three venerable West Coast companies with long histories and proven market leadership identities— Johnston Pump, PACO Pumps, and General Valve—were consolidated into Flow Technologies, Inc. The firm chose the rural community of Brookshire for its headquarters, bringing one of the world's most diverse pump and valve manufacturers into the local business community.

A Good Business Climate

J. Jack Watson, the founder and chairman of Flow Technologies' parent company, Newflo, Inc., recognized a better business climate in Texas, with easy access to domestic and international trade. General Valve and Johnston Pump had set up operations in Brookshire in the 1980s, and PACO joined them at the 53-acre manufacturing site in 1991.

The products of each of the Flow Technologies companies are designed and manufactured by a highly focused workforce of 325 local employees. (There are about 600 Flow Technologies employees worldwide.) Operating under ISO 9001 quality systems, the companies have a common goal: to produce superior quality products and to have the most pleased product-confident customers in the world. Through meeting that goal, they have built a worldwide customer base as diverse as the products they manufacture.

JOHNSTON PUMP: IT'S A VERTICAL WORLD

I. N. "Newt" Johnston built his first vertical pump in Los Angeles in 1909 to meet the irrigation needs of western farmers. The firm's growth has been assured by increased demands for vertical pumps in the chemical, process, petroleum, power, steel, mining, marine, water utility, and other industries.

Johnston Pump has pioneered many advances in vertical pump design, engineering, and application. The firm's advanced engineering staff uses the latest technology to match product design and manufacture to the application's requirements. The vertical facility at Flow Technologies features a large fabrication shop, full machining capabilities, and a 180,000-gallon test pit, all staffed by vertical specialists.

In addition to its manufacturing and engineering capabilities, Johnston offers the world's largest service organization devoted exclusively to vertical pumps. Through expert failure analysis, Johnston can recommend design changes, material upgrades, or system modifications as required. Johnston's emphasis on worldwide service starts "at home": It provides pumps and pump repair to numerous chemical and petrochemical companies and refineries on the Houston Ship Channel and along the Gulf Coast.

Johnston's focus on vertical pumps enables the company to tackle the most complex problems and applications. In addition to its Brookshire headquarters, the company operates nine U. S. and two international service centers staffed by vertical pump professionals who offer 24-hour service on all levels.

PACO: THE SMART PUMP COMPANY

PACO was established in 1907 by Samuel E. Huntting to support reconstruction activities in San Francisco after the earthquake and fire of 1906. Today PACO serves the worldwide marketplace with a

SITUATED ON A 53-ACRE PARCEL, FLOW TECHNOLOGIES, INC. CORPORATE OFFICES AND MAIN MANUFACTURING PLANT HOUSE THREE OPERATING COMPANIES WITH 250,000 SQUARE FEET OF MANUFACTURING SPACE (RIGHT).

ENSURING THAT THE PRODUCT MATCHES THE APPLICATION IN FUNCTION AND MATERIAL IS ROUTINE AT FLOW TECHNOLOGIES, INC. HERE, A GENERAL VALVE BODY NEARS COMPLETION PRIOR TO ASSEMBLY (BELOW).

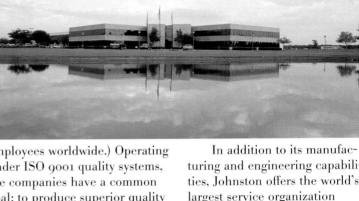

JOHN BERNHARD

complete line of horizontal, vertical, and submersible pumps.

PACO pumps are in use for such diverse applications as commercial heating, air-conditioning, and plumbing; farmland irrigation systems; fish hatcheries; food processing plants; municipal water and wastewater plants; waterscapes and pools; and shipboard use. Industrial applications are also broad, ranging from computer-chip and electronics manufacturing to contact water in steel minimills. Whatever the requirement, PACO has a pump to provide optimal performance.

PACO has built a reputation over the years for responding to customer needs through emphasis on lowering life cycle costs. Using CAD and CAM design since the 1970s, the company's innovations have led to lines that offer reduced operating, installation, and maintenance costs.

The company's entire product line—from small-end suction pumps to large multipump systems—is supported by a dedicated team of engineers, production specialists, and service personnel. PACO operates 11 sales and service centers across the United States. The centers and the entire PACO sales force of salespersons, representatives, and distributors offer a full array of software to assist in application analysis and troubleshooting.

GENERAL VALVE: SETTING INDUSTRY STANDARDS

General Valve Company was founded as a valve reconditioning shop in Southern California in 1929 by Joseph Heinen; but its future was fixed in 1951 with the introduction of the Twin Seal valve, invented by Heinen to meet the petroleum industry's rigid standards for leak-stopping, bubble-tight service.

The Twin Seal valve quickly became the industry standard because of the integrity of its sealing system, its ease of maintenance, and its extremely long life

in critical service. Today thousands of Twin Seal valves are setting records for reliability and long life in petroleum and petrochemical facilities worldwide; the company has more than 35 years of experience at applying them to a variety of fluid-handling requirements.

General Valve is now recognized as one of the world's leading manufacturers of high-integrity positive shutoff valves. The firm's various valves are ideal for any service requiring provable positive sealing and simple maintenance. They do industrial duty in food handling, pulp and paper, chemical,

gas compression, and off-site main pipeline applications.

General's Four-Way Diverter Valve and other products were designed by I. J. Heinen to provide dependability in meter proving, custody transfer, fuel distribution, tank isolation, and manifolds for the oil and gas industry worldwide.

General Valve is committed to continued advances in state-of-the-art sealing technology to handle new product formulations for its expanding customer base. In addition to its Brookshire headquarters, the firm operates a factory in Long Beach, California.

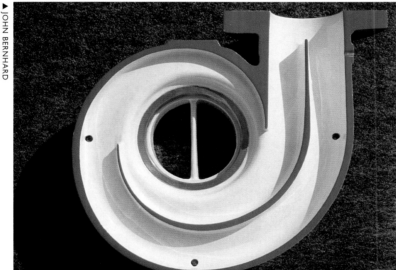

▲ JOHN BERNHARD

▲ JOHN BERNHARD

LOWERING LIFE CYCLE COSTS IS A HALLMARK FOR EACH OF THE FLOW TECHNOLOGIES, INC. OPERATING COMPANIES. THE PACO PUMPS COMPENSATED DOUBLE VOLUTE REDUCES RADICAL LOADS AND, AT THE SAME TIME, IMPROVES EFFICIENCIES, PROVIDING LONG LIFE WITH MINIMAL OPERATING COSTS (LEFT).

FLOW TECHNOLOGIES, INC. COMPLETE FABRICATION AND MACHINE SHOP IS STAFFED BY AN EXCEPTIONAL WORK-FORCE AND OPERATES UNDER AN ISO 9001 QUALITY SYSTEM. HERE, A SPECIALLY DESIGNED JOHNSTON PUMP DISCHARGE HEAD IS BEING MACHINED (BELOW).

FUTRONIX CABLE DEPOT

BEHIND THE GATED ENTRYWAY OF A NORTHWEST HOUSTON office building sits a pristine warehouse stacked high with hundreds of reels, each perfectly wound with electrical wire and cable. Along the shelves, fittings are organized by manufacturer, each one lined up carefully as if it were priceless crystal. The entire warehouse is dust free—a full-time vacuumer sees to that. ★ "There's not

a facility like this anywhere in the world," says Regional Manager Steve Sweat. "There may not even be another company like this in the world." The firm he is referring to is Futronix Cable Depot, a specialty distributor that has become one of Houston's fastest-growing companies.

LIGHTNING STRIKES TWICE

Futronix Cable Depot began operations in 1991. President and CEO Terry Hunt had previously helped build another company, Houston Wire and Cable, into an industry powerhouse. Named by the publication of the National Association of Electrical Distributors as one of 10 people who changed the electrical industry most in the previous 50 years, Hunt founded Futronix with the goal of shaking up the industry once again.

Because Hunt was bound to a three-year noncompete clause with his former employer, his company sold only electrical apparatus for its first few years of operation. However, the wait may have been a blessing

because, during the first three years of operation, the company was able to develop an extensive client base. "Lightning strikes twice," explains Hunt. In 1995, Futronix's first full year of wire and cable sales, the company's sales leaped from $6.9 million to $30 million. Wire and cable now account for 90 percent of Futronix's revenues, although Hunt doesn't want to be known strictly as a wire and cable company.

Futronix buys wire and cable by the mile from the world's finest manufacturers and then sells it to electrical wholesalers by the foot. Through these wholesalers, Futronix's inventory goes to petrochemical plants and refineries, pulp and paper mills, industrial automation facilities, and cogeneration plants worldwide.

"We don't make any products, but we sell a much broader basket than the manufacturers," says Hunt. "You can come to us to get everything rather than going through four different manufacturers." Futronix is also willing to meet even the smallest

needs. "If they want $50 worth of wire, they can get it here," Hunt says.

In addition to its Houston headquarters, the firm has distribution facilities in Baton Rouge, Chicago, Tampa, Charlotte, Philadelphia, Portland, and Dallas as well as Sparks, Nevada. Futronix also plans to open six more locations by 1997.

"Our product is service," explains Hunt. "We also have great products, a fair price, we're a lot of fun to do business with, and we deliver at the lowest overall transactional cost."

NOT JUST A VENDOR: A PARTNER

Futronix representatives are always available by beeper, even in the middle of the night and on weekends. "For every hour a plant or refinery is down, it could cost that company $100,000 or more. They don't want to hear 'It's going to be three weeks,' " says Hunt. Major clients often call Futronix during emergencies, knowing that the company will deliver immedi-

THE COMPANY'S HEADQUARTERS AND LOCAL WAREHOUSE OPERATIONS ARE LOCATED ON HEMPSTEAD HIGHWAY IN NORTHWEST HOUSTON (RIGHT AND BELOW).

FUTRONIX BUYS WIRE AND CABLE BY THE MILE FROM THE WORLD'S FINEST MANUFACTURERS AND THEN SELLS IT TO ELECTRICAL WHOLESALERS BY THE FOOT (RIGHT).

ately and bill through their wholesalers the next week.

"We ship most everything out the same day," adds Hunt. Futronix also offers a service called A.M. Express to regular customers at no extra charge. Through this service, orders received before 7 p.m. are delivered to the customer by 9 a.m. the next day. Says Hunt, "One customer said he could get material faster out of our warehouse than out of his own."

Hunt points out that all of Futronix's service features focus on helping customers find ways to be more competitive. "We don't just want to be another vendor, we want to be a partner," says Hunt.

The perfectly maintained warehouse is important to the company's philosophy. "The distributors have a high regard for us as a vendor partner because they know when the product gets to their customer, it's going to be a good representation of their company," says Sweat. "We act as an extension of their warehouse. Therefore, our packaging is immaculate."

A PLACE WHERE GOOD ATTITUDES THRIVE

Futronix is also a company where good attitudes thrive. "We want to provide an environment where people can use their talents at 110 percent or better," says Hunt. Even in the warehouse, there's a sense of ownership. "Nobody feels like just an employee," adds Hunt. "We work together."

Futronix also devotes attention to follow-up customer service. Twice a month, the Futronix staff members put on aprons and head out to a customer's office to serve a catered lunch. "There's no sales pitch involved. It's just our way of saying thanks," says Buddy Boyd. "The lunch is just one day, but we're on the phone every day."

In 1995 Futronix was one of the top 10 distributors in the world for Belden, a premier wire and cable manufacturer. Futronix also became the first supplier of excess electrical material ever to receive the coveted International Organization for Standardization

(ISO) 9002 certification. This certification sets a standard for Futronix as its wire and cable inventory continues to grow.

But the company is still committed to building for the future. Recently Futronix established a presence on the Internet in order to give customers another competitive edge. Hunt plans eventually to make Futronix a public company. "But we're going to keep it lean, mean, and technologically efficient," he says.

ISO 9002 CERTIFICATION SETS A STANDARD FOR FUTRONIX CABLE DEPOT (BELOW).

EXECUTIVE LIVING, INC.

FOR A CORPORATE EXECUTIVE RELOCATING TO A NEW TOWN OR visiting one on a temporary assignment, the idea of living for weeks or even months in a cramped expensive hotel room doesn't offer much appeal. Neither does the notion of hassling with hotel laundry service and eating every meal out. ★ Imagine this scenario instead: The executive stays in a spacious apartment,

condominium, town home, or single-family dwelling that has been decorated by a professional interior designer. It comes complete with such amenities as a washer and dryer, microwave, stereo, clock radio, color television, VCR, and perhaps even a fax and answer machine. Its kitchen is fully equipped with everything from dishes, silverware, and place mats to pots and pans, bottle opener, toaster, and measuring spoons. A plentiful supply of bed and bath linens is provided, too. All utilities and local phone and cable TV service have been connected, and maid service has been scheduled on a regular basis.

"All the executive needs to bring are clothes and a toothbrush. Everything else is set up for them," says Carol Gremillion, of Executive Living, Inc. "We have made our name offering such at-home surroundings to our guests."

HOME AWAY FROM HOME

During a 15-year career in sales and marketing, Gremillion recognized a growing demand for comfortable affordable housing alternatives for executives on the move. She founded Executive Living in October 1992 to address that need. Terry Gremillion became a partner in the company in 1995 after 11 years with Union Carbide.

Since then Executive Living has established a reputation for providing first-class accommodations for executives on temporary assignments, transferees who haven't found permanent space, and individuals whose homes are under repair or construction. "Typically corporate executives need housing for periods of a month to a year," Gremillion explains. "However, it's hard to find a high-quality apartment complex that's willing to sign a lease for only a month or two. It also takes a lot of time and effort to furnish the apartment and to arrange for utilities, telephone service, and cable TV to be turned on. That's why corporations call on us," she says. "We lease apartments on a long-term basis, furnish them, and then make them available to executives, hassle-free. We make things hassle-free for clients' corporate relocation departments, too. When an executive needs temporary accommodations, the relocators simply pick up the phone and call us. They know we'll take care of everything. They don't have to worry any more."

Comfort isn't the only advantage Executive Living offers. "There's a substantial cost savings as well," Gremillion says. "Our clients can reduce their corporate housing costs by as much as 50 percent by working with us instead of boarding their executives in a hotel."

PROVIDING A PERSONAL TOUCH

Executive Living's professional staff in Houston and Sugar Land prides itself on providing personalized service to its clients, some from as far away as Germany, Venezuela, Korea, and Kuwait. "We don't take the standard cookie-cutter approach," Gremillion says. "We listen carefully to the executives' needs and then customize each arrangement to address every detail. If they have children and they're working with a real estate agent to find a permanent home

EXECUTIVE LIVING CURRENTLY LEASES 120 APARTMENTS, RANGING FROM STUDIOS TO FOUR-BEDROOM UNITS, THROUGHOUT THE HOUSTON-SUGAR LAND AREA. THE FIRM ALSO OFFERS SPACE IN CONDOMINIUMS, HIGH-RISES, TOWN HOUSES, AND SINGLE-FAMILY HOMES.

in a specific area, we'll help them find an apartment nearby so the kids won't have to change schools again when they move," she says. "And since executives often arrive late at night and don't know where things are located, we provide a starter package with enough groceries to get them started. If our clients have any questions, we're available to assist them at any time, night or day."

The Gremillions and their staff make every effort to establish a relationship of trust and caring with their clients. They have taken clients' families on golf outings and to the zoo, and have even hosted Houston Rockets game parties to make them feel at home.

Most of Executive Living's business comes from referrals by satisfied clients. "That tells me we're doing a good job," Gremillion says. "In this business, you live or die by the service you provide."

The company has experienced steady growth. Beginning with only a handful of apartments, Executive Living currently leases 120 apartments, ranging from studios to four-

bedroom units, throughout the Houston-Sugar Land area. The firm also offers space in condominiums, high-rises, town houses, and single-family homes.

"We're continually growing and getting stronger in our markets," Gremillion says. In early 1996 Executive Living acquired another corporate housing company, and the transaction boosted

its business by about 25 percent.

"Our goal is to remove the burden of finding housing from the busy corporate executives' shoulders so they can concentrate on other, more important things," says Gremillion. "After all, if employees are happy in their surroundings when they're not at work, they'll be happier and more productive on the job."

EXECUTIVE LIVING HAS ESTABLISHED A REPUTATION FOR PROVIDING FIRST-CLASS ACCOMMODATIONS FOR EXECUTIVES ON TEMPORARY ASSIGNMENTS, TRANSFEREES WHO HAVEN'T FOUND PERMANENT SPACE, AND INDIVIDUALS WHOSE HOMES ARE UNDER REPAIR OR CONSTRUCTION.

HOUSTON-BASED WESTERN NATIONAL CORPORATION IS well known as a specialist in the annuity business. Its principal subsidiary—Western National Life Insurance Company, which is one of the largest life insurers in the United States—markets retirement annuities through a nationwide distribution network that includes financial institutions, independent agents,

specialty brokers, and direct marketers.

Western National Corporation became a publicly held company in February 1994 and established its headquarters in Houston. The company immediately set out to become number one in the sale of retirement annuities through alternative distribution channels, principally financial institutions. This objective is rapidly becoming a reality.

A LEADER IN THE FINANCIAL INSTITUTION MARKET

In the late 1980s Western National was among the first to recognize the potential of banks and other financial institutions as a primary distribution channel for annuities. Today

the company is one of the leading providers of individual fixed annuities through financial institutions—a market that now represents the life insurance industry's largest distribution channel.

Western National continued to build on its strong presence in the financial institution market with the 1995 launch of a proprietary fixed annuity program. "We were the first [in the annuity field] to develop a proprietary product that allows the bank to manage the annuity assets," says Chairman and CEO Michael J. Poulos. "This makes the bank more of a partner than strictly a sales vehicle, which we think speaks well in terms of the long-term nature and profitability of this business."

For most other insurers, banks are merely annuity product sales outlets. Western National's proprietary agreements allow financial institutions to manage the money generated from sales. "We are in the unique position of outsourcing the investment management," says Poulos, who sees the proprietary program as a natural complement to Western National's traditional financial institution distribution. In addition to its agreements with financial institutions, Western National's products are sold by telephone and direct mail through a direct marketing company acquired in 1994. Another important marketing channel is the company's army of general agents and managing general agents, many of whom have been

AS A SPECIALIST IN RETIREMENT ANNUITIES, WESTERN NATIONAL CORPORATION IS WELL POSITIONED TO CAPITALIZE ON FAVORABLE DEMOGRAPHIC TRENDS AND THE PUBLIC'S INCREASING CONCERN ABOUT OUTLIVING THEIR RETIREMENT SAVINGS.

▼ MICHAEL HART

selling Western National products for many years.

Western National has also entered into a joint venture with American General Life to sell and service structured settlements, which are specialty annuity products typically purchased for the benefit of injured claimants by property and casualty insurers following settlements with claimants. "We were one of the first companies in the structured settlement business, which today is a $5 billion per year industry. We have a tremendous level of expertise," says Poulos.

Western National is diversifying its product line beyond fixed annuities. In 1995 the company introduced a variable annuity. This product, which combines the characteristics of a mutual-fund-type investment with the tax-deferred feature of an annuity, positions the company to attract customers who are more return oriented and risk tolerant than its traditional senior saver customers. Another new product expected to be launched in mid-1996, a specialized life insurance product, will target the growing wealth transfer market.

PROVIDING FOR A FUTURE WITHOUT SOCIAL SECURITY

Annuity sales are growing across the nation because people are having to assume more responsibilities for their own retirement. Financial analysts predict that in the near future, Social Security payments will be inadequate to support individuals throughout their retirement years.

Other considerations that have attracted buyers to annuities include current trends, such as the fact that company pension plans are fading, and people are living longer. Indeed, the possibility for running out of money after retirement is a growing concern, which helps explain why annuities have outsold life insurance by growing margins for more than a decade.

STREAMLINED OPERATION

Poulos describes the company's management team as the best he has worked with in his 35 years in the business. Of the firm's 300 employees, approximately 70 make up the Houston office's marketing, legal, actuarial, financial, and investor relations departments. Most of the other employees work in the firm's service center in Amarillo, where the company has maintained a strong presence for more than 50 years.

Western National's service center is among the most efficient in the business. Poulos says the company's low-cost customer-focused operation provides a strong competitive advantage. The company's statutory operating expenses, excluding commissions, were 0.49 percent of annuity reserves in 1995, which compares favorably with the latest available industry average of 0.82 percent.

FUTURE FOCUS

Like its customers, Western National's focus is on building for the future. Strategic initiatives implemented in 1995 expanded the company's position in established outlets and enabled it to penetrate new markets. These accomplishments position Western National well for 1996 and beyond. The company's target market is growing, its market share is increasing, and its product line is diversifying. Poulos hopes to see a strong double-digit company growth rate by the end of 1996.

"Western National has an impressive track record, and we hope to improve on this performance with strong competitive products, great service, and a strong balance sheet," says Poulos. "Our long-term strategy is to build a company that is perceived as a good company by our customers, by our employees, by the banks that we distribute through, by our agents who we sell through, as well as our shareholders. It's that mix, that blend, and that balance that you have to maintain. And we think we've done it."

WESTERN NATIONAL'S MANAGEMENT TEAM IS LED BY (SEATED, FROM LEFT) CHAIRMAN, PRESIDENT, AND CEO MICHAEL J. POULOS; SENIOR VICE PRESIDENTS MICHAEL J. AKERS AND WILLIAM O. DANIEL; AND (STANDING, FROM LEFT) EXECUTIVE VICE PRESIDENTS ARTHUR R. MCGIMSEY, RICHARD W. SCOTT, AND JOHN A. GRAF.

THEATRE UNDER THE STARS

NE OF HOUSTON'S FAVORITE SUMMER TRADITIONS BEGAN ON a humid night in 1968 at the newly renovated Miller Outdoor Theatre, when a fledgling company called Theatre Under The Stars (TUTS) presented a single, free performance of *Bells Are Ringing*. The cast worked for free, created its own costumes, and even helped raise $4,000 to cover the total expenses. Today TUTS has

CLOCKWISE FROM TOP RIGHT: ROBERT GOULET, PATRICIA KIES, AND JAMES VALENTINE WERE ROYALTY IN TUTS' 1990 *Camelot*.

IN 1993 THEATRE UNDER THE STARS PREMIERED A LAVISH NEW MUSICAL BASED ON JAMES A. MICHENER'S CELEBRATED NOVEL, *Sayonara*, TO GREAT CRITICAL ACCLAIM.

THEATRE UNDER THE STARS (TUTS) WAS FOUNDED BY FRANK M. YOUNG, WHO IS ALSO ITS CURRENT EXECUTIVE DIRECTOR.

become the largest professional not-for-profit producer of musical theater in the nation. It is a leader in developing new musicals, with nine world premieres to its credit.

Among the shows it has developed are *Phantom, Sayonara, Annie Warbucks,* and *Jekyll & Hyde.* TUTS' international tours have included *Mame* with Juliet Prowse, *The Unsinkable Molly Brown* with Debbie Reynolds, and *Carousel* and *Man of La Mancha* with Robert Goulet. These shows carry the TUTS banner all over the United States and Canada to help support Houston artists and the acting community. The Walt Disney Company chose TUTS in 1993 to mount the world premiere of *Beauty and the Beast: The Musical*—for a record-shattering pre-Broadway run.

"The American musical is one of only two art forms indigenous to our country," says TUTS Founder and Executive Director Frank Young. It's his mission to make sure this art form not only survives, but flourishes. In the process, all of Houston benefits.

In Houston alone TUTS now draws audiences of 350,000 annually. In addition to its annual free summer shows at Miller Outdoor Theatre, the company mounts a yearly indoor season of musicals at the 3,000-seat Music Hall for a large subscription audience.

TUTS also established the Humphreys School of Musical Theatre, which it has operated since 1972, with 1,000 children annually taking classes.

In 1985 Young founded the National Alliance for Musical Theatre, a nonprofit national service organization, which today includes 90 producers across the United States.

In 1989 TUTS formed the 5th Avenue Musical Theatre Company in Seattle, which it now runs from Houston. The combined budget of all TUTS venues (including Seattle, the Music Hall, and Miller Theatre) approaches $30 million annually.

In addition to its free summer performances, TUTS donates thousands of complimentary tickets to local charities each season, conducts performance workshops at inner-city schools and neighborhood centers, sends students from the Humphreys School of Musical Theatre to perform at hospitals and nursing homes, and operates a graduate student intern program with the University of Texas at Austin and the University of Houston.

HOUSTON MUSIC HALL FOUNDATION

THE MUSIC HALL, BUILT IN 1936 AS A WORKS PROGRESS Administration (WPA) project, is owned by the City of Houston and has been the indoor performing home of Theatre Under The Stars (TUTS) since 1972. ★ After alterations and renovations over the years, little of the original building remains, and the Music Hall is once again badly worn, with a stage house too small for many

of today's state-of-the-art productions. TUTS paved the way for a new musical theater complex by establishing the Houston Music Hall Foundation in 1994. A 501(C)(3) not-for-profit organization, the Foundation is charged with raising the necessary funds to redevelop the Music Hall site and oversee its design, construction, and operation.

"Houston deserves a world-class state-of-the art hall to handle civic events as well as a rich variety of musical theater, including TUTS productions," says Bud Franks, Houston Music Hall Foundation executive director.

The redevelopment project was launched after feasibility studies showed it would be more economical to build a new performing arts center on the site than to try, once again, to save the old facility. "What was originally a $25 million renovation plan became a $55 million to $60 million redevelopment of both the Music Hall and Coliseum sites," says Franks.

The new Music Hall will include offices for TUTS, the Humphreys School of Musical

Theatre, ample rehearsal space, a small 700-seat theater, a state-of-the-art stage house capable of housing the most complicated theatrical technology, and a new 2,700-seat theater. Franks says it will also have a warm people-friendly atmosphere with "more than adequate comfort zones and people places, including spacious lobbies and rest rooms that double the city's standard."

No one who has attended events at the Music Hall in recent years would argue with the need for a new building. Those on the inside see an even greater urgency. "*Beauty and the Beast* almost didn't happen because of the small stage housing here," Franks says. If several more gen-

erations of Houstonians are to enjoy civic events and the tradition of musical theater that has been established at the Music Hall, a successful capital campaign to redevelop the venue is critical.

Governed by a civic board of directors under the leadership of Marc Shapiro, chairman and CEO of Texas Commerce Bank, the Houston Music Hall Foundation is actively engaged in planning the capital campaign and soliciting pledges of lead gifts. The success of this campaign will enable the Foundation to provide a modern performing arts center for Houston and future generations by the beginning of the new century.

CLOCKWISE FROM TOP LEFT: RICHARD WHITE AS PHANTOM AND GLORY CRAMPTON AS CHRISTINE STARRED IN THEATRE UNDER THE STARS' WORLD PREMIERE OF *Phantom* BY ARTHUR KOPIT AND MAURY YESTON.

TERRENCE MANN AND SUSAN EGAN PLAYED THE TITLE ROLES IN THEATRE UNDER THE STARS' WORLD PREMIERE PRESENTATION OF *Beauty and the Beast,* A RECORD-SHATTERING PRE-BROADWAY COPRODUCTION WITH WALT DISNEY PRODUCTIONS.

THEATRE UNDER THE STARS' MOST RECENT PRODUCTION OF BROADWAY'S LONGEST-RUNNING MUSICAL, *A Chorus Line,* TOOK PLACE IN 1994. "AUDIENCE POLLS REQUEST IT EVERY YEAR," SAYS TUTS EXECUTIVE DIRECTOR FRANK YOUNG.

JULIET PROWSE STARRED IN TUTS' 1989 MUSIC HALL STAGING OF *Mame* AND ITS NATIONAL TOUR IN 1990.

▲ MARTHA SWOPE ASSOCIATES CAROL ROSEGG

▲ JOAN MARCUS

▲ NATIONAL TOUR PHOTO 1991

BERT BRANDT (1915-1975) began his photography career as a White House photographer during the Roosevelt years until World War II began. During the war he was a correspondent for Acme News Pictures/United Press International and was the first photographer to return to the United States with photos of the actual D day landing mission. In 1953 Brandt and his wife, Liz, moved to Houston to start a family. Here Brandt launched his career as a freelance photographer working on corporate and advertising assignments, which included countless annual reports.

CAROLYN BROWN, a native of Fort Morgan, Colorado, is a freelance photographer specializing in architecture, fine arts, and travel photography. Having earned a bachelor's and a master's degree in art from Cornell College in Iowa and Texas Woman's University in Denton, respectively, she photographed the images in *Dallas: Shining Star of Texas* and is currently serving as the photography editor for Towery Publishing's book, *Dallas: World-Class Texas*. Brown's work can be seen in many exhibits at the Dallas Children's Hospital, Houston Museum of Art, Dallas Museum of Art, and Southeast Museum of Photography.

ROCKY J. BOUDREAUX has lived in the Houston area since 1951. He received a bachelor of science degree in industrial distribution from Texas A&M and currently runs Rocky J. Boudreaux Photography. Specializing in illustration and scenic, wedding, and stock photography, he has had work published in *Texas Highways* and *Texas Parks and Wildlife*. Boudreaux is a member of the professional photographers' guild and of Wedding Photographers International.

JIM CALDWELL, a 1971 graduate of Rice University, has been a commercial, editorial, and theatrical photographer based in Houston for more than 20 years. His work can be seen in several books, including *Houston: A Self-Portrait* and *Texas on a Roll*, as well as in many magazines and newspapers, such as *Time, Newsweek, Texas Monthly, U.S. News & World Report, New York Times, Houston Chronicle*, and *Los Angeles Times*. Caldwell is the past president of the Houston Chapter of the American Society of Magazine Photographers and has worked on the board of the Houston Center for Photography.

L.A. CLEVER, a freelance photographer, specializes in black-and-white photography as well as editorial and fashion photography. Clever has been featured in *Photo District News* and twice has been a FotoFest Featured Artist. She has won both the Gold Award and Silver Award for her work in *Houston Metropolitan*, and has had work published in *Houston City, San Francisco Focus, Boston Magazine, Modern Bride, Ultra, Houston Life*, and *Time*.

GEORGE CRAIG, a native Houstonian and sixth-generation Texan, is a self-employed photographer who specializes in corporate advertising, annual reports, and capabilities brochures. Some of Craig's previous clients are MCA, Warner Bros. Records, Epic Records, Procter & Gamble, G.E. Appliances, and such talents as Diana Ross, Clint Black, and ZZ Top. A graduate of the University of Texas with a bachelor's degree in journalism, Craig established George Craig Photography in 1976.

PAM FRANCIS, a native of Houston, studied at Kinkaid High School, Rollins College, and the University of Texas. The owner of Pam Francis Photography, her areas of specialty include editorial and advertising portraiture. Francis' work can be seen in such magazines as *Time, Parade, Sports Illustrated, Forbes, Newsweek*, and *Texas Monthly*. She has photographed several celebrities, including Kevin Costner, Lyle Lovett, and Dan Rather, and won an Addy award in 1996.

TERRY FOSS, who was born 30 miles outside Houston in Needville, moved to Houston 20 years ago. A graduate of the Brooks Institute of Photography, Foss' areas of specialty include commercial, industrial, and corporate photography. His clients have included Browning Ferris Industries, Shell, Toyota, and Air Liquide Corporation. He enjoys traveling in the Texas Hill Country, listening to live music, and canoeing.

ERIC FRANTZ, a native of Boston, graduated from Sam Houston State University with a bachelor's degree in photography. Employed by Foley's Photography Studio, he specializes in landscape, fine art, and studio photography. Frantz' previous clients include Austin Health and Fitness, Houston Food Bank, Current Computer Services, and Clanton and Company.

MARK GREEN is a freelance photographer based in Houston.

HESTER & HARDAWAY is a Fayetteville, Texas-based studio, owned and operated by Paul Hester and Lisa Hardaway. Hailing from Arkansas, Hester is a graduate of Rice University and of Rhode Island School of Design, while Hardaway, who is from Los Angeles, earned bachelor's and master's degrees in music from Rice. Specializing in architectural photography and images of people and art, Hester

& Hardaway has served clients including such national and international architecture magazines as *Architectural Review* and *Architectural Record*. The studio has also photographed Georgia O'Keeffe's house in Albuquerque.

DOUG HICKMAN, a native of Dallas, moved to Houston in 1987. A graduate of the University of Texas at Dallas with a bachelor of arts in psychology, he specializes in industrial, corporate, editorial, and environmental photography, as well as portraiture. Once nominated for a Cleo Award, Hickman's client list includes Exxon, Chevron, Shell, and Foley's. He enjoys throwing darts, camping, golf, reading, and fine-tuning his computer.

GEORGE D. HIXSON, the owner and operator of George Hixson Photography, specializes in photo illustration and fictional image design. A native of Endicott, New York, he moved to Houston in the early 1980s. Hixson has exhibited at several local galleries, including the Contemporary Arts Museum, Blaffer Gallery, Commerce Street Artist's Warehouse, and DiverseWorks. He is currently working on a series of photographs from his travels in Guatemala.

DAN HOLMES was born and raised in Houston and completed all of his formal education in the city. He earned a bachelor of science at the University of Houston and a master's degree from Sam Houston State University. Specializing in corporate and industrial photography, Holmes has worked with Pennzoil, Tenneco, Methodist Hospital, and Price Waterhouse.

HOUSTON METROPOLITAN RESEARCH CENTER (HMRC) is a department of the Houston Public Library with the objectives of locating, preserving, and making available to researchers primary source materials that document Houston's history. One of HMRC's most important components is its historical photographs. Consisting of more than 2 million images of Houston from its 19th-century beginnings to the present, the collection visually records all aspects of Houston's growth. HMRC operates a photo preservation lab with copying facilities on the premises.

WALTER JIMENEZ, a native of Mexico City, moved to Houston in 1988. He has earned a master's degree in communications and currently runs Walter Jimenez Photography, specializing in tabletop, stock, and black-and-white photography. Jimenez' clients have included the Greater Houston Partnership, Chevron, and Coca-Cola Foods, and he has won awards for his participation in the biannual juried exhibit *Windows on Houston*.

ROBB KENDRICK specializes in photographing people. A native of Spur, Texas, he attended East Texas State University (ETSU). Kendrick is a frequent contributor to *National Geographic, Life*, and *Sports Illustrated* magazines.

ROCKY KNETEN is a self-employed photographer specializing in shooting people in interesting environments. A graduate of the University of Texas in Austin, Kneten moved to Houston in 1984. His clients have included *Texas Monthly, Esquire*, and *Rolling Stone* magazines, as well as Southwestern Bell, Shell, and American Express. Kneten enjoys mountain biking and many different types of food.

SCOTT F. KOHN, a native of Morgantown, West Virginia, moved to Houston in 1976. Earning a bachelor's degree in photography from Sam Houston State University, Kohn specializes in advertising, serving such clients as Coca-Cola, Du Pont, the University of Houston, and the Houston Symphony.

HAL LOTT is a native of Houston and a graduate of Stephen F. Austin State University, where he studied photojournalism, business, and art. Specializing in still life, food, and architectural photography, Lott has worked for Hilton, Texaco, and *Woman's Day*. In addition to serving as president of TexStock PhotoInc. and as owner of Hal Lott Photography, he enjoys cycling, music, and Texas culture.

MIEKO MAHI specializes in corporate and industrial photography and video, specifically in the oil and natural gas industry. Originally from Tokyo, she lived in Alaska and Michigan before coming to Texas in 1974. Mahi has won numerous awards, including five gold and silver awards from Women in Communications for her work in video and photography. Her work can be seen in *Oil & Gas Journal, Oil and Gas Investor, Petroleum Engineer International*, and *Gulf Coast Oil World*.

STEPHAN MYERS is a self-taught photographer specializing in underwater, nature, and travel photography. His previous clients include *Audubon, Texas Highways, Smithsonian, Texas Parks and Wildlife, National Wildlife*, and *Ranger Rick*, and he served as a coauthor and photographer on *A Diving and Snorkeling Guide to Texas*. A native of Houston, Myers moved to Corpus Christi in 1994.

DAVID NANCE, a native of Charlotte, moved to Houston in 1965. Having studied photography at the Rochester Institute of Technology, Nance has several areas of specialty, including corporate, industrial, aerial, and public relations photography. Prior to starting his own business in 1979, Nance spent 17 years in the news business and was a recipient of many awards on the local, regional, state, national, and international levels.

JIM OLIVE was born and raised in Houston and attended Sam Houston State University, where he majored in biology. The owner of Jim Olive Photography, he specializes in corporate/industrial and environmental photography. An Addy winner, Olive has participated in *Windows on Houston* and *Houston: A Self-*

Portrait, and some of his previous clients include Kenner Manufacturing, Time-Life Inc., Desert Publications, and Guest Informant. Olive travels extensively and is actively working on a documentary on Christmas Bay.

TONY ROMANO, a native of Houston, now resides in Austin and works for Just Say "Cheese!" Global Productions. His client list includes Delta Air Lines' *Sky Magazine, Houston Metropolitan*, and the Ultimate Players Association. Romano claims to have started taking pictures in 1986 after buying a camera with an unemployment check; he started his career in photography in 1990.

JANICE RUBIN is an award-winning Texas-based freelance photographer whose work has appeared in numerous national and international publications, including *Smithsonian, Newsweek, Forbes, Town and Country, Fortune*, and *Rolling Stone*. Rubin was the recipient of a National Endowment for the Arts (NEA) fellowship for her participation in *The Ties That Bind: Photographers Look at the American Family*. Her photo exhibition and lecture series *Survival of the Spirit: Jewish Lives in the Soviet Union* toured 17 cities in the United States and Canada.

PAUL SCHMIDT is a native Houstonian and the owner of Paul Schmidt Photography. Specializing in photographing people, Schmidt won an Addy award in 1991 and has worked for Aramco and Butterworth Jetting Systems, among other clients.

STEPHEN SEEGER specializes in photographing people, lifestyle, and corporate culture. Born in Burbank, Seeger became interested in photography at age 12 and had his first photograph published when he was 15. He graduated with honors from Art Center College of Design in Pasadena with a degree in photography and moved to Dallas in 1981.

Seeger's previous clients include American Airlines, Andersen Consulting, Babbages, Inc., Cigna, Dr. Pepper, GTE, and Haggar Apparel.

F. CARTER SMITH is a photographer based in Houston.

RAY SOTO is a native of San Antonio who moved to Houston in 1963. Specializing in corporate photography, Soto has won numerous industry awards from the Houston Advertising Federation, the Art Directors Club of Houston, and the Public Relations Society of America. He earned an associate degree in photography in 1983.

JAY STEVENS, owner and operator of Jay Stevens Photography, was born and raised in Houston. His areas of specialty include people, still life, polaroid transfers, black-and-white infrared, studio and location shoots, editorial, commercial, and landscape photography.

BERYL STRIEWSKI is a native of Detroit who moved to Houston in 1985. She earned a master of science in art from ETSU and a bachelor of science in criminal justice from Michigan State University. Specializing in panoramas and people in their environment, Striewski has served such clients as Continental Airlines, IBM, Rice University, Shell, and *Texas Monthly*. She was awarded an NEA grant in 1987, and has won many Addy awards and Houston Art Directors Club awards.

TexStock PhotoInc. is a Houston-based full-service stock photography agency with a concentration of images in Texas, the Southwest, and the Gulf Coast. TexStock represents more than 70 photographers from Los Angeles to New York with images from the 1950s to the present.

C.S. VARLACK, a native of the British Virgin Islands, moved to Missouri City, Texas, in 1978.

Specializing in outdoor and nature photography, Varlack is employed by Brown & Root USA. His work can be seen in *Lindan Spot Lite, Island Sun*, and *Outdoor and Travel Photography*. His favorite subjects are macro shots of entomological subjects.

ELLIS VENER is originally from Corpus Christi and moved to the area in 1968. The owner of Ellis Vener Photography, she specializes in portraiture, panoramics, architecture photography, corporate photography, and photojournalism. Having won many awards from the Houston Art Directors Club, Vener has been regularly featured for the last six years in *Windows on Houston*. Vener served as the only non-New Yorker on the official photography team for the rededication of the Statue of Liberty in 1986.

GEORGE WONG, a native Houstonian, attended Bellaire High School and the University of Houston. Specializing in fashion photography, he is a freelance photographer for *United Press International* and *Country Weekly*.

ALLTEL Sugar Land Telephone 180

American Airlines, Inc. 178

American Rice, Inc. 244

Andersen Consulting 182

Associated Pipe Line Contractors, Inc. 188

BSG Alliance/IT, Inc. 246

Baker Street Group Inc. 253

Baxter & Swinford Realtors 191

Brown & Root 175

John Brown—Houston Technical Center 214

Burnett Personnel Services 218

Career Management International 224

The Children's Assessment Center 254

Entex, A NorAm Energy Company 160

Executive Living, Inc. 260

Flow Technologies, Inc. 256

Four Seasons Hotel 234

Front Office Business Centers 237

Fugro-McClelland 190

Futronix Cable Depot 258

Haldor Topsoe, Inc. 200

Halliburton Energy Services 174

Houston Coca-Cola Bottling Company 164

Houston Community College System 215

Houston Fuel Oil Terminal Company 232

Houston Grand Opera 198

Houston Music Hall Foundation 265

KTBZ—107.5 *THE BUZZ* 242

Kelsey-Seybold Clinic 194

Arthur D. Little, Inc. 238

Lorance & Thompson, P.C. 216

I.W. Marks Jewelers, Inc. 230

Maxim Technologies, Inc. 165

McDonnell Douglas Corporation 210

The Methodist Health Care System 168

NGC Corporation 240

New Era Life Insurance Companies 250

PaineWebber Incorporated 202

Pappas Restaurants, Inc. 208

Pepsi-Cola Company of Houston 184

Port of Houston 166

RE/MAX of Texas, Inc. 226

The Ritz-Carlton, Houston 248

Jack Roach Ford 171

Sanifill, Inc. 252

Shell Oil Company 172

Simmons & Company International 220

South Shore Harbour Resort &

Conference Center 247

Southwestern Bell 170

Sterling Bank 219

TeleCheck International, Inc. 222

Texas Chiropractic College 206

Texas Instruments 196

Theatre Under The Stars 264

Turner Collie & Braden Inc. 192

Martha Turner Properties 223

United Space Alliance 204

Unocal Corporation 186

Visible Changes Inc. 228

Western National Corporation 262

Westheimer Transfer & Storage Company, Inc. . . . 162

Wyndham Warwick Hotel 176